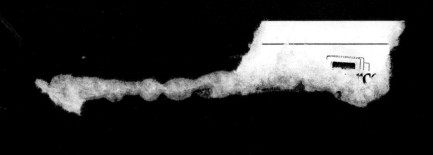

D0236700

3:59.4

*The Quest to Break
the Four-Minute Mile*

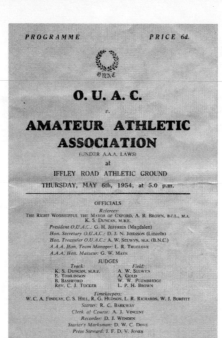

Running order: sixpence bought a programme,
and Event 9 brought four minutes of history.

3:59.4

*The Quest to Break
the Four-Minute Mile*

John Bryant

HUTCHINSON
LONDON

First Published by Hutchinson in 2004

1 3 5 7 9 10 8 6 4 2

Hutchinson
The Random House Group Limited
20 Vauxhall Bridge Road, London SW1V 2SA

Random House Australia (Pty) Limited
20 Alfred Street, Milsons Point, Sydney
New South Wales 2061, Australia

Random House New Zealand Limited
18 Poland Road, Glenfield
Auckland 10, New Zealand

Random House (Pty) Limited
Endulini, 5a Jubilee Road
Parktown 2193, South Africa

The Random House Group Limited Reg. No. 954009

www.randomhouse.co.uk

A CIP catalogue record for this book is available
from the British Library

Papers used by Random House are natural, recyclable products made from
wood grown in sustainable forests. The manufacturing processes conform to
the environmental regulations of the country of origin

Typeset by Palimpsest Book Production Ltd, Polmont, Stirlingshire
Printed and bound in Great Britain by Mackays of Chatham plc

ISBN 0 0918 0033 1

For Chris Brasher – who always believed that
a man's reach should exceed his grasp

Contents

Acknowledgements

This book could never have been written without the enormous contribution of those hundreds of athletes and athletics enthusiasts who shared their miles and memories with me over a lifetime of running.

The club runners of Achilles, the Thames Hare and Hounds and Lauriston have kept me running and writing when I might have slowed to a halt. Particularly, the friendship, help and encouragement of Sir Roger Bannister, Sir Christopher Chataway, Chris Brasher and their families have been inspiring, generous and the mainspring of the book.

My lifelong running companion, Donald Macgregor, Olympic marathon runner and poet, has shared every step of this work, tirelessly setting the pace through every chapter and every post-run drink.

In Australia, John Landy was generous with his time and as courteous as ever. In the United States, Wes Santee was energetically helpful and as competitive as always. In Sweden, the tireless Fred Smedberg was an invaluable link with the great Scandinavian runners of the past, and gave permission to use the picture of Arne Andersson.

Stan Greenberg, one of the world's foremost track statisticians, is the best fact-checker in the business, and Norris McWhirter has a memory that makes the *Guinness Book of Records* seem redundant.

I am indebted to Peter Radford, Olympic sprint medallist and one of sport's finest historians, for his research on the neglected milers of the eighteenth and early nineteenth centuries. My thanks, too, to athletes John and Sylvia Disley, Derek Johnson, Sydney Wooderson, Roger Robinson, Tim

Noakes, Dave Bedford, Nigel Miller, Ronnie Williams, Jan Hildreth, David Thurlow and to two great runners of the past who shared so many stories with me – Arnold Strode-Jackson and Jerry Cornes.

I owe a major debt to many who have written on athletics, and particularly on the mile. I was inspired as a boy by Roger Bannister's own remarkable book, *The First Four Minutes*, originally published in 1955 and now re-issued in a 50th anniversary edition. Few books on running can match its insights, and I am grateful for permission to quote from it.

My own book would have remained a dream without the skill and encouragement of my literary agent Mark Lucas and my editors at Hutchinson, Paul Sidey and Tiffany Stansfield.

Above all, for their unwavering support throughout the time it took to research and write this book, my thanks go to my wife Carol, who was with me every stride of the way, and to my sons Matthew and William, who are still sometimes kind enough not to outrun their father.

Preface

John Bryant, an ardent athlete himself, writes with great verve and has delved into the history of the mile with admirable diligence. This book will fire all those runners fascinated by the past and interested in its arcane lores. The modern reader will perhaps be taken aback by the amateur rules which brought to an abrupt close the careers of many runners like Paavo Nurmi and Wes Santee. The maximum prize for an amateur race at that time was fixed at 12 guineas and we can almost sympathise with Santee's problem of gazing at a collection of 57 watches, the usual prize for helping to fill a stadium with some 20,000 spectators. Today, the successful athlete can earn a very decent living and the very few ultra successful runners can earn millions.

Some nineteenth century training schedules were grotesque, like the diet of undone beef and raw eggs washed down by a tankard of strong malt liquor, with two glasses of port a day to relieve the monotony. This will amuse rather than instruct, but we cannot smile in complacent superiority as many athletes today, with or without drugs, may be making equal mistakes in trying to harness to the full their minds and bodies. The now fashionable sports science courses at universities may throw fresh light on the validity of different modern training regimens.

Many books have been written about the four-minute mile, drawing extensively on my own book, which has just been republished as a 50th anniversary edition, with a wide ranging review of the many changes in sport since then. But John Bryant's book gives an overarching picture of the history of the mile from its very early days. It will be absorbing not only for the dedicated runner, but also for historians and sports journalists, of which John Bryant is such a distinguished archetype.

No sports library should be without this book. Interest will be aroused around the world, from Australia to Scandinavia. Among the burgeoning scientific inquiries into sport, we should do well not to forget the romance that lies behind this enthralling story. I wish *3:59.4: The Quest to Break the Four-Minute Mile* every success.

Sir Roger Bannister

1

A Day in May

Bid me run, and I will strive with things impossible.

Shakespeare, *Julius Caesar*

Thursday 6 May 1954

You wake up half excited, half terrified. Like a man under sentence you have but one thought – the race. And the first thing you always do is go to the window and look out at the weather. Roger Bannister didn't need four minutes for that. A glance at the tree branches stiffening in the wind, the sky cinder-track grey, the rain spitting from the dark clouds made the whole idea preposterous. How could you run decent times on a day like this, let alone records?

For days and nights now he had existed in a state of tortured anticipation. This was far more than just pre-race jitters. He knew the climax was approaching, and the over-brimming tank of nervous energy that gave him the ability to wring everything out of his body and mind was threatening to wreck him.

All through the previous week he'd cut right back on his training, resting up, greedily hoarding energy for the trial to come. Without the running he had more time to think, more time to worry. Every little tickle in the throat, every imagined pain in the neck, half convinced him he was about to fall victim to a cold. He felt alternately ridiculously strong and impossibly weak. However hard he tried, he thought too much about the four-minute mile; and when he wasn't thinking about the mile he was fretting about the weather.

It was hopeless. He'd phone up Chris Brasher to say the attempt was off. Then he'd ring Chataway to say perhaps it's on. To run, or not to run: it was a crazy, impossible question.

After the weather, the legs. The day before, Bannister had slipped on the proudly polished floor of St Mary's Hospital. It was nothing really, but he trembled a little and spent the rest of the day limping, half dreading and half welcoming the idea that he might not be able to run after all.

Time, on the morning of a race, runs out of control. You have too many things to do, but too many hours to kill. You desperately hang on to routine and try to keep up. So it was off to St Mary's to find something, anything, to slow down the mind. Bannister took his running spikes with him to the hospital lab. These were the same black leather spikes that he'd had specially made for him in Manchester. He and a fell-climbing shoemaker had tinkered with the design until they'd pared the weight of each shoe from six to four ounces.

Now Bannister took these shoes to the laboratory grind-stone and methodically honed each spike into needle sharp-ness. A passing colleague smiled indulgently and asked, 'You don't really think that's going to make any difference, do you?' But Bannister knew the rituals he needed. He knew that there might be magic in sharpening the mind along with the spikes. He ached to control everything.

The weather was the first thing they talked about when Bannister bumped into Franz Stampfl on the train at Paddington. Half by chance, half by destiny, both men – the athlete and the coach – had decided to travel up early to Oxford, and to travel alone to focus their every thought on the race ahead.

Though he'd wanted to travel alone, Bannister was pleased and relieved to see Stampfl. The inspirational Austrian coach who had plotted so hard with Chris Brasher and Chris Chataway for this day was just the man to share and perhaps blow away some of his doubts. Behind the scenes Franz had worked tirelessly, using Brasher and Chataway to guide, nudge and shape Bannister's preparation. If ever there was a moment to ask for his help and guidance, this was it. But still Bannister could not ask.

He clung to the belief, arrogantly some felt, that he needed no coach. He had attended Franz's training sessions and run, when it suited him, with Franz's protégés. But he could never admit that Franz was his coach in the accepted sense – adviser perhaps, coach never. Bannister believed he could, and must, do it alone. If he won, the victory was his. If he lost, no one else could be blamed.

But on the train, with the rain flecking the windows, Bannister turned to the artistic, inspirational Austrian. What would be the cost of the wind? One second, half a second a lap? Could the barrier be broken in only the most perfect conditions? Franz knew with certainty that a man could run a mile in under four minutes, and he knew that Roger had the talent and the will to do it.

He argued that Bannister had time in hand, that he was capable of 3 minutes 56 seconds and that the wind could never slow him by more than half a second a lap. The evidence was there, he said, in the training, in the time trials that Bannister had run. It's all in the mind, argued Franz, the mind can overcome almost anything. And what if this is the only chance you get? Others want that record; tomorrow may be too late.

Bannister knew well that of all the factors which make up a runner, mental strength is the most important. If you lose that, you might as well lose a leg. The body is there for the ride; it's the will that does the driving. Scientists can talk of pulse rates, lung capacity and lactic acid, but Franz the artist spoke of resolution. His quiet, shrewd words hit home. Bannister got the message. This could be the only chance: reject it now and you might regret it for the rest of your life.

The crowd that made its way across Magdalen Bridge and up Oxford's Iffley Road to the running track was not large, 1,200 at the most. The match between Oxford University and the Amateur Athletic Association had attracted groups of schoolboys in their blazers and caps along with students, scarfed and duffel-coated against the wind and rain. Sixpence bought you a programme for the match that began in the quietest way with the pole vault at 5 p.m.

In the years to come, many thousands were to claim, or convince themselves, that they were present, too, that evening. 'At the very most there were 1,500,' Chris Brasher used to chuckle, 'and I've met every one of the 20,000 who tell me they were there.'

But among those who had made it to Iffley Road were a dozen sportswriters, a handful of photographers and a BBC television camera crew. The journalists and Paul Fox, from the newly minted *Sportsview*, had been tipped off by the McWhirter twins, Norris and Ross. This remarkable pair, later editors of the *Guinness Book of Records*, were deeply steeped in the lore and statistics of athletics, and from their lair in the Holborn offices of the monthly magazine *Athletics World* they had helped hatch the record attempt, and lured the press along to witness it.

It was the McWhirters who had been responsible for an abortive and controversial attack on the four-minute barrier by Bannister a year before, at Motspur Park. The race had been slipped into a schoolboy meeting. There was no mention of it on the programme, and the pacing and circumstances had been so artificial that the British Athletic Board had refused to ratify the time of 4:02.0. It was not, they said, a bona fide competition according to the rules. And, they added, 'the Board does not regard individual record attempts as in the best interest of athletics as a whole'.

This time, the event and the meeting seemed genuine enough. The pacemakers, Chris Brasher and Chris Chataway, had come along as legitimate competitors who would run the full distance and finish the race. This May evening it was not the pacemakers who were the problem – it was the weather. In the Parks that afternoon, where Oxford University's cricket team was being trounced by Yorkshire and the bowling of Freddie Trueman, the wind was strong enough to have blown over the sightscreen.

At Iffley Road, Bannister seemed to some almost paralysed by dithering doubt. It was as if he was unsure whether he dare unleash his finely tuned body, on a wet and sticky track, against the wind that tugged angrily at the St George's flag on the church tower that overlooked the sports ground. Despite Franz's words to him on the train, he still agonised through his warm-up. The pacemakers were baffled: was it on now, or off? Only Bannister could make that decision, and only Bannister knew how fleeting the chance was.

This dream had been born out of defeat, and Bannister knew that if he went for the record now and missed it he would be branded a failure again. The memory of the 1952 Olympics in Helsinki was still as raw as a freshly pulled muscle.

He had gone there hailed by the newspapers as the favourite, the golden boy, weighed down by the crippling burden of expectation that he would surely bring back a medal to brighten the austere gloom of post-war ration-book Britain.

But the organisers stuck in an extra round, an extra race. This threw him and destroyed his confidence. He ended up only fourth in the 1,500 metres and out of the medals. The headlines were savage, the hurt deep. He dreaded those headlines now.

But this dream could save him. This dream that many considered impossible – the breaking of a barrier erected in front of a set of figures of pleasing symmetry, the running of four laps on a quarter-mile track in a time of four minutes or less. Some believed it was only a mental barrier, others that it physically couldn't be done. It intimidated runners with its very arithmetic – four laps in four unforgiving minutes.

There were those who feared the human body couldn't take it. After all, those two super-fit Swedes, Gunder Haegg and Arne Andersson, had broken or equalled the record six times but had stuck at 4:01.4. The four-minute barrier had withstood assault after assault, from John Landy in Australia, from Wes Santee in the United States, and from Bannister himself.

But to bring the dream alive you had to be the first. Others are lining up to try it, warned the McWhirters. What if this is your only chance? Franz's words rattled round in Bannister's head. The wind came in gusts; he glanced up again at the flag flying on the squat, square tower of St John's Church. It had dropped and was gently slapping the flagpole. He was dreaming again; the record attempt was on.

They lined up in those silent moments of tense uncertainty that every runner knows too well. From the centre of the track, Alan Prentice, the lone TV cameraman, caught them in his lens. They crouched, leaning forward, fists clenched, their arms already bent as if frozen in full stride. You could hear their breathing above the wind now, and Bannister wondered how long the flag would lie low.

Suddenly Brasher broke. Too eager to hit the front and set the pace, he had jumped the gun. For a moment you realised how cosy, how intimately low-key this whole Oxford meeting was. 'Sorry, Chris,' said Ray Barkway, the starter, a fellow Blue, calling Brasher back to the line like a housemaster restraining a fifth-former.

The false start made Bannister a little angry; his precious lull in the wind was not to be wasted. Once more the starter raised his gun. This time the dream mile was on.

> Blink and you miss a sprint. The 10,000 metres is lap after lap of waiting. Theatrically, the mile is just the right length – beginning, middle, end, a story unfolding.
>
> Sebastian Coe

How fast can a man run a mile? No other athletic question has so haunted the sporting imagination. No other single athletic event has ever had such a build-up as the assault on the four-minute-mile barrier, and no other event has received such acclaim. The mile race has always held a special place in the hearts of athletes and spectators in the English-speaking world. There is magic in the single unit of one, in the simple measure of distance rooted deep in Britain's history. In an age of metrication, the mile run is now the only non-metric distance still officially recognised for world records.

For years milers had been striving against the clock, but the elusive four minutes had always beaten them. It had become as much a psychological barrier as a physical one. And like an unconquerable mountain, the closer it was approached, the more daunting it seemed.

In the middle of the nineteenth century the then leading authority on athletics, Sir Montague Shearman, noted, 'The mile is usually considered *the* race of the day.' And it is still the most intriguing and watchable of all track events. It is a favourite with spectators because it is neither a sprint, over in the blur of an eye and too fast for the brain to catch, nor is it a drawn-out drag where the competitors reel off lap after weary lap, waiting for grinding attrition to win the day.

The mile is the classic middle distance – the perfect meeting of speed and stamina. Sir Roger Bannister says that the secret of its appeal lies in the twin and balanced demands made upon the aerobic and anaerobic systems of the athlete.

Anaerobic running is what the dash men do, their legs full of fast-twitch fibres that fire like pistons at the crack of the starting gun. Aerobic runners, by contrast, have the heart and lungs of the long-distance animal, the low pulse rates and lightweight frames that can carry them at a lope beyond the horizon. When these two characters meet you get the drama and excitement of the mile – described by John Landy, the second man to conquer the four-minute barrier, as a perfect drama in four acts. Take your eyes off the mile for a moment and you're liable to lose the plot.

Derek Johnson, a superb middle-distance runner himself, and winner of an Olympic silver at 800 metres, was, as secretary of the Oxford University Athletic Club in 1954, responsible for the preparation of the cinder track on which the mile barrier was broken. He says the mile is 'a distance you can get your head around. It is not too short and it goes on just long enough to suit the attention span of the spectator. With the 5,000 metres you'd be switching off, but the mile is just the right length to get you involved – to catch your emotions.'

In the mile more than any other distance, a knowledge of pace and strategy matters, along with the ability to wring out of the human body every last ounce of energy and the talent to produce, as if from nowhere, that final burst of acceleration and speed.

The mile is the perfect distance, and four minutes the perfect time. Above all, the mile is not an event to be treated lightly. Whenever Roger Bannister was gearing himself up to race the distance, his friends used to say he looked like a man going to the gallows. 'Few understand,' said Bannister, 'the mental agony through which an athlete must pass before he can give his maximum at the mile, or how rarely he can give it.'

The idea that a mile might be run in four minutes had lurked in the minds and legs of athletes since the distance was first contested in the eighteenth century. In races staged between milestones, the landed gentry would back footman against footman for vast purses, and wagers would be made against the watch, with the wise money saying that four minutes would probably never be broken.

In a more regulated world of early cinder tracks and well-wound stopwatches, men measured themselves against the mile and gradually amassed and unlocked the secrets and tactics of training that would, second by second, bring the magic four minutes closer. On occasion a rare athlete, as if inspired, could seem for a moment about to defeat the sweeping hands of the watch and come close to breaking the barrier. The great Walter George, running a ridiculously ragged race of bravado, courage and uneven pace, set the mark as a professional in 1886 at just over 12 seconds short of four minutes, establishing the Mile of the Nineteenth Century. Many believed this was a time that would never be beaten.

But George himself knew better and, soon enough, other giants were showing that it was possible to match it. Arnold Strode-Jackson, Paavo Nurmi, Jack Lovelock, Sydney Wooderson: the names echo around the stadiums and down through the years as the men who threatened the four-minute barrier and left their mark on the mile.

As the times came down there was increasing speculation about which athlete and which great duel might produce four minutes. They dreamed of it with Strode-Jackson before the shrapnel of the Great War tore at his legs. They hoped for it from Paavo Nurmi in the 1920s before age and the laws of amateurism chipped away at his invincibility. They expected it in the '30s from Jack Lovelock – and expected it so achingly that there were rumours he'd already been beyond the barrier in his secret training.

As the legends grew, the size of the barrier also seemed to increase. Then, in the 1940s, the Swedes produced two phenomenal runners, Gunder Haegg and Arne Andersson, who trained with the air of pine woods in their lungs and raced with the loose-limbed fluency of thoroughbreds. In head-to-head battles they made assault after assault on the peak that the four-minute mile had become. They came within strides of the summit, but always it seemed just a few feet out of reach. Every attempt that fell short made the four-minute Everest seem more unconquerable.

For eight long years after the Swedes – a lifetime in athletics, the length of two Olympiads – no runner could match their times. And the summit seemed to recede into the mists of impossibility. Then, in the post-war years after the 1952 Olympic Games, as the warmth of peace returned to the world and the chill of austerity melted, a new generation of runners took to the track and the race for the four-minute mile was back on.

The fascination with the simplicity of four laps in four minutes, the idea that somehow this feat might represent some new benchmark in human achievement, grabbed the imagination of the watching public as few other attempts on an artificial barrier have done before. People were used to the idea of the Poles being reached, mountains being conquered or the sound barrier broken. Yet neither they, nor the experts who chose to pontificate on record-breaking, knew if it was really possible that a man might cover a mile on foot in under four minutes.

If Gunder the Wonder, the great Swedish world record-breaker, had fallen short, who could say for sure that any man could pull it off? Others, though, believed it was a certainty.

By the 1950s, men like John Landy in Australia, Wes Santee in the United States, and Britain's long-legged, coltish thoroughbred Roger Bannister were threatening the barrier with practically every run they did. No longer was this a simple race of man against man on some cinder track in Oxford, Melbourne or Kansas. Using radio, film or ticker-tape, these men and their advisers scanned the world for results. They watched anxiously each time a man with four-minute hopes toed the line in his spikes.

The question of whether the four-minute mile was possible had been asked so often and for so long that the barrier had taken on an almost mythical power. Bannister himself wrote: 'The four-minute mile had become rather like an Everest, a challenge to the human spirit.' If the barrier could be breached, the coaches wondered, what might be the ultimate time possible for the distance?

Of course there must be limits to any human performance. And the answer to the simple question of how fast a man can run a mile must lie somewhere in the undreamed-of future. But on a grey and blustery May evening in 1954 the question was given new meaning by the revolutionary suggestion that maybe there are almost no limits to human endeavour.

The man who challenged the 'impossible' that evening was the 25-year-old medical student, Roger Bannister, who had broken through as a miler while a teenager at Exeter College, Oxford. His preparation and much of his approach to his sport seemed firmly rooted in the classic amateur ethos of the pre-war world into which he was born. There the part-time Olympian, taking a break from his studies or his work to carry off a gold medal, was the ideal hero. But by the time Bannister was athletically weaned, sport was glimpsing a future of full-time athletes, where it would take years of hard unbroken work to get anywhere near an Olympic final, let alone challenge a world record.

Bannister, for all his fine performances, was not of that world. He emerged from the mists of Oxford and academia's dreaming spires, and when his work on the track was done, that was the world to which he returned.

Many experts believed the barrier could be broken only in perfect and exceptional conditions. They predicted the race would have to be run in Scandinavia. The track would be hard, dry clay and rolled cinders. There would be not a breath of wind and the temperature would be an ideal 68 degrees Fahrenheit. A large and enthusiastic crowd would lift the runners psychologically. The pace would be perfect.

But Bannister did it on a wet track on a windy day, before a small crowd in the relative backwater of Oxford. Much of the enduring fascination of his triumph is that this seemingly superhuman effort was apparently achieved with the most amateurish approach. On a grey day at Iffley Road, this self-contained student doctor, a genuine part-timer with his own training methods, made what the more professional athlete Gordon Pirie dismissed as 'a fleeting appearance on the scene' to steal the Crown Jewels of the sport – the four-minute mile.

The barrier that fell that May evening might have been an artificial one, an accidental coming together of time and distance, but it kept Bannister's name as part of folklore for half a century.

Fifty years ago, the quest to be part of that folklore was played out before a global audience. The prize was simple, easy to understand, there for all who dared to run against the clock. But only one man would have the honour of being the first, of standing where no man had stood before, and knowing that however many followed, the four-minute mile would belong to him.

In Australia, John Landy had the four-minute mile thrust upon him by a public and press who willed the young Melbourne student to try and try again to achieve the time they longed for. In America, Wes Santee chose the four-minute mile like Jack Kennedy chose the Moon – as a target to shoot for, so that it could for ever be claimed as a prize belonging to him and the United States.

In England, Roger Bannister thrust the four-minute mile on himself. He was a driven man who pushed himself to the limit in his work as in his sport. He was devoted to both. He and his training companions had forged their friendship and learned their craft as runners while at the two greatest universities in the land. Theirs was a long tradition. Somewhere in their passion for running you might catch the slapping of oars from an Oxford–Cambridge boat race that for a century had irrationally divided Britain into instant supporters of the Dark or Light Blues.

Bannister himself had long let it be known that his real ambition was to be a doctor. He and his fellow runners were not professional athletes. The mile to them was what the mountain is to the climber. They were tackling it because it was there. If the world thought a four-minute barrier existed, why shouldn't they have a go at being the ones to crack it?

It could be fun as well as hard work. And they might get there first. That would be a triumph for Oxford, and for Britain. Perhaps they could even think their way through the barrier – plot, plan and pace their way into folklore.

Afterwards Bannister was to say, 'We had done it where we wanted, when we wanted and how we wanted.'

2

The Four-Minute Gamble

My favourite diet was a glass of beer with some bread and cheese.

Walter George, greatest miler of the nineteenth century

The crowd which kicked and shoved its way towards London's City Road through the dusty heat of the late afternoon of 26 July 1785 was there for just one reason – to watch and enjoy the great mile race. The betting on the result had been the talk of the town for weeks.

Most of the men, women and children were on foot. There were kitchen maids and grooms, tradesmen and tinkers, mingling freely with the quick-moving pickpockets and the elegantly dressed fashionable young followers of sport, known as 'The Fancy'. Many of these forced their way through the crowd in carriages, from where they were guaranteed a seat and a better view of the action.

According to the account in *The London Chronicle*, there were at least 5,000 spectators that day in the City Road. What had brought them out in such numbers was the spectacle of two men running head to head over a mile. It would be a bit of fun, a contest to bet on and talk about, something to liven up a long summer's day.

Yorkshire Joe was the man they fancied. They knew his form. He always ran hard and usually won. You could put your faith and your money on him. Up against Joe was The Welshman – a dark horse, they said, but even The Fancy didn't seem to know too much about him.

The purse was fifty guineas a side, which had the grooms shaking their heads in wonder. You could live for ever on fifty guineas, they reckoned. It was a fortune to a working man. But if the purse was beyond their imagining, the distance was familiar enough. It was one English mile, a concept readily understood when milestones marked every road out of London. They had all walked the dusty miles between the stones. Throughout the land coaching roads were marked by milestones, and pretty accurate they were – the distance from stone to stone was usually measured using agricultural chains.

Side-betting on the City Road mile was heavy, fuelled by those who had heard about Yorkshire Joe's reputation as a runner. The crowd was so dense in places it seemed impossible that a gangway could be cleared wide enough for two men to slip through side by side.

They toed a line scratched in the dust by the milestone. For a moment the thousands hushed and stilled. Then, at the drop of a scarf, the pair thrashed off at a sprint, panting their way through the narrow corridor left by the spectators. A swell of sound followed them as the crowd, screaming and cheering, heaved like a wave trying to keep the runners in sight.

In the mêlée one young boy, scarcely more than a child, was kicked over as dozens surged forward. Before he could scramble to his feet, the wheels of a coach had rolled over him, crushing his body and killing him on the spot. The accident was hardly noticed as the race reached its climax, with the Welshman pulling away to win by twenty yards. In the excitement, nobody bothered to record the time.

But there were plenty of races where the time on the clock

was the *only* thing that mattered. One of these contests has particular interest in the saga of the long quest for the four-minute mile, for it was reported in the pages of the *Sporting Magazine* of November 1796 that a man called Weller had done something quite remarkable.

The Wellers were a family famous for their running, and three of them raced regularly in the Oxford and Woodstock area. They used to boast that the family trio of athletes could take on and beat any other three runners in the land. On 10 October 1796, one of the Wellers undertook a wager to run a measured mile – not against a man, but against the clock.

According to the *Sporting Magazine*, the challenge he threw out was that he could cover the mile in four minutes. The boast attracted wagers and side-bets and the gamblers were naturally wary of dirty tricks. They didn't know if Weller could do it, or indeed whether such a feat could be achieved at all. The distance would have to be re-measured, the watches double-checked. Weller's own purse was set at three guineas. If he could go the distance in the round four minutes or less, he would collect.

When Weller sank to his knees after his flat-out solo effort, the judges who had scrutinised the distance and the watches declared that he had covered his measured mile in two seconds *under* the four minutes. So on this October day in 1796, a century before the first modern Olympic Games, and more than a century and a half before the first authenticated sub-four-minute mile, we have a tantalising glimpse of a man reported to have covered the distance in 3 minutes 58 seconds.

Of course such oddities are easily dismissed by subsequent generations as totally meaningless. These races, they are quick to point out, bear little resemblance to the events of today. Conditions weren't standardised, competitors were professionals, and the scope for cheating and skulduggery was a mile wide. 'Every now and then,' says Sir Roger Bannister with a smile, half a century on from his own four-minute mile, 'I hear from someone who finds an old cutting suggesting that someone ran it in the far-off past. But an authentic four-minute mile does presuppose that man can measure a mile properly and has an accurate watch.'

Clearly Bannister's legacy has nothing to fear from these old-time milers, but while the quest for the magic four minutes did not end in the eighteenth century, that is where it began. For a number of well-documented and recorded performances do make it clear that however bizarre and unstandardised the conditions surrounding the races, the idea that four minutes might be the ultimate breaking point of a man up against a mile had entered the public consciousness as early as 1770. Highly trained 'pedestrians', whose full-time business was running, were to tackle the distance often enough to get a good idea where the limits lay. And by the time of the first manuals offering advice on how the human body should be trained for sport, early in the nineteenth century, the experts were observing that a mile in four minutes has 'perhaps never been done'.

Foot racing is a simple pastime that enjoys a long tradition. But it was in the eighteenth century that men, the mile and the watch first came together, and the guesses became gambles as to how fast the distance might really be run. It was a time when the sporting culture of Britain was increasingly dominated by heavy gambling. It grew from a fashionable pastime – centred around horse-racing and prize-fighting – to an obsessional activity among many of the aristocracy.

Men with vast estates, and fortunes to match, would wager huge sums of money on the outcome of a race or fight. They would trek between town and country houses, their coaches accompanied by footmen whose duties included the carrying of letters and documents, running ahead of the family coach to make arrangements for food, drink or rooms at wayside inns, and racing to alert country-house staff that their guests were soon to follow.

With the gambling culture ablaze, it became almost inevitable that aristocrats began to back their footmen, one against another in races, sometimes with thousands of pounds riding on their speed and stamina. Competition between footmen gradually gave way to the idea of one man racing against the clock over long distances. Men could win huge sums walking or running dozens or even hundreds of miles within a given time. Side-bets were rampant – and so no doubt were the dirty tricks that accompanied them.

But while many performances may have been suspect, some were conducted under the most rigorous of rules and scrutiny. The very act of setting up a wager ensured that checks were put in place to stop gamblers being cheated of their money. Both stakeholders and referees had to be satisfied that the terms of any wager could be met. Times and distances had to be carefully measured and the athlete monitored throughout the performance. Specialist watchmakers provided properly regulated and checked timepieces that had already been in use for decades in horse-racing. It was quite common to set up contests between men on measured coach roads or on race-courses, and many took place between milestones.

The great landmark challenge of the pedestrian era involved covering one thousand miles in one thousand hours, the catch being that you were only allowed to run one mile in any given hour. This meant activity round the clock, twenty-four hours a day, for almost six weeks. Rather like the build-up to the four-minute mile a century and a half later, there was intense speculation as to whether the human body could survive such a test.

When Captain Robert Barclay Allardyce attempted it on Newmarket Heath in 1809, crowds of many thousands flocked to see for themselves whether the barrier could be broken. Barclay did it, losing four stone in the process and becoming an instant national hero. A fortnight later he was off fighting in the Napoleonic Wars, but his performance, and the tough training methods that made it possible, had a profound and lasting influence on the sport of athletics. His training, supervised by a tough old Yorkshire farmer, Jackey Smith, set the standard for decades.

Barclay's regime was certainly not for the faint-hearted or the part-time dabbler in sport. It began with the taking of emetics, to 'purge and cleanse' the body of toxins, which was followed by a prodigious amount of running and walking. Even the athlete's sleep routine was rigidly controlled. Barclay would be woken up at 4 a.m. to be moved from his bed into a hammock for an hour or so. The theory was that rounding off the night's sleep in a hammock loosened the leg and back muscles, ready for the early morning run.

Running started at 6 a.m., and Barclay was expected to exercise beneath a mountain of clothes, to work up a powerful sweat. He wore two pairs of breeches, two waistcoats and an overcoat. The run was followed by a massage, and a half-hour rest in a bed heated by a warming pan filled with red-hot coals, under blankets and a feather quilt. The moisture lost by all this sweating would be replaced by a tankard of strong malt liquor.

The afternoon brought yet more running, and Jackey Smith would make his athlete sprint repeatedly up a grassy hill. The old farmer would throw stones and abuse at him to get the adrenalin flowing. Barclay's diet was predominantly protein – underdone beef, mutton and raw eggs – and to break the monotony a glass of port, morning and evening.

But beyond all the quaint talk of emetics and sweating, the trainers of the professional pedestrians built up an enormous store of expertise and knowledge about physical conditioning. They knew the value of big mileage training and they knew about speedwork. They had to know their business. With fortunes of thousands of pounds wagered on their men, they could not afford to get it wrong.

When it came to betting on mile races, the gamblers as well as the athletes had to know what was a likely time, and from the earliest contests in Britain there were indications that four minutes might be close to the limit. The references to the 'even' four-minute time are too frequent to be ignored.

So the *Sporting Magazine* reports that for a 15-guinea bet on 9 May 1770, James Parrott, a costermonger, ran the length of London's Old Street, from the Charterhouse Wall in Goswell Street to Shoreditch Church gates, a measured mile, in exactly four minutes. Seventeen years later, the stakes on 'a four-minute mile' had risen enormously. In 1787 *Jackson's Oxford Journal* reported that a wager of 1,000 guineas was made that a man called Powell could not run a mile in four minutes, and that in training for it he ran a trial 'entirely naked within 3 seconds of the time'. Whether he ever won his four-minute wager was not recorded.

Such times and distances, of course, may have been hopelessly inaccurate, but the idea that the mile might be run in something around four minutes, by these full-time professional athletes, was evidently part of early pedestrian lore. The first book on running, in 1813, Walter Thom's *Pedestrianism*, half history and half coaching manual, treated all record claims with care. It reported that in 1803 John Todd ran from Hyde Park Corner to the first milestone on the Uxbridge Road – one measured mile – in 4 minutes 10 seconds, and clearly believed the performance was authentic.

The Hyde Park Corner milestone was a famous one and was used by mapmakers to calculate distances for coach travel, but by the 1850s the professional runners were moving off the roads and on to the even more accurately measured running tracks. Again, the driving force behind the move was commercial. Promoters could enclose the tracks and make spectators pay, and soon track running was a full-time business. To keep up interest among the public and make sure the gate money rolled in, the early athletic impresarios also quickly learned how to put on a show.

When an American runner named Louis Bennett turned up to run a series of races in Britain in 1861, the promoters had a great idea: they would make him run in fancy dress. They made sure that when he appeared on the track he did so wearing feathers in his hair (he was part Seneca Indian from New York State). They wrapped him in a wolfskin blanket and put moccasins on his feet. They announced that he spoke no English, that he had done all his running on the hunting field, and that his name was Deerfoot. Despite some very mixed performances, and many charges of race-fixing, the tour was a sell-out success. Deerfoot's backers got their money back many times over.

But time was running out for the promoters, for such stunts and for the old professional pedestrians, however fast they might have covered their miles. The professionals were about to find their performances deliberately written out of history and the record books by the generation of athletes and their chroniclers who followed. For with Victorian self-confidence at its height, there was to emerge a new creed of athletics, dedicated to amateurism, and bringing with it a powerful backlash against the evils of betting and professionalism that had haunted the sport in the past.

The new middle classes, with time and money to spare, were about to clean up and codify sport in Britain, rewrite the rules and teach the world to play their games. They were developing a new philosophy, which saw sport as physically and morally beneficial to its participants, with the emphasis on competing for glory not for gold.

Champions and historians of the new amateur athletics, obsessed with the purity of their ideal, set out to dismiss and ridicule the performances, and the training methods, of their predecessors. They deliberately selected patently absurd examples from the past and trotted them out to demonstrate the superiority of the new 'gentleman amateur' of the Victorian era. But in their zealous enthusiasm for the purity of their new sport, the amateurs, and the new propagandists of their code, airbrushed out of their histories many fine performances of genuine athletic achievement.

One such achievement was an amazing mile run by William Lang, a professional athlete from Middlesbrough. Lang was dismissed by the historians of the new amateur sport with a sneer, particularly, they said, because he was reputed to have run a mile 'in the preposterous time of 4 minutes 02' in 1863. But they deliberately chose to ignore the circumstances of Lang's '4:02 mile'. It was done over a measured point-to-point mile in Newmarket, but it was openly acknowledged that the course was slightly downhill. Since Lang also ran a well-authenticated mile on an established cinder track in 4 minutes 17 seconds in 1865, the downhill 4:02 was far from impossible.

For the new breed of amateur, it was not Long's perform-ance that was the problem; it was his 'professionalism'. The forefathers of the amateur code re-invented their games for a generation of educated but part-time dabblers. They ensured that their athletic clubs were open only to gentlemen by birth and education, and devised new definitions of amateurism that were as much about class prejudice as professionalism.

The new amateur establishment tore up the history of running and invented a new 'year zero' for their sport. A century after Lang, athletics historian Roberto Quercetani wrote that 'probably the most important date in the history of modern athletics is that of March 5 1864, when teams repre-senting two different universities, Oxford and Cambridge, met for the first time in an athletics match. The meeting was held in Christ Church ground, Oxford.' Christ Church cricket meadow is still there today, separated by just a hedge from Oxford's Iffley Road track. The winner of the one mile on that March day in 1864 was Charles B. Lawes, in 4 minutes 56 seconds. Three years earlier he had won his school mile on the playing fields of Eton.

Lawes was the living embodiment of the Corinthian amateur. A magnificent all-round athlete, he was the Cambridge University stroke in the Boat Race of 1865, he won the mile in the first English Amateur Championship in 1866, was winner of the Diamond and Wingfield Sculls, and was a champion cyclist and renowned sculptor.

But while Lawes was being hailed as a champion for breaking five minutes for the mile, William Lang, the profes-sional pedestrian who had once run 4 minutes 2 seconds down-hill, was dead-heating with William Richards running the mile on level ground in 4 minutes 17.

It would take years for the new amateurs to catch up with

what the old professionals knew about the mile. But at least the new breed of university gentlemen amateurs like Lawes were up and running – and the long quest for the four-minute mile was still on.

3

First Glimpses

The man who made the mile record is W. G. George . . . His time was 4 minutes 12¾ seconds and the probability is that this record will never be beaten.

Harry Andrews, athletics coach, 1903

It is always difficult to pin down that moment when someone first looks up at a mountain peak, sees the clouds clear and daydreams of what it would take to stand on the very top.

On the afternoon of 22 October 1883, in the Polo Grounds in New York, a hundred or so hard-core athletics enthusiasts braved a raw and blustery afternoon to watch a bizarre exhibition of running that depended entirely on the interplay of one man, one mile and one stopwatch.

The event was slipped into an athletic match that was being staged to raise money – a retirement payoff – for two long-serving and loyal sports coaches from the American and Manhattan Athletic Clubs: Mr Goulding and Mr Badger, the formality a sign of respect for the wealth of athletic lore that these two old-time trainers carried beneath their ever-present hats and overcoats. These were the men who were always there for the athletes, to rub strange liniments into their legs before races, to hold the watches while they trained, or to wonder with them just how fast a distance might be run.

The crowd that huddled around the home straight and wrestled with their umbrellas in the swirling wind that day was unexpectedly small. There hadn't been much of a build-up in *The New York Clipper* or the other sporting press. But even so, the organisers must have hoped there would be quite a turnout – for appearing on the track that afternoon was the great Lon Myers, universally hailed as the finest runner in all America.

Myers, a deceptively frail athlete, skeletally thin, looked an unlikely sports star. He was born to a Jewish family in Richmond, Virginia, in the days before the great Civil War when Richmond was the capital of the South. As a baby, consumption robbed him of his mother, and the doctors shook their heads at the sickly child and reckoned fresh air and exercise were his only hope of holding off the same fate. So Myers ran. By the time he was coming up to 20, those who knew him well noticed two things: his speed was phenomenal – and his cough was alarming.

But if his lungs were suspect, it was generally allowed that Lon Myers' body was perfect for running. He stood a breath shorter than 5 foot 8 inches in his spiked leather shoes, and looked even lighter than his 112 pounds. When he was stripped for the track, the first things you noticed about him were his legs. They were ridiculously long, so far out of proportion that they seemed to belong to somebody else. One observer described him as having 'practically no body at all above the waist'. A pair of long, strong legs with a tiny light body perched on top of them might have appeared freakish to some, but to those who knew about sport, Lon Myers was simply the perfect running machine.

There were less favourable mutterings about Myers in the British press. The man was not a true amateur, they said. He took appearance money and prizes that he could sell on for cash. In England the Amateur Athletic Association had been born in the Randolph Hotel, Oxford. Its very first words were those laying down the law on amateurism – there was no place for the paid full-timer in this newly codified Victorian sport, and the charge of professionalism was one that was to haunt the world's best milers for decades.

But Lon Myers knew that the promoters of athletics meetings were making fortunes out of his talent, for he could usually guarantee to pull in plenty of gate money whenever he raced. He had an aura about him that caused a frisson of excitement every time he stepped into an arena, for not only could he break records, seemingly at will, but his strange physique and his eccentric appearance meant that once seen he was not easily forgotten.

For one thing, he habitually ran with a knotted white handkerchief covering his dark hair. His drooping moustache gave him a serious, sometimes quite lugubrious look, and made him seem far older than his years. But when he ran he looked young enough, and he moved like no man you had ever seen. He seemed to prance, his tiny body held very upright, while his legs kicked out a long raking stride that devoured distance and seemed to grow longer if he tired. He demolished the American records at every distance from 50 yards to the mile, with the versatility of an uncoached schoolboy who hasn't been told that you don't become a champion that way.

In only his second season as an athlete, in 1878, at the age of 21, Myers had become the first person to run the quarter-mile in less than 50 seconds under well-documented conditions – clocking 49.2 – and two years later, at the US National Amateur Athletic Union championships, he won the 100, 220, 440 and 880 yards. Within seven days he won the same four events in the Canadian national championships. Anyone who could capture eight national titles in a week had to be a crowd-puller.

In those infant days of track and field the athletes and promoters played inventively with men and distances – always seeking to entertain, often seeking to push back the boundaries. The tracks were rough – grass, beaten earth or cinders – but the watches were good. Performances were scrupulously monitored using stopwatches that had been developed to measure fractions of a second for horse-racing. They were accurate, reliable and remained virtually unchanged until the introduction of electronic timing in the 1960s.

Such sophisticated timing devices meant that right from the start there was great interest in how fast a distance might be run – not just simply in who might win a race. Often enough promoters would leap at the chance to stage a race over a novelty distance or to serve up some new challenge that might see new records set and provoke robust betting on the outcome. The bookmakers lurked around the running tracks on both sides of the Atlantic, and Myers was always happy to make a few more dollars by wagering on himself or any other runner of promise.

That cold October afternoon he agreed to give an exhibition of his running ability by running a mile 'off four starts'. This was a peculiar event, dating back to the days of the professionals, in which the athlete ran four separate quarter-miles, with an agreed interval between each one. The times of the four quarters would be added up to give the end result.

The challenge that day for Myers was to beat a feat that had reputedly first been performed by a man named Charles Westhall 40 years earlier – to run four separate quarters of a mile at intervals of 15 minutes, covering each quarter in a minute or less. Already, teased by their stopwatches, the athletes and promoters were toying with the magic of the numbers of the mile. Four straight laps and four simple minutes: that was the challenge. Everyone could understand it, anyone could have a bet on it.

Charles Westhall, known on the tracks of Britain as the 'London Clipper', was the first of a remarkable breed – a medical student and a miler supreme. His career as an athlete covered that twilight period between the decline of the old professional sport of pedestrianism and the rise of the Victorian sport of amateur athletics.

Westhall's range as an athlete was impressive. He had sprinted 150 yards in 15 seconds, but had also walked 25 miles in 3 hours 58 minutes. In 1852 he competed for and won the inaugural One Mile Championship Belt. This was a magnificent trophy, seven feet long, incorporating 43 ounces of sterling silver and valued at £50. The Westhall Feat, the mile off four starts that Myers was about to tackle, had been accomplished by Charles Westhall himself in a total running time of 3 minutes 52 seconds.

For Myers the challenge was ridiculously easy. With the recovery time allowed between the efforts he knew he could do it in any time he wanted. But, as ever, he knew the trick of turning the routine into a special performance, and the speed at which he chose to do each quarter-mile was impressively reckless. Prancing round the track, upright as always and appearing to onlookers as if he was hardly trying, Myers knocked off the quarters in $51^{2}/5$, 55, $52^{3}/5$ and $52^{4}/5$ seconds. Only the hacking little cough at the end of each quarter-mile showed that it had been any strain at all.

The track was sodden and sticky, the weather bitterly cold, the wind raw and his clothing was heavy. But still Myers had cruised through the challenge with energy to spare – looking as if he had scarcely needed the minutes between the efforts to recover. Around the track old athletes and trainers shook their heads in awe at the potential of such a man. What if he could put quarter-miles like that together? they wondered. What if he slowed down a little to cut out the need for the rest period? What if the hands on the stopwatches and the legs on the track just kept moving instead of pulling up to restart again?

The spectators walked away buzzing with the possibilities of it all, for they had just seen Lon Myers run four quarter-miles that added up to 3 minutes 31 seconds for the full distance. On a fine day with a firm track, out of that biting wind and with other runners to pace and race against, was the notion of a non-stop mile in four minutes such an outrageous dream? Could a man like Myers ever do it?

Intriguingly, the time of 3:31 is remarkably close to the 3:30 that Roger Bannister predicts as the ultimate limit for the miler of the future – beyond 3:30 even Bannister sees a barrier.

Lon Myers was certainly the athletic wonder of the age. He could run the 100 yards in 10 seconds, covered the 440 in 48.6, and set an American record for the mile at 4:22.6. He ran more 880-yard races under two minutes and 440-yard races under 50 seconds than all the rest of the amateur and professional athletes of his era put together. But despite his power on the running track, he was never robust. He relied on nervous energy and mental strength to perform at his best, and was frequently sick both before and after his races.

He was slapdash about his training methods, relying on his frequent races to keep him in good shape. He would defy advice by staying up until dawn drinking and gambling. A hand of cards could always keep him away from his bed, and friends used to chuckle over the story of how he had got up from an all-night poker game, taken a hearty breakfast and a stroll to freshen up, and then set off for the track to break yet another world record.

But even Myers had his breaking point – and it was the mile that found him out. The mile, as Myers discovered, is the true measure of a runner. It calls for a unique blend of speed, strength and endurance. If you're a little short on any ingredient, the mile will have no mercy. Lon Myers was a sprinter. They say sprinters are born, not made. He had the speed and he had the courage; what he lacked was the science, the coaching, the knowledge that could give him the condition he needed for the complex demands of the mile.

Back in England, the British had a man who they reckoned was more than a match for Myers. They called him the Wiltshire Wonder. Walter Goodall George, from the West Country town of Calne, was the man who would influence mile racing for the next seventy years, and who fired the starting gun on the race for the four-minute mile that was to end a lifetime later.

He loved to go fast. You could see him sometimes kicking up clouds of dust careering around the lanes outside Devizes on his penny-farthing bicycle. Maybe the heavy contraption strengthened his young legs and conditioned his heart and lungs. He was certainly a fit enough 19-year-old, tall and willowy, when, as a complete novice, he entered a walking race in the Midlands in 1878. He finished in joint first place, unflustered and with a broad smile.

Brimming with confidence and enthusiasm for his newly discovered passion, George joined the local Moseley Harriers. They were a well-established athletics club with a solid Victorian clubhouse in Birmingham's Lower Aston Grounds.

Moseley Harriers boasted some of the best track and cross-country runners in the land. They knew how to run races and how to train for them. Hanging around that clubhouse, soaking in a steaming hipbath or getting a rubdown from the trainer, you could learn all there was to know about running and runners. So they smiled at one another knowingly when, just three months after he had joined their club, young George told them about his dream for the mile.

George had done a few weeks of training, and taken part in that one walking event, but so far he had never even toed the line in a running race. That didn't stop him. Sitting on a bench in the comforting warmth of the clubhouse, he casually informed anyone who would listen that he had drawn up a schedule for the mile to be run in 4 minutes 12 seconds. Some laughed, some snorted, some pretended not to hear.

But the scoffers started to take notice soon enough. George entered a one-mile handicap race in Nottingham. In the early days of track and field athletics many, if not most, of the events were handicaps. It made for exciting finishes and guaranteed that no race was a foregone conclusion. The fastest man, on known form, would start at the back of the field, off 'scratch'; each lesser runner would be given a carefully calculated start, and the race would get underway with runners already strung out around the track. The idea was to produce a perfect blanket finish, and the handicappers prided themselves on their skill and knowledge of runners, their form, and the tricks they might use to get a more favourable handicap.

In his first mile race, like the novice he was, Walter George was given a forty-five-yard start on the scratchman. It was a bad mistake. The handicappers had been made to look stupid and were furious. George won the race easily in 4 minutes 29 seconds, and the result sent the stewards into a huddled inquiry.

It was over an hour after the finish before they begrudgingly declared him the winner and gave him his prize. But it was the first and last time that the handicappers ever allowed him a start. From that day on Walter George was always the man starting from scratch.

For more than five years George was the outstanding amateur athlete in Britain, breaking world records from one mile to 10 miles and setting a world best by covering 11 miles 930 yards in an hour on 28 July 1884. Between 1880 and 1884, in the new series of championship meetings devised by the Amateur Athletic Association, he won no fewer than 10 titles at distances ranging from 880 yards to 10 miles. His fame crossed the Atlantic, and there was an inevitable clamour for the great Englishman to line up against America's Lon Myers to determine who was the greatest runner in the world.

In the autumn of 1882, George and Myers met in three 'test matches' at New York's Polo Grounds. On 4 November Myers won the first contest, coming from behind to outkick George at the end of a half-mile in 1 minute $56^3/5$ seconds. On the 11th the Englishman evened the score, beating Myers over a mile in 4 minutes $21^2/5$ seconds. Finally, on 30 November George won the deciding race over three-quarters of a mile in 3 minutes $10^1/2$ seconds. Huge crowds ranging from 30,000 to 50,000 attended each of the races. The hype surrounding the contests was enormous and the betting was fierce.

At the height of his power, in 1886, George had simply run out of men to beat. He had triumphed over every amateur in Britain and America and the only thing the public wanted settled was whether he could beat the best professional miler in the world – William Cummings from Paisley. Cummings was George's professional counterpart, holding all the professional records at the same distances as the Englishman, and was reputed to have run the mile in 4 minutes 16 seconds. George begged the Amateur Athletic Association for permission to race as an amateur against Cummings. He reckoned that if he promised to give his half of the gate money to the Worcester Infirmary they could hardly refuse him.

When they did, George turned professional. For a man who had just stepped out of the amateur ranks he was in remarkable shape. Although he worked a 12-hour day in a chemist's shop, he devised a system of training whereby he would chalk a line on the floor in the pharmacy and prance on the spot whenever he got the chance, lifting his knees high in what he called 'the hundred-up exercise'. This exercise was still being demonstrated to Oxford University athletes by Steve Ovett's coach, Harry Wilson, a century later.

For the first six years of his running career the 'hundred-up' was George's chief method of training, though by 1882 he was running every morning and afternoon, alternating slow runs of one to two miles with faster stretches of 400 yards to three-quarters of a mile and a series of short sprints. His remarkable endurance was based on miles of cross-country running. He was English cross-country champion three years in a row and trained at varying speeds over hills and open country. When he did manage to get to a track, his training was formidable and consisted of more varied paced running and time trials. In one of these, according to news that leaked from his training camp, he was said to have recorded 4:09 for a solo mile in August 1886 – run in secret on a track in Surbiton. The world record at the time stood at 4:18.4.

But the ambition that George had shared with his clubmates back in the summer of 1878 had never been forgotten. He carried with him a notebook in which was written: 'Timetable for Possible Record, written June 1, 1878. First lap 59 seconds.

Second lap, 2 minutes 2 seconds. Third lap, 3 minutes 8 seconds. Fourth lap, 4 minutes 12 seconds.' It is said that he kept the piece of paper with his plan for the 4:12 mile in his pocket all his long life.

He certainly stuck to his theory – and boldly went for an opening lap of less than a minute every time he raced the mile. For his battles against Cummings, George did a series of formidable time trials over three-quarters of a mile and one and a quarter miles. The track equivalent of a sparring partner was brought in to pace and push him – William Snook, a champion athlete in his own right and a one-time rival of George. As an amateur, Snook had run the mile in 4:20.

The venue for the duels between George and Cummings over the mile was the Lillie Bridge ground, which had been the setting for the second FA Cup final in 1873 and was west London's major stadium before the building of Stamford Bridge. In their first meeting, before 25,000 spectators, George led throughout and won easily by 50 yards in 4:20.2. But in their next two meetings, over four and six miles, Cummings came out as the winner.

The two met again for a showdown in what was billed as 'the Mile of the Century' on Monday 23 August 1886. The crowd, estimated at 30,000, was so dense that according to an eyewitness, 'George was forced to reach his dressing room at the top of the old grandstand by means of a ladder from an adjoining courtyard.'

It was a fiercely fought race, with the first quarter run in 58½ seconds and the half-mile in 2:02. The crowd went wild and invaded the track as George pulled away to win in 4:12¾. Cummings, a beaten man, collapsed with 60 yards to go.

Such was the standard of George's running that the world record set that day was not touched by any runner, amateur or professional, for 29 years. And when it was shaded in 1915 by American's Norman Taber, it was in a specially paced race and then by only a fraction of a second. Walter George's 'Mile of the Century', with its first half at four-minute pace, was so far ahead of its time that many believed it would never be beaten.

4

Jackers and the Oxford Creed

Give me that boy, and I'd have had what I always wanted,
the four-minute mile.

Jack Moakley, US coach, 1913

For a while after Walter George's magnificent mile record at
Lillie Bridge, it seemed that the gap between the old professional pedestrians and the new amateurs was so great that the
quest for the four-minute mile must die.

The new breed of part-timers, the men who regarded their
sport as nothing more than a pleasant pastime, a youthful
interlude of play, had turned their backs on the grinding
training regimes of the professionals. Performances inevitably
slumped, and any man who could better four and a half minutes
for the distance was considered a crack athlete. The Americans
were to chip away at the amateur world record, but no one
could touch the Wiltshire Wonder's time.

At the turn of the century, Britain's Joe Binks was about as
cavalier as they come. His idea of training was to go along to
the track just one evening a week for half an hour or so. 'My
training was always light, I would run half a dozen 6 x 60- to
100-yard bursts of speed and finish with a fast 220 or 300
yards," he said. But on this playground training Joe Binks set
a new British record time of 4:16⁴/₅. In his later life no man

did more than Binks to promote athletics. As a journalist, working for the *News of the World*, he would constantly whip up excitement about the prospect of the four-minute mile.

But while Walter George fired the imagination and set some speculating about even faster miles, there were plenty of experts who thought athletes had already hit a barrier. One such was Harry Andrews, in his day a renowned professional runner and in his later days one of the most respected coaches in the land. He coached the mighty Alfred Shrubb, who held every record from two miles to 10 miles. Eventually banned as a professional, Shrubb wrote a manual on how to race and train – a book that was given to Roger Bannister as a schoolboy by his father.

Shrubb was a legendary and sophisticated trainer. He ran twice a day and tested himself with frequent time trials, usually close to racing pace. Shortly after a record-breaking spree in 1904 he was suspended from the amateur ranks for taking prize money. He continued to run for years as a professional, at one time beating a mixed relay team of men and horses over 10 miles.

For all his hard training, Shrubb was never a great miler, and his coach, Harry Andrews, reckoned that in Walter George the world had seen the greatest miler ever. 'His time', Andrews confidently stated, 'will probably never be beaten.' But there were other, shrewder coaches who believed that Walter George, far from representing the ultimate, had thrown open the door on the four-minute mile itself. The most far-sighted of these was the best respected of American coaches, Jack Moakley.

Moakley became the University of Cornell's first full-time track coach in 1899, and held the position for 50 years. His most famous pupil was John Paul Jones, who held the world mile record of 4:14.4 from 1913 to 1915. So good was Moakley that he earned the nickname 'miracle man' for his coaching skills at Cornell. He became chief track and field coach to the US team and one of the finest athletic pundits in the world. Jack Moakley believed not only that four minutes could be broken, but also that he had seen the man to do it.

The athlete who inspired his confident prediction was Arnold Strode-Jackson, the archetype of the amateur university runner. He was an icon who was to set the pace for generations of Oxbridge milers yet to come, and beat a path for Roger Bannister, Chris Chataway and Chris Brasher to follow.

Even in old age, in the late 1960s, Arnold Nugent Strode-Jackson cut an impressive figure as he haunted the bar of Vincent's, Oxford University's elite sporting club. There he would peel off his Sherlock Holmes-style cloak, order a pewter tankard of beer, and hold court about the glories of Oxford's miling tradition.

When he had first arrived at Oxford over half a century before, in the years leading up to the Great War of 1914, he was just one among a huge pack of privileged, dilettante students. From school at Malvern College he went up to Brasenose College, where he became part of a dazzling group of sportsmen, all ex-public school boys, determined to enjoy themselves in the playground of an Oxford and an England floating through the heyday of Edwardian prosperity.

Strode-Jackson was at once one of the most extraordinary and one of the most privileged athletes ever to line up for the mile. As a schoolboy he had been an outstanding natural athlete, excelling at every sport and game he tackled. Cricket, football, boxing, hockey, golf, rowing, athletics – he tried them all, and at all of them he was a winner.

He played football and hockey for the college, but what he enjoyed most during his first summer as an undergraduate were the cool breezes and lapping water of the river. Every afternoon he would take himself off to the boathouse. At 6 foot 3 inches, and well muscled, he cut a powerful and elegant figure in the Brasenose eight, and every afternoon he would ask his fellow rowers back to his rooms in college. There the college servants would ply the young gentlemen with afternoon tea – on cold days plates of toast and crumpets, on hot days cool drinks and fresh fruit.

His uncle, Clement Jackson, a don at Oxford at 23, and already a mover, fixer and leading committee member of the newly formed governing body of amateur athletics, had been charged by Jackson's family with keeping an eye on the young undergraduate known to everyone as 'Jackers'. Uncle Clemmy did not approve of everything he saw.

To start with, the bills that were being run up for afternoon tea were excessive. The young Strode-Jackson would order up vast quantities of grapes, which went down well with his rowing friends. But Uncle Clemmy soon tired of having to underwrite the cost. Not only that, the shrewd observer of sport, who himself had been a world champion high hurdler in 1865, believed that the young Strode-Jackson was wasting his time and his talent.

Clement Jackson urged his nephew to go to the Iffley Road track to stretch his legs and try his luck at running. And there, with training regimes that even in those far-off days looked casual, Strode-Jackson, with a long, elegant, raking stride, found himself winning mile races for Oxford.

With practically no training, Jackers displayed unbelievable talent. At the Oxford–Cambridge match at the old Queen's Club, on the three-laps-to-the mile track, he romped ahead of the field to win in 4:22. In the royal box, King George V was so impressed that he presented Jackers with a special cup. As he broke the tape that afternoon, Jackers was embraced by his proud uncle, Clemmy, wearing a frock coat and top hat.

About the only training technique that Strode-Jackson had been taught was that he should cultivate long striding, in the belief that the fewer strides taken in a race the less energy would be expended. As a result of his run against Cambridge, he found himself selected for the team for the Olympic Games in Stockholm in 1912. There were nine competitors from Britain taking part in the 1,500 metres, and in those days entrants were expected to pay their own way.

Even so, nearly 4,000 competitors turned up for the 1912 Games, which were described by Baron de Coubertin, founder of the modern Olympics, as 'enchanting'. The stadium, specifically built for the Games, was used for the first time in May of 1912. Its cinder track, jumping pits and throwing circles had all been designed and built by a veteran British groundsman, Charles Perry, and were reckoned to be the finest in the world.

In Stockholm, Jackers teamed up with a Cambridge Blue, Philip Baker (who later changed his name to Noel-Baker), who was also running the metric mile. On their second night the pair decided to dine at the Opera Café and were completely baffled by the Swedish menu. Instead of being served with the simple dish of the day, which they thought they had ordered, they were confronted with two waiters bearing vast silver trays stacked with the largest lobsters they had ever seen. The Englishmen were rescued by a Swedish diner and his wife, who took pity on them, bought them each a steak, and every evening for the rest of the Games drove them out into the cool of the Swedish countryside for dinner at a lakeside restaurant.

Prior to the Games, few seemed to hold out much hope for the prospects of the British runners in the 1,500 metres. A couple of the world's shrewdest coaches, however, took a different view. The Americans Jack Moakley and James E. Sullivan had seen Strode-Jackson running in the preliminary heats and warned the US squad that the tall Englishman was the man to look out for. And Britain's Sam Mussabini, later immortalised in the film *Chariots of Fire* as the trainer of Harold Abrahams, chuckled that the big Oxford Blue was the man to bet on.

Strode-Jackson's preparations for the Olympic final were, even by his standards, eccentric. He had decided to make the most of Stockholm by dining out and party-going as often as possible. He spent four days celebrating the Fourth of July on board the SS *Finland*, which had been set up as a floating American Olympic headquarters. Three days later he reckoned that he should try himself out on a track in preparation for the 1,500-metre heats. A fellow Oxford Blue had set up a flight of hurdles for a time trial over a quarter of a mile. Jackers announced that he would test his own speed by running on the flat alongside the hurdler. The result horrified him. 'The damned fellow was going over the sticks, all I had to do was keep up on the flat,' said Jackers, 'but I could hardly hold him. I decided I was tired, so I just went off to bed and stayed in bed for twenty-four hours.'

Forty-eight hours later he was Olympic champion. His giant loose strides, unleashed in the finishing straight, enabled Strode-Jackson, shepherded and paced by his friend Baker, to outkick the best of the American milers, who had seemingly ganged up against him. The Americans fielded seven of the 14 finalists, and they included the world record holder, Abel Kiviat, the defending Olympic champion, Mel Sheppard, as well as two of the world's top milers, Norman Taber and John Paul Jones.

Despite running as a well-schooled squad and forcing Jackers to run wide much of the way round, the Americans were well beaten. Strode-Jackson, wearing his Oxford blue shorts, a Union Jack on his vest, and his black leather hand-made spikes, went from seventh to first in the home straight, to finish well clear of the Americans running three abreast behind him.

Jack Moakley could only shake his head in admiration. So impressed was he by Jackers' run that as early as 1913, just a year after the Games, he went on record as saying, 'Give me that boy, and I'd have had what I always wanted, the four-minute mile.'

Jack Moakley was part of, and part-founder of, the American college system that produced so many of the USA's finest athletes. His was a structure that nurtured world record breakers and Olympic champions by the score, a world of highly competitive, heavily coached college boys, living on athletic scholarships, training and racing as hard and as frequently as their coaches dared and demanded. So it is intriguing that he picked out Strode-Jackson as the man with the glint of the four-minute mile in his eye. For though Jackers had an abundance of physical potential, with his rangy, well-balanced frame and his renowned long stride, he was from a very different tradition. He raced infrequently, he never took part in the AAA Championships, and he turned up only occasionally for Oxford races. In April 1914 he took part in his last competition, the Penn Relays in the United States, anchoring the Oxford quartet to victory in the 4 x one mile relay.

At the outbreak of war, Strode-Jackson became a brevet major in the regular army, before joining the King's Royal Rifle Corps, where he won four DSOs – a distinction shared by only six other officers throughout the war. While serving on the Western Front he was badly wounded three times and, when demobbed, as an acting brigadier, he was never to run again. His war wounds left him with a lifelong limp.

He served on the British delegation to the Paris Peace Conference and was awarded the CBE. In 1921 he married an American girl, left the army and emigrated to the United States, where he lived in Madison, Connecticut, and ran the family business. He became an American citizen in 1945 but spent his last years in England, where he died in his beloved Oxford in 1972.

Bannister had left Oxford before Strode-Jackson returned in the 1960s, but in his old age, Jackers was fond of swapping drink, and anecdotes about his days as an athlete and a soldier, with the latest crop of Oxford Blues. He would tell how, in the years after the war, when he settled in America, he was made an honorary British consul. This gave him powers to conduct weddings. On one bizarre occasion, aboard a liner heading for New York, the bride, a Roman Catholic, asked him to include a prayer in Latin.

'I was never much good at Latin,' said Jackers, 'and not much good at praying. So I gave 'em the only Latin prayer I knew – the Brasenose College grace, the one I'd heard every evening before dinner in hall at Oxford. So what they got was: For what you are about to receive, may the Lord make you truly thankful.'

Strode-Jackson always claimed that 'the clever men at Harvard' had used their new-fangled computers to calculate that because he had run in the fourth lane for most of the Stockholm race in 1912, he had in fact come very close to the metric equivalent of the long-dreamed-of four-minute mile. But he was very much the Oxford man, totally unlike the hard-gambling Myers or the methodical George. To Jackers, like Roger Bannister half a century on, running was fun, a relaxation, but merely an interlude. There were, he said, far more important things to do in life once the running was over.

On 16 July 1915, Norman Taber, who had finished third in the 1912 Olympic race, made an attack on the world mile record, officially held by fellow American John Paul Jones at 4:14.4. Taber's real aim was to break Walter George's long-standing professional record of 4:12¾, set back in 1886.

The attempt was made in the Harvard stadium, and three men were given handicap starts to help pace him. With their aid Taber just managed to shave George's time, with 4:12.6. 'On the very day Taber made his record in 1915,' said Strode-Jackson later, 'my battalion was relieving the French dismounted cavalry in Picardy. The statisticians of the London *Times* informed us then that the average life of a second lieutenant at the Front was eleven days.'

'What we did in the war, in the trenches,' said Strode-Jackson, 'that was really important. The running, even the Olympics, was just fun.' Pastime it may have been, with little effort devoted to training, but Strode-Jackson – like so many champions – never abandoned his fascination with the mile. 'Are you a miler?' he would ask Oxford students in the 1960s. 'Can you run even pace? How long's your stride? What have you run today? You young lads are running yourselves into a tizzy,' he would chide, rebuking his successors for running too hard, too far and too often. This attitude to training became a central part of the Oxford tradition. Decades later, Chris Chataway would say, 'What we tried to cultivate at Oxford, and at Iffley Road, was the image of effortless superiority.'

The amazing blooming of Arnold Strode-Jackson took place in an environment of an Oxford where athletics, and in partic-ular middle-distance running, had already begun to flourish. As the backlash against the old-time professional pedestrians gave rise to the birth of the new creed of amateurism, it was the young privileged classes of Oxford and Cambridge who took the lead and set the pace.

If Jackers was a legendary icon and role model, he was not alone. The tracks of the universities were churning them out. They almost seemed to specialise in producing athletes who could combine athletic success with a great war record. The Chavasse twins were sprinters. They competed together in the Varsity Sports over 100 yards. Both went on to represent Britain, in the London Olympics of 1908, over 400 metres. Christopher Chavasse later become Bishop of Rochester; his brother Noel was killed while serving as a medical officer in the First World War. He was the only British soldier to be awarded the Victoria Cross twice.

Intriguingly enough, it was Exeter College, the very college whose quadrangles would be graced by Jack Lovelock and Roger Bannister in later years, that nurtured the first stirrings of the Oxford tradition of athletics. There, over drinks one evening in 1850, a bunch of students hatched the novel idea of holding a 'college grind' – a steeplechase without horses. They had endured a particularly bad day riding and were bruised and weary from falling off too often. They drew up the rules while the beer and wine went down, and advertised their event as if it were a horse race. The runners turned up dressed as jockeys.

As well as the steeplechase across two miles of country, they agreed a contest or two on the flat. With races over 100 yards, a quarter of a mile, 140 yards hurdles and one mile, the similarities between these first sports and a modern-day programme of events are quite apparent. Their success led to the standardising of many of the athletic events that nowadays are practised around the world.

The flat races were held on Oxford's Port Meadow on unlev-elled turf. One student, Halifax Wyatt, whose fall from a horse had prompted the idea of a steeplechase on foot, had already won the 100 yards. So when he lined up for the mile he had to carry several pounds of lead shot in an old-fashioned shot-belt around his waist. Thus handicapped, he was beaten into second place.

It was not long before Cambridge was throwing out a chal-lenge to Oxford for an athletics match modelled on the pattern of the Boat Race, which had been taking place regularly since 1839. The Boat Race had given birth to the first inter-university competitions that were to play such a leading role in the devel-opment of athletics in Britain. The first Inter-Varsity Sports were held on the Christ Church Ground, Oxford, on Saturday 5 March 1864, and already the mile was a centrepiece. The *Times* considered this inaugural match as worthy of a leading article, commenting that 'the development of athletics at the universities would do much to counteract the evil effects of rowing on the physique of undergraduates'.

The year 1880 saw Oxford University Athletic Club involved in the inauguration of the Amateur Athletic Association. The members of the club who were prime movers in this venture included Strode-Jackson's uncle Clement Jackson, a tutor at Hertford College. Clemmy Jackson had been a formidable sportsman in his own right, as 110-metre hurdle champion of the world in 1865. His career had ended in a race against W. G. Grace, the great cricketer. W. G. was not always the rotund figure who lives on in popular imagination: as a young man he was a fine athlete and a champion quarter-mile hurdler. When Clemmy Jackson tried to match strides with him he injured his foot badly, cutting it on an oyster shell that was buried in the rough cinder track.

On 24 April 1880, Jackson, together with Bernhard Wise, 21, a scholar at Queen's and President of OUAC, and Montague Shearman, 22, a graduate of St John's, booked the banqueting hall of the Randolph Hotel in Oxford and invited delegates from athletic clubs all over England to dine with them. Over dinner, the Amateur Athletic Association was born.

Clemmy Jackson and his young Oxford team helped formulate the very rules of amateurism which were so often invoked when it seemed the four-minute mile might fall to men who ran on the fringes of professionalism. Clemmy Jackson too guided and nurtured, in the figure of his own nephew, the man who set the pace and pattern for generations of light-training but wonderfully confident milers, who seemed to share the belief that the mile belonged in some mysterious way to them, and to Oxford.

Whenever he feared the British might lose their domination of the mile, old Arnold Strode-Jackson was there with a warning. Writing in the *Times* in 1919, in the run-up to the Antwerp Games, he said, 'So far as next year's Olympic Games are concerned America seems to have beaten us already. A fortnight ago, at the annual meeting of the Senior National Amateur Union Championships at Philadelphia, Joie Ray won the mile in the championship record time of 4 minutes 14.4 seconds. As for ourselves, while in less than a year the Antwerp Games will be all over, we have not yet heard a word as to what our plans are.'

Yet Strode-Jackson himself had won gold at the previous Olympics with a complete lack of planning. He muddled through to victory, embodying an approach to his sport and his life that many later compared to that of Roger Bannister. Jackers trained lightly, raced infrequently and had great self-belief. He considered his subsequent career and achievements far more important than anything he did on the track. He was exciting to watch with that 'long raking stride' and he pioneered the powerful finishing burst 300 yards from the tape that was to become the trademark of so many great Oxford milers.

Years later, in 1944, as another great war was raging, Strode-Jackson wrote a penetrating prediction of what would subsequently happen to the mile record. 'The four minute mile will be run,' he said, 'probably by someone alive today.' And, he added ten years later, with all the unchallenged hindsight of an ageing Olympic champion, 'I always believed it would be done by an Englishman.'

5

The Golden Thread

In our business, son, we have a saying: You can't put in
what God left out.

Sam Mussabini in *Chariots of Fire*

Arnold Strode-Jackson may have been right that the Americans
had the money, the organisation and milers like Joie Ray who
could run close to the world record. But they reckoned without
Britain's secret weapon – a coach who was decades ahead of
his time in understanding men and methods.

Scipio (Sam) Africanus Mussabini was born in London in
1867. His ancestry was a mixture of Arab, Turk, Italian and
French. Initially he followed his father into journalism; then,
in the 1890s, he took up professional sprinting. Standing no
more than 5 foot 8 inches tall, he was strong and aggressive.

Mussabini was always a keen observer of human movement.
In his early days he was particularly inspired by Harry
Hutchens, the professional sprinter, whom he described as 'the
fastest thing ever to operate on two feet', and the great Walter
George, the miler who had set the record at 4:12¾ back in
1886. Mussabini is unique in Olympic history as the only coach
to have trained the winners of both the 100 metres and the
1,500 metres.

In the early 1890s in Britain professional cycling was all the rage. The winner of the National Cycling Union's first professional championship was Bert Harris of the Polytechnic Cycling Club, and he was trained by Sam Mussabini. By 1896 Sam was employed professionally by Dunlop to take charge of their cycling squad.

He took an equally keen interest in athletics in the run-up to the Olympic Games in London in 1908. As a former professional sprinter himself, he went to work on the South African sprinter Reggie Walker. He improved Walker's starting technique so effectively that he was the winner of the Olympic 100 metres in the 1908 Games. Mussabini had been associated with the Polytechnic Club since he had worked with cyclists in 1894, and by the time of the next Olympics, in 1912, he had been appointed official coach to the Polytechnic Harriers, a job which he stayed in until 1927.

Mussabini was nothing if not innovative. He saw the potential of moving film in the coaching of sport and seized on the latest craze for cinematography. By the early 1920s he had bought his own tripod and camera and was busy shooting film of athletes in action. He used his home-made movie sequences to improve the start, the dip finish and the stride pattern of his athletes. He insisted he should be called a 'coach' and not a 'trainer'. He saw the 'trainer' as being little more than a towel-holding masseur, a rubber of legs, not a sophisticated technical adviser like himself who understood the finer points of the sport.

In the film *Chariots of Fire*, Sam agreed to coach the Cambridge University athlete Harold Abrahams, after watching him suffer a humiliating defeat by his great domestic rival, the Scot Eric Liddell. 'I can find you two yards, Mr Abrahams,' he promised. And he did.

Mussabini was obsessive about making improvements to a

sprinter's technique, and spent hours working with Abrahams. He used to make him run holding corks in his hands, which he said provided a more powerful arm action. Hours, too, were spent shortening his stride and perfecting what Mussabini labelled the 'drop' finish. 'We paid infinite attention to my length of stride,' Harold Abrahams later wrote. 'I shall always believe that the vital factor in my running in Paris was that by conscientious training I had managed to shorten my stride an inch or two.'

No aspect of running escaped Mussabini's analytical eye and he turned easily from coaching world-beating sprinters to producing champion milers. 'Good running means easy running,' he said, and 'Ease stands for action and speed. There is no surer way of putting the brake on yourself and retarding progress than by straining and struggling with every nerve and muscle at full stretch.'

'A very great proportion of failures are due to trying to do too much,' he warned. 'Most try to run faster than their own particular speed limit allows. The result is far too often that they do not get the best out of themselves. The sprinter, for instance, in a frantic effort to get every ounce, and often a few ounces more out of himself, goes all to pieces and is no faster over 100 yards when racing all out, than at three-quarter speed in a training spin.'

'The miler must learn his speed limit per lap just as the ten miler and marathon men do. Briefly,' Mussabini declared, 'the better the running style, the less energy expended.'

'Absolutely the most smooth and effective movement I have ever seen for covering long-distance, up hill, down hill, on the King's highway or across the fields,' he also noted, 'was carried out many a long year ago by a company of the famous French troops know as the Chasseurs des Alpes. Carrying enormous packs on their backs, stacked up to a point a foot or so above the tops of their heads, wearing their military overcoats looped open in front to allow freedom of knee action, they travelled along at a standard gait of nine miles per hour.

'Their way of covering the ground was a cross between a run and a walk, with the smallest perceptible amount of foot lift, the knees being always kept more or less bent. Their bodies were carried in a loose, half-squatting position with their head and chin dropped noticeably forward. The effect of this loose-limbed, though heavily laden company has never faded from my memory.'

Mussabini was to start a relay of coaching lore that led to the very brink of the fabled four-minute mile. He found the perfect pupil on whom to try out his theories of middle-distance running in Albert Hill.

Hill was not one of the gilded university boys schooled in the belief of effortless superiority. He was born into working-class south London and was employed for much of his life on the railways. 'Sam used to appreciate the efforts I was making,' he recalled later. 'I would have to rush from my job as a railway guard to get to the track – and often Sam gave up his time freely.' Sport was in Albert Hill's bones: his father had been a keen rower, and young Albert began competing at the age of 15 as a cyclist and a swimmer.

When he ran in a local half-mile handicap race, his second place whetted his appetite for more. Soon he was winning junior cross-country events and enjoying success as a distance runner on the track – winning the AAA four-mile champion-ship in 1910. In 1913 he made a great leap forward by joining the country's leading athletic club, the Polytechnic Harriers, where Sam Mussabini was well installed as professional coach.

The Olympic Games scheduled for 1916 in Berlin were abandoned in the smoke of the Great War, and Albert Hill spent most of the next four years as a soldier, serving as a wireless operator in France. When he was finally demobbed in the spring of 1919, he presented himself to his old coach back at the Polytechnic Harriers track and, at the age of thirty, threw himself back into training.

Mussabini was delighted by Hill's form, and particularly by the speed he showed as he returned to fitness. He was staging a magnificent comeback. Mussabini had him working to a strict schedule night after night on the Herne Hill track, where he made him lap endlessly until Hill could guess accurately, to within half a second, the precise pace he had run for any single circuit.

'A sound steady time schedule, that's the secret,' Sam would repeat. 'You have to run as evenly as a mechanical engine. Run in comfort and you can do 62 seconds a lap all the way. Run close to the inside edge of the track, carry your arms loose and low, keep your fingers closed around the corks in your hands' – no detail was too small for the great Mussabini.

With his slow-motion cine camera, his stopwatch and his analytical brain, he realised that record-breaking was still in its infancy. 'But the mile', he said, 'is undoubtedly the hardest race of any, where first-class and well-matched runners are concerned.'

By the run-up to the 1920 Olympic Games in Antwerp, Albert Hill and Sam had their eyes on not just one event, but two. The selectors were dubious, but Hill and his coach argued strongly that he should be allowed to attempt both the 800 and the 1,500 metres. The result was a sensational double. Hill finished first, seemingly completely fresh, in the Olympic 800 metres in 1:53.4. Two days later he was ready for the metric mile, in pouring rain on a churned-up and waterlogged track.

Joie Ray from the USA led the charge to the first bend, but then Philip Noel-Baker, who had helped Strode-Jackson eight years before in Stockholm, hit the front and set the pace for Hill, who won quite easily in 4:01.8.

Once again Jack Moakley, the chief coach of the US team, had seen his finest milers defeated by an Englishman. And once again he was generous in his tribute. 'I regard Albert Hill as the wonder man of the meeting,' he declared. 'He is in his thirties yet he scalped young American athletes in two events. I backed him and I am glad I did so. He is a grand chap.'

Hill's lack of pre-race nerves, a quality carefully developed by Sam Mussabini, was the envy of his rivals and their coaches. Before a race, while others would agonise over imaginary aches and pains and waste valuable nervous energy, Hill would take an early lunch and calmly sleep for two or three hours.

Back home from his double Olympic gold medal triumph, Albert Hill sat down with Sam Mussabini and old Walter George, the great nineteenth-century mile champion, to plan an assault on the mile record at the AAA championships of 1921. The British amateur record was still held by the happy-go-lucky Joe Binks at 4:16 $^4/_5$. Mussabini believed his level pace schedule would bring Hill home in 4:08, which would be well inside the existing world record.

The problem with level pace, as Hill and Mussabini were to discover, is that in a highly competitive race other runners are not there to help your master plan. In a ridiculously large championship field, where 44 runners had been allowed to enter, Hill was stampeded into covering the first lap at below four-minute-miling pace. He paid dearly for going off too fast, but a furlong from home he was out on his own and still looked certain to beat the old record.

Up in the stands sat old Joe Binks, and the crowd, sensing that his mile record was surely doomed, broke into a spontaneous parody of a popular Negro spiritual:

> *It's going, it's going,*
> *His head is falling low,*
> *I hear those unkind voices calling,*
> *Poor old Joe.*

Albert Hill had failed to stick to Sam Mussabini's even pace schedule and get the world record he had hoped for. Nonetheless, he had still knocked three seconds off the British record, clocking 4:13.8.

Mussabini, though, knew that the mile record was nowhere near its limit. Running to an even pace schedule, he used to say, that was what would bring the time down. And as later runners ran fast times, but still with ragged, uneven laps, old Sam would shake his head sadly and say, 'If only he'd stuck to one of my even pace schedules, we might have had the four-minute mile.'

When it came to records, no one took more delight in seeing them tumble than Joe Binks. For years he was to urge British athletes to stage attempts to crack the four-minute mile, and at the Antwerp Olympics he approached Albert Hill with a lucrative offer to attack the world three-quarter-mile record. There would be generous expenses and tempting prize money on offer, said Binks.

But Albert Hill, ever the true amateur, turned it down, choosing instead to run for nothing in the London and North Western Railway AC 28th Annual Sports. The annual works sports were part of a long-vanished world of athletics, a world of handicap racing, where the only rewards were cups and medals, clocks and cigarette cases.

At the Silvertown Rubber Works Sports, held at Canning Town on 23 May 1914, in the early summer of the year of the war to end all wars, the list of prizes reads like the inventory from a pawnbroker's shop. A champion could take his pick from a 14-day French mahogany clock, Morocco and silver cigarette cases, Gladstone bags, gold cufflinks and studs, Wedgwood bowls and servers, silver watches and endless canteens of cutlery.

The race programmes of the time tell of an era when sport was pure play. Among the track and field events were skipping races, tug-of-wars and veterans' events. In one 100-yard handicap race an 83-year-old walked home in third place. This was a world where sport was genuine recreation – far away from the serious business of work and war.

With both war and Olympic victories behind him, Albert Hill quit the track in 1921 and turned to coaching. He worked first with runners at Blackheath Harriers, but when Sam Mussabini died in 1927 Hill was offered his old coach's job at Polytechnic Harriers. He immediately took over the coaching of one of Mussabini's sprinters, Jack London, and helped him win a silver medal in the Olympic Games of 1928.

Just over a decade later Hill took on the coaching of Sydney Wooderson. Using the methods that he had learned from Sam Mussabini, he guided Wooderson to world records in the 880 yards and the mile. Working with Hill, Wooderson was to dream of breaking the four-minute barrier. He was to set others dreaming too.

As a schoolboy at Rugby, Chris Brasher saw the puny-looking Wooderson run and win, and vowed, 'If he can do it, anyone can.' And at the age of 16, another schoolboy was taken by his father to watch Sydney Wooderson battle it out with one of Sweden's world-record-breaking milers. That boy, inspired by what he saw that day, was Roger Bannister.

6

The Phantom Finn

Mind is everything: muscle – pieces of rubber. All that I am,
I am because of my mind.

Paavo Nurmi

At the end of his days, with all his races won, you could catch
the great man easily. He shuffled through the streets of Helsinki
on a stick, half blind, more than half bitter, they said, racked
by rheumatism, tamed by heart attacks. But when he was in
his power they hailed him as immortal, peerless Paavo, the
Phantom Finn.

If world records and Olympic medals are the criteria for
measuring athletic greatness, one man knows no master – Paavo
Johannes Nurmi. During a track career that lasted from 1913
to 1934, he won nine Olympic gold medals and set so many
world records that statisticians still argue over the number
(there were 28 in one ten-year period).

In an era before television Nurmi became not just an unbeatable champion but a star who ranked alongside Hollywood's
finest. His legend was known to millions. In sophisticated pre-
war Berlin there was a fashion among jokers to call their pet
tortoises 'Nurmi'. Chris Brasher, who was to pace Bannister
in the first four-minute mile, named one of his racehorses
'Dream of Nurmi' in homage to the master.

Nurmi's claim to be the greatest rests not only on his track record but also upon the effect he had on the world of athletics. He marks the watershed that divided the nineteenth century from modern athletics. He was born in 1897, just one year after the revival of the modern Olympics. Before him attitudes to training and competition were very different. After him nothing could be the same.

Paavo was born into a family that was poor and knew about hard work. His father, a carpenter, was always physically frail, and friends of the Nurmis said he worked himself to an early death at 50. His mother lived to 80. Nurmi's brother and two sisters never raced a step. But Paavo's approach, even as a child, was a good 50 years ahead of his time. Somewhere in his half-lost childhood he became at first inspired, and then obsessed, with the feats of his countryman Hannes Kolehmainen. Hannes was the first of a long line of legendary Finnish running masters. He won three Olympic gold medals in 1912.

The Finnish love affair with running began with small pockets of young people inspired by reports of the infant Olympics. One family in particular became infatuated with the idea of running the new-fangled marathon distance – an event that had been dreamed up by a French aristocratic friend of Baron de Coubertin and which had sparked something of a distance craze in both Europe and the United States.

In August 1906 Finland staged its first marathon, in Helsinki. The winner went on to finish eleventh in the London Olympic marathon of 1908. The Kolehmainen family liked the sound of the event and, in an age and a land where training knowledge was in short supply, they went for it head on, using their own hit and miss methods. Young Hannes Kolehmainen, for instance, started competing in marathons with abandon. He ran two when only 17 in 1907, a third in 1908, and five more in 1909. It was an incredibly heavy workload for the period, but the family were used to working hard and playing hard. Hannes and his brothers, Wiljami, Tatu and Kalle, were already fit from covering enormous distances on cross-country skis. This winter exercise was one of Finland's secret weapons – the long ski journeys strengthened both their legs and their heart–lung systems, providing an ideal background for distance running.

By 1912 Hannes Kolehmainen was ready to make a mark in the Stockholm Olympic Games and to plug into the growing awareness of Finnish nationalism. Finland was still a state within the great Russian empire, but the Finns ached for their freedom, and anything that could get the national flag waved and put their country on the map was greeted with excitement.

In Stockholm Hannes began by winning the 10,000 metres with a front-running performance that burned off all challengers. He romped away with a world record in the 3,000 metres team race, and he won by inches from France's Jean Bouin in the 5,000 metres, in what was reckoned to be the greatest race of the Games. His time of 14:36.6 was nearly half a minute faster than anyone had run before.

When Kolehmainen saw the Russian flag hoisted to honour his victory, he turned to a British competitor, Philip Baker, and said, 'I would almost rather not have won than see that flag up there.' But the national rejoicing in Finland set alight a tradition that made Finnish distance runners unbeatable in the years between the two world wars. As every detail of the race was reported back in Helsinki and Turku, hundreds of Finnish schoolboys began running in the forests and along the rough roads of Finland, dreaming of emulating their hero.

Hannes was certainly an inspiration to the young Paavo

Nurmi. Paavo had been fascinated by sport, particularly running, even before the Stockholm Games. As early as 1908 he would hang around the track in Turku, and it was said he begged one athlete, Fabian Liesinen, to time him over 1,500 metres. Liesinen told Paavo he had run 5 minutes 2 seconds – a sensationally fast time for an eleven-year-old, but not fast enough for young Nurmi. This strange, single-minded child, with the patience that would eventually make him a saint to the runners who followed, vowed to undertake a long-term training programme that called for three or four sessions of easy running each week for five years.

Nurmi was ever the innovator. He must surely have been the first to use a mechanical pacemaker when he ran beside the trams of Turku for speed work. At 13, with his father dead, he became the family breadwinner, an errand boy for a local wholesale dealer, spending hours pushing a heavy cart uphill to Turku railway station. He loved the effort, happy that the hill work would give him great leg strength. He was decades ahead of his contemporaries, too, in becoming obsessed with details of fitness. For a while, it was said, he became vegetarian. He neither smoked nor drank and would not touch coffee or tea.

The Olympic Games of 1916, scheduled for Berlin, had been suspended because of war, but Nurmi, with a fixed sense of his own destiny, stuck to his master plan, training much and racing little. By the time he began his military service in 1919 legends were already growing around his name. It was said he had route-marched almost ten miles, carrying a rifle and full pack, in less than an hour. By the spring of 1920 he was running at near world record pace for 3,000 metres and was sent off to the Antwerp Olympics with Finland's team aboard the steamship *Oihonna*.

Paavo was violently seasick for five days and had hardly recovered when he came up against the new French hope for the 5,000 metres, Joseph Guillemot. Nurmi chose to lead, but the Frenchman shadowed him every inch of the way. Guillemot was a strange and unlikely athlete. Only 20 years old, he smoked heavily and was just 5 foot 3 inches tall. Bizarrely, his heart was on the wrong side of his chest, and he had almost died in the war from gas poisoning, lying unconscious for several days. Somehow he had recovered sufficiently to become a top-class runner, and as the front-running Nurmi began to tire, Guillemot passed him and took revenge for France's defeat in Stockholm. The Frenchman turned to greet the vanquished Finn – only to vomit all over Nurmi's shoes as he finished.

Three days later, in the 10,000 metres, Nurmi got his revenge. He had concluded that faulty pace judgement had cost him the 5,000 metres. It was a mistake he would never make again. He always thought his way through such problems, and to solve this one he took to carrying a stopwatch in his hand. It became his trademark, always there, whether he was training or racing. He would peer into his palm, as if for inspiration, so that many believed it was not a watch at all, but a silver medallion with a picture of his mother.

By the time of the 1924 Olympics, Nurmi was so dominant that the organisers scheduled the 1,500 metres and the 5,000 metres within 75 minutes of each other, in an attempt, it was said, to stop him running both. It made no difference. He won both easily anyway, with a light massage and a snooze in between. The next day, in a heatwave, he added the 10,000 metre cross-country gold. Of 39 starters, only 15 finished, and 18 ended up in hospital.

As if training three times a day, incorporating interval speed work and monitoring every step with a stopwatch, were not enough to establish Nurmi as the first modern athlete, he also pioneered the athletics tour, with a schedule as tough as any found on the Grand Prix circuit today. In 1925, in the United States, he raced 55 times in five months, winning 53 and losing just one (at 880 yards). When he dropped out of one race with stomach trouble, rumours swept Finland that the great Nurmi must have died.

As he dedicated himself totally to his sport, Nurmi became the most famous Finn in history. He became a star among Hollywood stars. Valentino, Garbo, Chaplin: they all wanted to be photographed with the wonder of the world's tracks. More was written about him than about any other athlete, but at the same time he became austere and withdrawn. People said that he was grim, that he never smiled, that he was cold and unapproachable.

Nurmi's training increased. Races were won. The legend grew. He was the silent, dour, secretive, Garbo-like enigma. Just occasionally a fellow athlete might, for a moment, break through the protective shell. One such was Otto Peltzer – known as Otto the Strange, and one of the few men to defeat Nurmi and rob him of a world record.

A great admirer and follower of Nurmi, Peltzer, like most athletes of the period, picked over reports of Nurmi's training, in search of any secret that might be useful. A tortured bohemian character, Peltzer had a doctorate in social anthropology, and was Germany's top middle-distance runner of the 1920s. In 1926 he was invited to England to compete in the British AAA championships against Douglas Lowe, the 1924 800-metre Olympic champion. Peltzer's winning time of 1:51.6 snipped 0.3 seconds off the world record.

Always a globetrotter, Peltzer travelled in 1929 to China, where he met Eric Liddell, the 400-metre gold medallist at the

1924 Olympics and hero of the film *Chariots of Fire*. Liddell was working as a missionary, and in November 1929 the two men raced over 400 metres in Tientsin. Liddell came home in front in 49.1 seconds.

Sadly for Peltzer, life became impossible when the Nazis came to power in Germany in 1933. A fierce critic of their policies, he was charged with having broken their laws on homosexuality, and in 1941 was arrested and spent the next four years in a concentration camp.

In the autumn of 1925, Otto Peltzer had travelled to Helsinki to meet his hero, Paavo Nurmi. The two athletes had arranged to meet in a restaurant near Helsinki Zoo, where there was a sports arena. When Peltzer arrived he was somewhat surprised to find Nurmi, who was supposed to be a vegetarian and who never touched stimulants, seated at a table consuming a huge ham sandwich and a large cup of coffee. 'Is that ground coffee?' asked Peltzer. 'Yes, of course,' said Nurmi. 'I only drink ground coffee. If I haven't had proper coffee I am much too lazy when I train.'

'So it's not true when they say you reject all stimulants?' said Peltzer. 'And I can see you are not a vegetarian.'

'You know these vegetarians are great idealists,' replied Nurmi. 'When they came and asked me to write how useful vegetarian food was for the sportsman I did them a favour. To tell the truth, I've always liked meat. Perhaps meat makes you a bit temperamental and high-spirited, but anyway I eat it.'

Peltzer went on to learn that Nurmi ran every race strictly to the stopwatch to make sure he did not shoot off too fast at the start. Nurmi revealed, too, that he would never begin his training without having had a massage to shake his muscles loose. The two athletes trained for a while together, Nurmi clad in an undervest and long johns with a pair of black shorts

over the top and a thin pullover over his vest. He ran in black
leather spikes with thick white laces and took no notice of the
pace Peltzer set in training, preferring always to check his own
with the stopwatch that never left his hand.

As soon as the training session was over, Nurmi would drive
away from the track without so much as a goodbye. 'What
made him so popular', said Peltzer, 'is not that he so often
defeated his opponents. It was more the magic of his personality. Silently he entered the stadium, silently he ran his laps
and silently, almost shyly, he returned to his changing room.

'He has often been called the "magician of the track" and
there really was something mysterious about his appearances.
His face never betrayed a grimace during a race; in his impen-
etrability Nurmi was a Buddha gliding between the white chalk
markings on the track. Stopwatch in hand, lap after lap, he
ran towards the tape, clearly subject only to the laws of a
mathematical table.'

The following year the two athletes met again, but this time
in competition. Peltzer's 800-metre world record had made
him a national hero, and a special challenge race was set up
three months afterwards in Berlin. Four runners were invited
to race over 1,500 metres: Peltzer, Nurmi, Edvin Wide of
Sweden and Herbert Bocher of Germany.

Nurmi's reputation at this time was at its peak. The stadium
was sold out. The seemingly invincible Finn led all the way
until 1,200 metres. Suddenly Wide hit the front and held the
lead until the finishing straight, when Peltzer launched a fierce
drive which took him past Nurmi and Wide in the last few
strides of the race. His winning time of 3:51 lopped 1.6 seconds
off Nurmi's world record and the crowd went wild. It was the
biggest moment of Peltzer's career, while Nurmi, for the first
time in his running life, had finished third.

It was a rare defeat for Paavo, racing at a distance well below his best, but any defeat came as a shock to a man who had been on a world-record-breaking spree for more than a decade. In his tireless quest for running perfection Nurmi had uncovered every detail he could find about the methods of the great Walter George and the former British amateur mile record holder Joe Binks. In the 5,000 and 10,000 metres Nurmi was the undisputed champion of the world, but what, many wondered, might he do, stopwatch in hand, to the mile?

What he did was to bring some of his mastery of even-paced running to the distance, and set coaches buzzing at the prospect of a mile in an even-paced four minutes. Nurmi flirted with the mile rarely, but when he did, this long-distance lover broke the hearts of those wedded to the middle distances. The best of them, in 1923, was Edvin Wide, the Finnish-born Swede. Out of love, or some said fear, of his homeland's athletes, Wide always refused to run against Finland in international matches between the Scandinavian countries. But he *was* talked into challenging the greatest of them all, Paavo Nurmi, to a duel – that rarest of contests in track and field, a head-to-head two-man race. Nurmi, said Wide, could choose his distance. The easy way, Paavo knew, was to opt for 5,000 metres. That was his forte, that was where victory was to be found. But what, he wondered, if he took on Wide where *he* was strongest – in the classic English distance, the mile?

Nurmi had in his sights the mile record of 4:12.6 held by Norman Taber of the United States since 1915. He was convinced he could cruise 62 seconds a lap all the way without too much difficulty, to run 4:08.

As ever, his preparations were meticulous. The track in Stockholm, the venue for the head-to-head duel, was 385 metres around. So weeks before the race Paavo marked out a

385-metre track of his own back in Finland, where he ran day in and day out, rehearsing for the battle with Wide.

The race was on home territory for the Swede, who was greeted with a roar from the 18,000 crowd. The first quarter-mile was fast. At 60.1 it was four-minute pace with Wide in the lead. Nurmi knew it was too fast for the 4:08 mile he had plotted, but he hung on anyway, and in the third quarter, where most runners of the day took a breather gathering for their sprint finish, he pushed hard, completing it in 3:06.7. He kept pushing and came home 18 yards clear of Wide in a new world record of 4:10.4.

Just over 10 seconds now separated Nurmi from the four-minute mile. Those who watched were amazed at the ease with which he had done it. Get the pace right, they said, keep it even, find him some more opponents, and we'll see the barrier broken. If anyone could do it, it had to be Peerless Paavo.

By late 1928 Nurmi was the holder of every world record from one mile to the greatest distance run in one hour, and still winning gold in the Olympics. But his international career finished with a row that seems as strangely modern as his approach to training and racing. He had dreamed of a grand finale in the 1932 Olympic marathon in Los Angeles, but was disqualified on the eve of the Games when the International Olympic Committee, under pressure from his Swedish and German rivals, ruled that he had taken inflated expenses in Germany. Nurmi denied the charges and said he had claimed the money for loss of earnings. He kept training alone, convinced to the last that he would be allowed to run the marathon.

His old opponent Otto Peltzer, who renewed his friendship with Nurmi in Los Angeles, said that Paavo ran solo around the Olympic marathon course as a trial in 2 hours 29 minutes.

But when the real race began, Nurmi was 'left sitting forlornly on the stone steps of the stadium'. The old Oxford code of amateurism had been rolled out again to end the international career of the world's greatest distance runner.

Nurmi returned home to run as a 'national amateur', but became increasingly bitter and reclusive. He had always been a loner, and though he married in 1932, his wife, Sylvi, was seeking a divorce before the marriage was 18 months old. The Finnish people, though, continued to love and revere him.

Nurmi's world, the sporting arenas of the 1920s, was far away from modern athletics with its overwhelming whiff of drugs and dollars. But Nurmi himself ended up a millionaire, and a decade or so after his death a Swedish newspaper ran a story that purported to show that even the great Finn might somehow be linked to drugs. It had been known that Nurmi had endorsed a German health drink in the 1930s. A picture of him, glass in hand, could guarantee to sell any liquid. But half a century later, after the fall of the Berlin Wall, records from East Germany apparently showed that the very drink he had endorsed contained an extract of bull's testicles, high in testosterone. The Swedes, ever ready to put the spike into a Finnish track hero, gloated that they had uncovered the secret of Paavo's success.

It was rubbish, of course. Nurmi's secret was that his training methods were decades ahead of his rivals'. He had shown that single-minded dedication could achieve the impossible in sport. He did it again and again. Generations of athletes who followed him were to learn from his example and from the training methods he pioneered.

He had shown the way in dedicated all-year-round training, in the balance of speed and distance work, in the relentless superiority of even pace and, above all, in self-belief in his methods and planning. He had stepped down to the mile and walked away with the world record. Before Nurmi, the prospect of a four-minute mile might have been a dream; after him, it was a certainty.

Nurmi's 4:10.4 represented a tantalising barrier. Just as four minutes became the barrier in the 1940s, so the 4:10 was there waiting to be broken. Study the running of Nurmi closely enough, other runners believed, find your pacemakers, and surely the barrier must fall. It was a new approach to miling, and there were plenty willing to try it.

A young French boy, Jules Ladoumègue, had an all-consuming desire to be a runner. His walls were plastered with pictures of Nurmi. He modelled his stride and style on the master. Ladoumègue shared Nurmi's burning ambition to explore every detail of his sport.

Nurmi had lost his father at the age of 13; Ladoumègue's father was crushed to death by blocks of timber on the Bordeaux docks just a few days before Jules was born in 1906. There was worse to come. Seventeen days after his birth, his mother died in a fire. Jules grew up with an aunt and uncle. At the age of 12 he was apprenticed as a gardener to an architect who had large plantations alongside the Talence racecourse.

It was said that the young Ladoumègue watched the horses exercising and began to copy them, trotting along like a thoroughbred. 'Often,' Ladoumègue said, 'I watched the horses training. I loved their stride. I observed attentively their leg movements. I owe to them the high knee lift that was part of my style.'

Sometimes his boss would catch him imitating the horses, and once his aunt was said to have been horrified to find him perched precariously on a table in front of a mirror studying his rear leg extension. At the age of 15, Jules could outrun all his friends, and they took him along to the Union Athlétique Bordelaise. Always his role model remained Nurmi, whose running technique he studied from photos. By the time he was 18, the boy they called Julot could, it seemed, beat anyone in France.

They hailed him as 'the new Nurmi', but Ladoumègue brought another quality to his racing that reminded some of the American Lon Myers – an excruciatingly painful pool of nervous energy. Although he was practically invincible in middle-distance races from 1929 to 1931, he usually vomited badly both before and after his races. His coach, Charles Poulenard, often had to drag him to the starting line. He had to convince Ladoumègue that he was never so ill as he imagined, and that the pains he experienced existed only in his mind. It was said that Jules had the sensitivity of a Stradivarius, and that if left to his own devices he would have run away before the start of every race.

From 1929 onwards Ladoumègue was rarely beaten. He went 24 months without losing a race over 1,500 metres. In 1930 he attacked and broke Otto Peltzer's 1,500 metres world record by 1.8 seconds. It was a specially arranged and paced affair, held in the Jean Bouin stadium around a 450-metre track following a rugby match. Ladoumègue finished in 3:49.2 to become the first man to run under 3:50.

In the way that he used his countrymen as pacemakers, and his ability to harness his mental energy, Ladoumègue foreshadowed the approach of Roger Bannister two decades later. In Paris, on 4 October 1931, in his favourite Jean Bouin stadium, Ladoumègue made a deliberate attempt on Nurmi's one-mile record. In a race with seven Frenchmen and two false starts he took 1.2 seconds off the record. He was actually 1.3 seconds down at the three-quarter-mile mark but ran his last lap in 61.2 seconds, compared with Nurmi's final lap of 63.7.

Ever the emotional runner, Julot said he had heard 'sweet music' on the last lap of his mile. 'That's where my real race began. I felt fresher than ever before. I broke 450 metres from home, with only one thought in my head, to catch up the time lost. I lengthened my stride, stuck out my chest, raised my head slightly. I was astonished that the last straight came so quickly. Going through 1,500 I heard them shout 3:52.4. I knew then I was going to do better than Nurmi.' Ladoumègue's winning time was 4:09.2.

He was now the toast of all France and was expected to win the 1932 Olympic 1,500 metres title. But to the horror of his countrymen, he was accused by the French Athletic Federation of receiving illegal payments for his races. The penalty was disqualification for life. Once again those old ghosts from the Randolph Hotel in Oxford had appeared to haunt those who dared to edge close to the four-minute mile. The strict amateur code, drawn up in 1880, put paid to Ladoumègue's record-breaking hopes, just as it had to Nurmi's career.

On 10 November 1935, an estimated 400,000 people flocked to the Champs Elysées to see their hero demonstrate his graceful stride. But it was all too late. For it was as an athlete already banned for life that Ladoumègue ran that day. He confessed that he was consumed by bitterness following the ban, and despaired at the 'all too short life span of an athlete'. 'A singer, a musician, a writer can fill their entire lifetime thanks to the gift heaven has granted them,' he said. 'Athletes are like dogs. They don't live long enough.'

As a professional Jules Ladoumègue tried in vain to improve the records he set as an amateur. But his spirit was broken, and the magic had vanished. Late in 1932 he and Paavo Nurmi planned to stage a series of professional races in the United States, but they found no commercial backers and the races never came off. Jules ran some exhibition races against horses and toured the tracks of the Soviet Union. His final public appearance was in a circus act, with Maurice Chevalier, just before the outbreak of war.

The boy who had covered his bedroom walls with posters of Nurmi ended up on a poster himself, but this one showed him prancing on a circus track, demonstrating his seven-foot stride. The man who had been the first to break the barrier of four minutes ten seconds for the mile finished his career being paraded each night under the canvas of the big top.

The continental takeover of the quest for the four-minute mile – with its barrier-breaking runs from Nurmi and Ladoumègue – had, it seemed, ended in the circus of commercialism. And for Jules Ladoumègue, in the sawdust of the circus ring itself.

7

Born to Win

It was the amateurs who built Noah's Ark, but it was the professionals who designed and built the *Titanic*.

Sir Arthur Gold, former Chairman
of the British Olympic Association

There was nothing of the commercial circus about the Oxford and Cambridge tracks of the twenties and thirties. This was the era of *Chariots of Fire*, where the leisured and self-assured student runners shrugged with mock amusement at the relentless hard work of a Nurmi, and recoiled with horror and contempt at the prospect of illegal payments. These were the gentlemen amateurs to whom winning came easily or not at all. Many were aristocrats, already at the pinnacle of the English class system. Others aspired to be, and even thought they might run or jump their way a little up the social ladder.

Lord Burghley needed no leg-up. He was a blue-blooded aristocrat who seemed born to win. He was depicted in the film *Chariots of Fire* balancing glasses of champagne on the hurdles while he trained. In fact, the real Lord Burghley's party trick was far more practical, but no less impressive. He would balance a matchbox on top of each hurdle, then run the flight with the object of knocking the matchboxes off with his leading leg, while leaving the hurdles trembling but upright.

As a training technique, producing a low, skimming, efficient hurdling action, it was inspired. It was not until coaches started using video cameras, a lifetime later, that a hurdler could get such sophisticated feedback about his action.

Lord David George Brownlow Cecil Burghley, son, heir and later successor to the Marquis of Exeter, first appeared in the Olympics in 1924, when he was eliminated in the first round of the 110-metre hurdles. In 1927, during his last year at Cambridge, he caused a sensation by running around the Great Court at Trinity College in the time it took the Trinity clock to strike twelve. Again, a distorted version of this event was presented in *Chariots of Fire*, in which the feat was credited to Harold Abrahams. Lord Burghley, who was then 76, was apparently so piqued that he refused to watch the film.

At the 1928 Olympics Burghley won the gold in the 400-metre hurdles using, he said, the technique of treating each hurdle as if it were the winning post. He was elected to Parliament in 1931, but was granted leave of absence to compete in the 1932 Olympics in Los Angeles, where he was placed fourth in the 400-metre hurdles.

His active athletic career ended just before the outbreak of the Second World War, when he snapped an Achilles tendon while attempting to show off his hurdling technique when 'not in training'. Shortly after his retirement from active sport he became President of the British Amateur Athletic Association, a post he held for 40 years. He was also President of the International Amateur Athletic Federation for 30 years and a member of the International Olympic Committee for 48.

Burghley moved effortlessly and gracefully from competing as a Cambridge Blue to lording it over Britain's athletics establishment. As a leading light in the Olympic movement, it seemed inevitable that he would be the man his country would turn to when called upon to stage the Games. The Olympics of 1940 and 1944 had been wrecked by the war, and London was asked to step in at short notice to stage the 'Austerity Games' of 1948. As Lord Burghley rose to the task with style, one of his most enthusiastic assistants was getting his first taste of the Olympic movement. That assistant was a young Oxford student – Roger Bannister.

While Lord Burghley seemed to glide effortlessly through his sport and his life as if destined to win, his contemporary and fellow Cambridge Blue, Harold Abrahams, considered winning a far more serious business.

Abrahams was born in Bedford at the turn of the century, the son of a Polish Jew and a Welsh mother. His brothers, Adolphe and Sidney – both later knighted – were also fine athletes. His father had arrived in Britain as a penniless 15-year-old, but he had great business acumen and ultimately set up as a highly successful money-lender. Abrahams said of him, 'He couldn't write a letter until the day he died, but he could sign a cheque. It was through his efforts that we were given such a fine chance in life.'

By the time Abrahams arrived at Cambridge University from Repton, he was already an established athlete, a sprinter and long-jumper in the classic mould of C. B. Fry, who had been at the same school. 'I was training hard by my standards,' said Abrahams in the 1950s, 'but at the most three times a week. I fear there is a grave inclination these days to over-train.'

At Cambridge Abrahams made steady progress under the eye of the long-time university coach Alec Nelson. He was the star of the annual Varsity Match with his sprinting and long-jumping, and he competed in the 1920 Olympic Games. But he was hungry for gold. So in the run-up to the 1924 Games in Paris, he employed Sam Mussabini as his personal trainer.

Sam worked endlessly on Harold's conditioning and technique. He changed his arm movement, sharpened his start and orchestrated his swooping dip to the finishing tape. For weeks before the Olympic Games Abrahams could be seen with Mussabini, working on his start and his finish at Paddington Recreation Ground, the Queen's Club or the old White City track. He was taught to know exactly how many strides he took to cover 100 metres, and Mussabini, who was always experimenting with athletic gear and techniques, even built special shoes for his star sprinter. The heels and toe-boxes were made in two parts and stitched together without a sole. They moved with the foot like a well-oiled hinge.

In Paris the odds seemed heavily stacked against Abrahams. The young sprinter was very nervous before his race, and to kill time Mussabini used to insist on him going on long drives around the suburbs of the city. Mussabini realised the importance of keeping Harold's mind occupied so that he wouldn't get over-anxious about the forthcoming Olympic final.

For the 1920s, this professional preparation was way ahead of its time, and it certainly raised eyebrows in Cambridge, where, like Oxford, it was not done to be seen to be too keen on your training. But it worked. And despite the fact that the highly fancied Americans had four men in the six-man final, Abrahams won the race. He had to wait for his gold medal, though. It was posted to him some weeks later, by which time he was resting on his laurels back in London.

With his active athletic career over, Harold Abrahams went on to distinguish himself as an athletics administrator, writer, broadcaster and statistician. He was shrewd and humane enough to give a job and refuge in the late 1930s to the émigré would-be coach Franz Stampfl, whose planning and methods were to set the pace that made the four-minute mile possible. He was also the most ardent supporter of Jack Lovelock, the Oxford medical student who so many thought might run the first sub-four-minute mile. His broadcast commentary on Lovelock's gold-medal-winning 1,500 metres in 1936 was as unforgettable as the race itself.

Abrahams was among the most influential of those commentators who sensed that the battle for the four-minute mile was hotting up. Above all, he wanted the prize claimed for Britain and, if possible, for Oxford or Cambridge. He ceaselessly encouraged Roger Bannister in the quest. Abrahams, Burghley and others from their generation still guarded closely the old amateur ideals. They played their games and danced their way through international sport, running and jumping as if convinced they were born to win. Perhaps, they believed, the perfect mile could be theirs for the taking.

One man from that golden age of British athletics knew all about perfect miling. Jerry Cornes, a lean, elegant Oxford student, with muscles like whipcord, was 22 when he stepped on to the Olympic rostrum in Los Angeles. He had just run the race of his life to carry off the silver medal in the 1,500 metres. Today an Olympic performance like that would set an athlete up with sponsorship, agents and rich rewards. However, sport and the world were very different in 1932.

In the spring of 1931, Cornes had set a new record of 4:22 for the Oxford University Sports mile, which had lowered by four-fifths of a second the time set by Arnold Strode-Jackson almost twenty years before. Cornes was straight out of the Oxford miling tradition. He won the Varsity Match, was elected President of the University Athletics Club and took under his wing a promising New Zealand Rhodes Scholar and medical student called Jack Lovelock. They both trained very lightly, under the watchful eye of the university coach Bill Thomas.

In the Oxford–Cambridge match in March 1932, Cornes and Lovelock glided in together in first place, and from there it was off to run together at the Olympic Games. A 12-day journey from Southampton, first by boat, the *Empress of Britain*, then by train, took the British team to a Los Angeles that was determined to put on a show despite the Depression.

The Americans feared that the Games would be a flop because it was so far to travel, but to the visitors the welcome seemed fabulous. The Olympic stadium, which held 104,000, was so good that it was used for the next Games in Los Angeles, 52 years later. The track was the fastest that most athletes had ever run on. There was the first purpose-built Olympic village and, with a touch of Hollywood, even the first appearance of the 'Olympic flame'.

Olympic sportsmanship, too, burnt with a brightness that might seem quaint today. In the 400-metres hurdles, for instance, Britain's Lord Burghley and Morgan Taylor of the United States were reckoned to be the best in the world. Taylor had been given the task of carrying the American flag at the opening parade, a tiring job in the baking Californian sunshine. So, in order not to gain an unfair advantage, Burghley carried the British flag at the same time. Both lost in their race to Bob Tisdall, an Irishman.

To Cornes it was all great fun. He was off to serve in the Colonial Service in Nigeria, and because he had won a place in the British team, he was allowed to travel there via California.

On 4 August 1932, Cornes finished second in the metric mile final to Luigi Beccali, the fast-kicking Italian, who ran 3:51.2, an Olympic record. Beccali covered the last 300 metres in around 41 seconds, a killing pace. Cornes ran 3:52.6, the fastest by a British athlete to that time. Jack Lovelock, his friend from New Zealand (who was to win gold four years later), trailed in seventh. Cornes had prepared himself for this performance on training that would be considered inadequate for a schoolboy athlete today. 'I ran only twice a week through the summer,' he said over half a century later. 'Absurd, compared with what they do nowadays.'

Cornes trained according to the classic English system, a method of preparation that had served generations of middle-distance runners, particularly from the old universities. Its ethos assumed that no coach could teach a man as much about himself as he might discover through his own self-initiated study and practice. Its aim was to produce a well-rounded person. Its ideal was a sound mind in a sound body. Its tradition suggested that great competitive success might be attained through determination, intelligence and confidence, even if training was kept to a minimum level.

The true sportsman in this tradition practised running because it was simply enjoyable, and competed purely for the joy of association with other sportsmen. Acclaim and the rewards of victory were just a bonus. It was a philosophy central to such books as *Athletics*, written in 1929 by Douglas Lowe and Arthur Porritt.

'In training of all kinds it is never wise to do too much,' they declared. 'The object of training is not to break records or to exhaust oneself, but to improve style and technique and to store up energy for the race. For this reason, it is an excellent thing, once stamina is assured, to practise over distances which are shorter than the race. There is no question about being able to stay the course in races – excitement and fitness will always carry one home.

'One should avoid running oneself out in practice – that is

not the aim of training. If possible, one should seek final polish and have all-out runs only in actual races. The frequency of training depends largely upon the individual. But three times a week at the most should suffice. When racing begins only one run a week besides the Saturday race is necessary, or indeed wise, else there is a risk of staleness. Slight under-training is better than too much, which nauseates. Should it happen that the athlete is anxious to attempt two or more middle-distance events, the first advice is that of *Punch* – "Don't.'"

After this kind of recreational running, Douglas Lowe defeated the world at 800 metres in the Olympic Games, not only in 1924 but again in 1928; and Arthur Porritt came third in the famous *Chariots of Fire* 100 metres in Paris in 1924. Other great runners, such as Strode-Jackson, Albert Hill, Jerry Cornes, Jack Lovelock, Sydney Wooderson and, in time, Roger Bannister, were all hugely influenced by the beliefs and methods outlined by such champions as Lowe and, despite their light training, proved great performers in world competition.

This training regime was a great contrast to the almost non-stop strenuous work advocated by the European and American systems, yet it was able to produce some excellent competitive results. It seemed to prove that, provided an athlete didn't try to race further than a mile, and provided that he didn't undertake competition seriously week after week, it was possible to run extremely well on such a part-time programme.

With the Olympic Games over, Jerry Cornes set out for Nigeria, where his arrival coincided with the staging of an annual 'round the wall' event – a cross-country race between two gates of the ancient city of Katsina. Cornes ran, but was out-kicked by a local; perhaps the first time, but certainly not the last, that a British middle-distance champion was to be beaten by an unknown African.

In 1936, Cornes was back in the Olympic team, and in the 1,500 metres in Berlin he sacrificed his own chances to set the pace for his friend Jack Lovelock, who won the gold in world record time. Cornes himself, in sixth place, ran a full second faster than in Los Angeles.

That was virtually his last track race, but the old chariot of fire kept rolling. As late as 1949 Cornes was turning out in the Southern Counties cross-country championship, trailing in twenty minutes behind the winner, to make up the team for his club, the Thames Hare and Hounds.

Towards the end of his life, flickering newsreel footage transported Jerry Cornes back to that August afternoon in 1932, and a simpler age – an age when winning a medal brought you not a big payday, but memories enough to enrich you for a lifetime. He had never before seen the film of the race that he had run more than 60 years earlier. As he watched, he shook his head with sadness and apology. 'I made a mistake,' he said. 'I was too busy looking out for the Finns.

'The middle distances, especially the mile, were the British events, and as the first string it was up to me to win,' he explained. 'At Oxford I was expected to beat Cambridge. And then together, in the Achilles Club, we were expected to take on the world. I was very disappointed not to win the gold. I felt I let the side down a bit. At the finish I was hardly tired. Oxford men don't like losing in the mile.'

8

Come on, Jack!

It came like electricity, it came from every fibre, from his fingertips to his toes. It came as broad waters come through a gorge. He called on it all.

Norman Harris, on Jack Lovelock's
finishing kick in the 1936 Olympics

Jerry Cornes always believed that Jack Lovelock was the true architect of the four-minute mile. In his later years Cornes would speak lyrically of the shy, smiling New Zealander whom he had taken under his wing at Oxford.

'Jack's permanent contribution to mankind', he said, 'lies in his paving the way for the four-minute mile. That achievement, to my mind, was as great as the conquest of Everest. Both achievements were much more than the climbing of a high mountain or the winning of a race against the clock. Achievements like these can inspire people everywhere.

'Jack was the pioneer. He kept very detailed records. He studied and analysed everything about the mile. Jack Lovelock contributed a lot to the ultimate achievement – Roger Bannister's breaking of the "sound barrier" of the four-minute mile.'

But even the admiring Cornes would have been amazed by the claims that were to be made about his one time protégé.

Myth, legend and mystery often hover at the heels of the world's great athletes. A Nurmi or a Zatopek, because their performances seem so often beyond what is possible, inspire strange stories of mythical feats in competition and training.

Jack Lovelock, the fair, wavy-haired world mile record-breaker from New Zealand, was as secretive as he was gifted. In the golden age of the mile he won the 1,500 metres gold medal in the 1936 Berlin Olympics, Hitler's games, in a world record time and in what many believed to be the perfectly executed race. The run brought Hitler to his feet in admiration and caused one eyewitness to declare that it was 'a race magnificent beyond all description'.

But as if this were not enough to secure Lovelock's place in the history of middle-distance running, half a century later an erstwhile training companion came up with a story which, if true, had the potential to completely rewrite the history of the quest for the four-minute mile. 'Did Roger Bannister really run the world's first four-minute mile?' asked London's *Sunday Times* on 11 September 1994. 'Or was he beaten to the record almost sixty years ago by a middle-distance runner few people have heard of?'

The question was prompted by a new edition of a book called *Lovelock* by James McNeish, a New Zealand author. Originally published in 1986, the book was, says its author, 'faction, an autobiographical novel', a strange blend of reportage and fiction covering the enigmatic life of a New Zealander hailed by many as the greatest genius in the history of mile racing.

In June 1987, shortly after the first edition of McNeish's book was published, a letter appeared in the *British Medical Journal* headlined 'Four Minute Life', which claimed that on two occasions in the mid thirties Jack Lovelock had actually broken the four-minute mile barrier. The letter came from Dr John Etheridge, a Hampstead GP and former international steeplechaser, who had trained with Lovelock in London in the 1930s.

Dr Etheridge said that he had timed Lovelock himself on both occasions, and subsequently he wrote to McNeish offering to substantiate the claims with records from his papers and diaries. He offered tantalising details. He talked of stopwatches being double-checked and heavy-duty steel tape measures being used to verify distances. He even recalled standing on the infield, watch in hand, shouting: 'Run, you Kiwi, run!' The time trials had taken place on cinder tracks in Paddington Recreation Ground and Motspur Park. As if further to convince, Etheridge added that he and Lovelock were no great friends. He found the medical student difficult to work with and an impossible social snob.

Dr Etheridge had been secretary of the United Hospital's Athletic Club when Lovelock was the captain. Of the Motspur Park run he made the fantastic claim, 'I cannot be quite sure without my athletic notes, but I think his time for the mile that Friday afternoon was 3 minutes 52.2 seconds unpaced.'

Sadly, the mysterious diaries chronicling these 'four-minute miles' were unavailable immediately because they were locked away in storage, and Dr Etheridge died in August 1988, apparently without having located them. Roger Bannister, who certainly carried out secret time trials of his own, and some of them at the same London tracks, has always been dismissive of Etheridge's claims. 'This sounds rather fantastic,' he said. 'Where are the race officials and the records of the time?'

Certainly no records have been found and no other witnesses produced, though McNeish said he was convinced by Etheridge and believed that the diaries chronicling these time trials do exist. After the '3:52.2 mile' at Motspur Park, Dr Etheridge says Lovelock 'was in no way short of breath or distressed. We then went in together and checked the written records, etc.' Of the Paddington run he said, 'Jack's time was four seconds under four minutes, when we had adjusted the length of the track.'

Lovelock himself never claimed publicly before Berlin to have broken four minutes, but he would certainly not have wished to have given away any of his training secrets. He ran a final time trial before the 1936 Olympic Games, at Herne Hill, and there were reports then that he ran a three-quarter mile in under three minutes. This would have bettered the official world record of the time and is far more credible than the suggestion made by Etheridge that Lovelock was running below four minutes for four laps.

There was much talk in the press in 1935 of the 'mythical four-minute mile' and how it might be run when Lovelock came up against the Americans Glenn Cunningham and Bill Bonthron. But when they met, in June 1935, Lovelock raced home an easy winner in 4 minutes 11.2 seconds – a long way off the sub-four-minute trials that Etheridge said he had been witnessing.

Even if you accept that Lovelock may have wished to keep secret the details of time trials before his 1936 Olympic victory, by 1941, when he was asked for his views about the possibility of a four-minute mile, there would seem little reason to stay silent if Etheridge's claims were true. By that time Lovelock had retired from racing and the Americans had come up with a new star in the mile, Walter Mehl, who in June 1940 broke the United States 1,500 metres record, running 3:47.9, while defeating Cunningham. In 1941 Mehl began talking openly of his plans to break the four-minute barrier, saying, 'I think I can do it this season or next.'

Jack Lovelock, asked to comment at the time on the prospect, said that he believed the four-minute mile was possible. 'I have been well under three minutes for the three-quarters,' he said, 'and I know that in competition, if pressed severely enough, another quarter could be done in 60 seconds or less.' Lovelock added that as a medical man he had never believed the feat to be physiologically impossible. 'There is a more important side than the physiological one, which is holding back athletes,' he said, but he gave no hint that he knew from his own experience that the barrier had already been broken.

The most likely explanation for the reported performances is that these were time trials over three laps, and that what the doctor witnessed were sub-three-minute performances. But what such reports, and the credence given to them, really demonstrate is the power of the myth that surrounded Jack Lovelock.

As a schoolboy athlete back in New Zealand, he was solitary, small and skinny, a boy with a 29-inch waist, nicknamed by his schoolmates 'Matchstick'. By the time his father died, when he was 13 years old, young Jack had already been running for two years. He did not tell his parents about his new-found activity; he simply trained in secret with a stopwatch. He was also a good rugby player and way above average in boxing. But running was his passion and he worked constantly to develop the silky, effortless style that was advocated by the training manuals of the 1920s.

One technique he would use to stop himself from bouncing up and down while he ran, and thus wasting valuable energy, was to run alongside a brick wall. He would get a fellow pupil at his boarding school to watch him run and to shout if his head did not keep absolutely level with the horizontal layer of bricks in the wall. It seemed to work, and Lovelock would often run at speed so smoothly that his body seemed to be moving on wheels. His running style was in time to be likened to the perfection of Mozart.

Lovelock shone both in his schoolwork and at his sport. By the time he had made up his mind to study medicine he was already winning area and university titles. While at Otago University he was nominated for a Rhodes Scholarship to Oxford, and he arrived at Exeter College in 1931.

At Iffley Road, Jerry Cornes, already twice winner of the inter-varsity mile, was king of the middle distances. On a late October afternoon in 1931 he stood beside the veteran Oxford University coach Bill Thomas, watch in hand, to observe the newcomer from New Zealand win the freshman's mile by a clear 60 yards in 4:37.6. They liked the look of their new miler, and Lovelock very much liked the style of his new home.

The concept of the gifted amateur was one that had lapped the university tracks at Iffley Road and Fenners since the days of the legendary Arnold Nugent Strode-Jackson. A succession of heroes had nurtured the idea of the man who could play the game for the sake of the game. The batsman who could hit a century and then move on to run an army or an empire, deliver a speech or preach a sermon was a model of excellence, much admired.

This ideal of effortless perfection helped develop the theory that sport was a part, an essential part, of a full and rounded life, and that sport might be a useful force in bringing together the youth of the world. There had been much of this idealistic thinking behind the pronouncements of the Baron de Coubertin, the young French aristocrat who in the 1890s engineered the revival of the modern Olympic Games.

De Coubertin was profoundly influenced by the approach to sport in the great English public schools and universities. His infant Olympic Games, delivered to the world in 1896, embodied many of the qualities that had begun to emerge from Oxford and Cambridge. There the students traditionally took a little time off from the studies that would turn them into doctors, businessmen, teachers or empire builders, to play their games. When the whistle finally blew or the tape was reached, they would leave their games to live out their lives and fulfil their destinies.

During a visit to Britain in the 1890s de Coubertin visited Rugby School and the village of Much Wenlock, where a splendid Victorian, Dr Penny Brookes, was running his own version of 'Olympic sports'. In search of a blueprint for his great Olympic revival, de Coubertin also turned up to witness a cross-country race on Wimbledon Common.

There the oldest cross-country running club in the world had been established in 1866 by a bunch of rowers from the Thames Rowing Club who wanted to keep themselves fit through the long dark months of winter. Taking their cue from the paperchases that were held at such schools as Rugby, their club, the Thames Hare and Hounds, was soon flourishing. Nearly a century later, athletes like Chris Brasher and Chris Chataway were to run regularly for the club on the same courses across the Common, scraping the mud from their legs afterwards in Victorian hip-baths in a steam-filled upper room at the King's Head in Roehampton. Chris Chataway, in his seventies, runs with them still.

Jack Lovelock sank easily into this world of steaming hip-baths, lofty ideals and effortless victories. He cut a romantic and debonair figure in the university world of the thirties. He loved and aped the blazered, flannelled, scarved image of the polished Oxford student about town. He still boxed, well enough and often enough to make the university boxing team, and whenever he ran, he seemed capable of producing a flashing burst of speed that made spectators watch in wonder.

Behind the jaunty straw boater and perfectly rolled umbrella, though, Lovelock was sensitive and obsessive about his running. He trained surreptitiously at night, clambering over the college walls to run alone in the silent parks. He concealed how much training he was doing in an Oxford where trying too hard might attract more sneers than cheers.

He kept a meticulous diary, noting every detail of his training, his weight, his races. He explored like a scientist his theories on diet, on tactics, on relaxation. He noted that he often ran best after a night in bed with a woman. The effect of his self-analysis was that when he raced it was evident he did so as much with his head as with his legs. Spectators would wait in tortured anticipation for that moment when he would bring the intellect and the body together to produce a devastating winning strike.

In the summer of 1932, Lovelock suddenly sprang to world fame at the annual match between Oxford University Athletic Club and the AAA. He was almost certainly aware that a good performance there might show the New Zealand authorities that he was worth a place in their Olympic team for the Games in Los Angeles. Jerry Cornes had opted to race the half-mile that afternoon, so Lovelock made up his mind, it seems, to go for a very fast mile – probably sub-4:20 if he could manage it.

Immediately before the race he asked his second string, Michael Alberry, to take the pace out fast over the first lap. This Alberry did, running the opening quarter in 57 seconds, with Lovelock audibly urging him to go faster. Twenty-two years later, in the same meeting at the same venue, Roger

Bannister would hurl the same command of 'faster' to Chris Brasher, his pacemaker, on the first lap of another record-breaking mile. Alberry held the pace until the 600-yard mark was passed, then Lovelock took over to complete the half-mile in 2:02.

Skipping and floating round the old Iffley Road track, Lovelock dropped the two experienced AAA runners and passed the three-quarter-mile mark in 3:13. Bill Thomas, the OUAC coach, dark-suited and bowler-hatted, who was to play a leading role in Lovelock's athletic life, held a stopwatch in trembling hands and with only 100 yards to be covered was telling the press reporters that four minutes had not yet been clocked.

The official timekeepers could scarcely believe their own watches, but Lovelock burst through the tape 50 yards ahead of Aubrey Harris, a 20-year-old trooper who had won the 1931 Army Championships in 4:24. Lovelock's time was 4:12. He had broken Jerry Cornes' Iffley Road track record of 4:17 made two years earlier, and the British All-Comers Record of 4:13.4, achieved by Reg Thomas of the RAF in 1931.

F. A. M. Webster, a leading athletics writer of the era, watched the performance in awe. 'What Lovelock would have done with opposition from Taffy Thomas, Jerry Cornes and Jules Ladoumègue, the French world record holder, one hesitates to think,' he wrote, 'but I still believe that the inspired Lovelock might have produced that afternoon the so far mythical mile in four minutes. He ran like a man possessed and wasted much breath, urging Alberry to run faster after that first lap.'

The difference between Lovelock's fastest and slowest lap was 14 seconds. So much for even-pace running. Bill Thomas, the coach, muttered sadly that an even-pace lap schedule might have got the four-minute mile. Nevertheless, Lovelock had knocked 8.8 seconds off his previous best mile time, and Arthur Porritt, the New Zealand Olympic Games bronze medallist, immediately wrote to the New Zealand Games selectors to tell them what the stylish freshman had done.

That race alone was enough to make Lovelock one of the most fancied runners for the Olympic 1,500 metres. In this respect, as in so many others, there were parallels with Roger Bannister. Bannister went as a favourite to the Games of 1952 and it was out of his 'failure' there, where he finished in fourth place, that the drive to break the four-minute mile was born.

In Los Angeles in 1932, the talented but inexperienced Lovelock came unstuck. His legs had suffered as a result of having run on the deck of the ship that carried him to America. And although he won his heat in 3 minutes 58 seconds, in the final he had a disastrous race. While his fellow Oxford Blue, Jerry Cornes, came within a stride of winning Olympic gold behind the Italian Luigi Beccali, Lovelock was a well-beaten also-ran in seventh. He noted in his diary that he would have to plan 'to even the score with Beccali and Co.'.

Lovelock believed he lacked the strength for two such races on consecutive days. This was the same belief that troubled Bannister in the Olympics of 1952. But many of Lovelock's colleagues reckoned his poor result was due to nerves. Either way, this 'failure' became the turning point in his career.

With the Games over, the self-analytical Lovelock plotted how he could spend the next four years preparing himself for the 1936 Olympics. He worked ever more closely with his coach Bill Thomas and became ever more dependent on him. He had strong theories that a body could be brought to a peak only once or twice a season, that style mattered above all, that burnout and staleness from too much heavy training should be avoided at all costs. He became a master at building himself up to an annual climax, but once it was over he appeared physically and mentally exhausted, and it would take him months to recover.

This theory on peaking meant that, even when he was beaten, Lovelock would often finish with a smile on his face. In his training diary he could write happily of defeat, as he did after Beccali had beaten him again in the World Student Games of 1933: 'It is probably rather good for one to take an occasional drubbing and though I would naturally have preferred to win, I did not in the least begrudge Luigi Beccali his win. He is a delightful opponent. Two wins to him, the third is mine!'

Lovelock's victories were delightful to watch, and he was a popular athlete, particularly with the journalists and athletics administrators of the day like Harold Abrahams, seeming to dance through his running and his life.

Lovelock's training involved numerous time trials, many of them in secret. He rarely liked to show his hand to his competitors. He experimented continually, sometimes with devastating bursts of speed on the last lap of his miles, sometimes during his fascinating duels with Sydney Wooderson, sometimes during races held amid much ballyhoo in America.

On 15 July 1933, Lovelock was in the United States as a member of a combined Oxford and Cambridge team. There he faced Bill Bonthron of Princeton, a fine miler who had held his own with Glenn Cunningham, at that time the most consistent miler in the world. In his race with Bonthron, Lovelock set a new world record of 4:07.6, while Bonthron, too, finished under the previous world record in 4:08.7. An entry from Lovelock's diary describes the occasion: 'That is the sort of race which one really enjoys – to feel at one's peak on the day when it is necessary, and to be able to produce the pace at the very finish. It gives a thrill, which compensates for the months of training and toiling. But it is the sort of race that one wants only about once a season.'

Those who saw this race say that Lovelock was poetry in motion. The *New York Herald Tribune* reported: 'It was all so easily accomplished, with so little outward evidence of stress and strain as to make a four-minute mile seem just around the corner – or at least at that time when Lovelock finds the conditions as perfect in every detail as they were today, with a runner of equal stature to force the pace all the way as Bonthron did.'

In 1935, Lovelock met, and beat, Glenn Cunningham in the 'Mile of the Century' in America. But when asked in early 1936 whom he feared most in the Olympics, Lovelock named Sydney Wooderson, in view of his devastating finishing sprint. In the event Wooderson did not make the Olympic final, having broken down in his heat with an injured foot.

By the time of the Berlin Olympics, Lovelock was in the greatest shape of his life. At 5 foot 7 inches, weighing less than 10 stone, the fair-haired New Zealander was described as 'perfect running machinery'. His centre of gravity seemed to be so low that he glided along as if on rails and his pulse rate was low, too, often well below 40. They said he was the perfect athlete, and his heartbeats, like a slow-thudding drum, were broadcast to every wireless set in the British Empire.

He was programmed to bring his body and mind to a single climax in a season, and his biggest build-up of all was timed to coincide with the Olympic Games in Berlin in 1936. These were the so-called 'Nazi Olympics', Hitler's Games, full of strange gimmicks and rituals and hijacked for propaganda purposes at every turn.

The plans for the German Games and the building of the Berlin Olympic stadium long pre-dated the rise of Adolf Hitler; and despite the Nazis' best efforts to control the spectacle, Jesse Owens, the black American athlete, and others like him cocked a golden snook at Hitler's belief that a master race of Aryan sportsmen would sweep all before them.

The Berlin stadium owed its existence not to any political leader but to Dr Carl Diem, a German sporting fanatic turned scholar and historian. He had been involved in sport since the 1890s, and he led German contingents to the Athens Games of 1906 and the Olympics of 1912 in Stockholm. He was a classical scholar and one of the most prolific sports historians of the twentieth century.

Diem's greatest disappointment came when the outbreak of the First World War aborted the 1916 Olympics, which were to have been held in Berlin. Like Baron de Coubertin, the founder of the modern Olympics, Diem believed that the Olympic movement was a force for peace and yearned for the ethos of the ancient Olympics, when warring states would declare a truce to allow the Games to take place.

Germany was excluded from the immediate post-war Games of 1920 and 1924, but thanks mainly to furious lobbying by Diem, they were allowed back into the 1928 Games in Amsterdam. Diem repeatedly pressed for the Olympics to be held in Berlin, pointing out that the facilities intended for 1916 were still there, and was delighted when in May 1932 Berlin's bid beat off Barcelona.

The 1932 Games were awarded to Los Angeles, where the organisers set a new pace for innovation, including a purpose-built Olympic village, subsidised food and transport. Diem stalked the American Games, notebook and tape measure in hand, vowing that everything he witnessed would be done on a grander scale in Germany. He was sure that the Berlin Games would be the most spectacular ever. If he was alarmed by the rise of the Nazi Party he did not show it. He was never a party member, but he was consumed by his vision of the Games and did not particularly care who his masters were as long as the bills were paid.

With the Games safely secured for Germany, Diem was able to indulge his love of pageantry and classical legend. He sent an archaeological expedition to the site of the ancient Olympics in Olympia, paying for much of it out of his own pocket. Focusing on Olympia, Diem was able to resurrect a pseudo-classical stunt he had toyed with for the Games that never were in 1916.

This involved a troop of Greek virgins kindling the 'sacred Olympic flame', using a mirror and the rays of the sun at the ancient site, and starting a relay of lighted torches that would end in the great stadium in Berlin. Every detail was recorded by Leni Riefenstahl, the great German film-maker known as Hitler's favourite director, who wanted the torchbearers to run naked, though Greek peasant boys recruited to run with the torches were having none of it. Even so, the relay became an instant publicity success.

The Berlin stadium, built by Werner March, was in its day the biggest and best in the world. But Hitler sniffed at it, and wrote it off as being far too small and cheap, with too little marble. Even a bit of touching up by Albert Speer, his favourite architect, could not make the Führer enthuse about it. But on 6 August 1936, nothing could have kept him away.

A record crowd of 112,000 waited in mounting excitement as the 12 finalists for the 1,500 metres marched to the starting line. It was said that Hitler was so keen to watch this clash of the world's greatest milers that he had cut short his lunch with the King of Bulgaria.

Britain's hopes of victory had vanished the previous day when Sydney Wooderson broke down in the heats because of his injury, but nevertheless many British expectations were centred on the wavy-haired Jack Lovelock, who was wearing the all-black of his birthplace, New Zealand. The British public and press had come to regard Lovelock as one of their own – after all, he was from the Empire, and for the past five years he had been at Oxford and at St Mary's Hospital, where he was studying medicine.

In the lead-up to the race Lovelock seemed to be in a terrible state of indecision. He was entered for both the 1,500 and the 5,000 metres, and prepared for both. Some thought he might try to dodge Wooderson by going for the longer race. In the event, he turned to Bill Thomas and to Arthur Porritt, the New Zealand team manager, for advice. With Wooderson hobbled by his injured foot, Lovelock opted for the 1,500 metres.

His rivals, in what was the greatest assembly of middle-distance runners yet seen, included two Americans: Glenn Cunningham – known as the 'Iron Horse of Kansas' – who by now held the world mile record at 4:06.8 and was the favourite; and the 19-year-old new wonder runner Archie San Romani. Also at the starting line were the experienced Italian Luigi Beccali, the holder of the Olympic record; the black Canadian Phil Edwards; and Lovelock's fellow Oxford Blue, Jerry Cornes, who had finished second in Los Angeles four years previously.

It was Cornes and the Italian Beccali who took up the early running. Lovelock, light-footed, relaxed and graceful as always, pattered along in fifth place. After one lap, the well-muscled Cunningham took the lead and Lovelock, wearing a smile of complete confidence, eased his way into third.

The cheering rose to a climax as 300 yards from the tape,

long before even his supporters thought possible, Lovelock unleashed a fantastic turn of speed that left the shocked Americans floundering 10 yards in his wake. Though he was tiring, Lovelock rounded the home bend and hit the finish five yards clear of Cunningham. The stopwatches read 3:47.8 – the new Olympic champion had sliced a second off the world record, and the next four men home, Cunningham, Beccali, San Romani and Edwards, all beat the old Olympic record.

For Jack Lovelock and those who witnessed it, this metric mile was the perfect race. It was regarded by many as the greatest race in Olympic history. Lovelock had jumped the field brilliantly and taken the gold in great style. It was considered such a classic that Leni Riefenstahl featured the whole event, from gun to tape, in her film of the Olympic Games.

Lovelock commented in his diary: 'Even Cunningham, strong though he is, could not live up to the strain of setting such a pace, combined with the mental worry of having a lightly stepping black shadow right on his shoulder, locking strides with him, almost breathing in his ear – for the trick of shadowing an opponent within sight and hearing is one of the more maddening and distracting forms of tactics that one can use in any race.'

The BBC covered the race live by wireless, with Lovelock's old friend Harold Abrahams responsible for a notoriously over-excited and non-objective commentary. As Lovelock burst clear of the field on the last lap and the excitement grew, Abrahams completely abandoned his English upper-class poise, urging Lovelock on to win and cheering him home: 'Lovelock leads! Lovelock! Lovelock! Cunningham second, Beccali third. Come on, Jack! A hundred yards to go! Come on, Jack! My God, he's done it. Jack, come on! Lovelock wins. Five yards, six yards, he wins. He's won. Hooray!'

Hitler presented all the Berlin gold medallists with an oak seedling. Lovelock sent his back to New Zealand with Cecil Matthews, a fellow athlete, and it is now a large oak tree in the grounds of Timaru High School. His near-perfect race had put the four-minute mile realistically within reach, but after the Games, again foreshadowing Roger Bannister, Lovelock announced that he would now be concentrating on his medical career.

He also became caught up with the riding and hunting set. He had always idolised Lord Burghley, who at one time ran his own private pack of foxhounds, and in October 1940 he was badly thrown from his horse while out cub hunting in Oxfordshire. His collarbone was broken, but worse still, his vision was permanently affected by a blow on the head.

In 1945 he married Cynthia James, a girl from the US Embassy, and at the end of the war took himself off to the States. He had had a strange, unsatisfactory war, working as an army medical officer. His running was sporadic and his athletic career was virtually over.

Only thirteen years after his great triumph in Berlin, Lovelock died beneath the wheels of a Coney Island subway train in New York, one cold December morning. He had been ill with flu, but insisted on going to work, and with his bad sight and reports of giddy spells it seems most likely that his death was an accident. But the myth-makers still looked for hidden motives for suicide. Dr Mendel Jacobi, New York's police medical examiner, reported, however, that the death was accidental, and that Lovelock was suffering from bad eyesight and heart trouble. He was only 39.

The pioneer of the perfect mile had left a remarkable legacy. As the 1936 Olympic champion and world record holder at the mile and 1,500 metres, Lovelock had been invited to write the chapter on middle-distance running for the *Athletics by Members of the Achilles Club*. This was the volume read avidly by Chataway, Brasher and Bannister. In it Lovelock pointed the way to the four-minute mile. He showed how training, planning, peaking and mental attitude would see the barrier inevitably broken. In his running and his writing he brought to the business of miling more thought, more pains and more science than anyone had ever done before.

Chris Chataway said that when he went up to Oxford in 1950, all the training was based on what Lovelock had done. That was what they talked about at Iffley Road. 'And Roger Bannister', he said, 'wanted to do exactly what Lovelock had done – win an Olympic gold medal and then quit competitive athletics to get on with his medical career.

'Failing to get gold like Lovelock,' said Chataway, 'which seemed at the time like the worst of luck, turned out for Bannister in the end to be the best luck in the world. If he had won the Olympics like Jack Lovelock, he would never have gone on to try for that four-minute mile.'

9

Cyclone Syd

It is the ambition of my life to be the first to do it.

Sydney Wooderson, May 1938, on the four-minute mile

When Jack Lovelock won the Empire Games mile at London's White City in 1934, the unlikely-looking athlete breathing down his neck was Sydney Wooderson.

A very British hero, no man looked less like the popular image of a champion than Wooderson. Standing 5 foot 6 inches and weighing under nine stone in his running kit and spectacles, he appeared fragile and undernourished. The black vest and baggy shorts of Blackheath Harriers that he loved to run in merely emphasised the whiteness of his legs. His health was shaky and he would frequently turn up at tracks looking as if he had been mugged for his ration book.

'If someone were to point out Sydney Wooderson to you on the running track and tell you he was the athlete who had run a mile more quickly than any other human being, you just wouldn't believe it,' said Harold Abrahams. 'If you were to see that tiny figure running with a dozen others, buffeted and almost apologising for occupying any space at all, he would be the last person you would pick out as a king among milers. That is until he releases that incredible burst of stored-up energy. Then, and not until then, he looks what he has proved so often to be – unbeatable.'

Within his modest shell blinked the spirit that endeared Wooderson to wartime Britain. He looked and behaved like Mr Ordinary – but on the track he could pulverise the best in the world, and he became a symbol of British pluck and determination.

In May of 1938, while the clouds of war were gathering over Europe, this shy solicitor's clerk stepped out into the sunshine of the White City track to begin his summer training and announced to the world that he was hoping to run the four-minute mile. 'It is the ambition of my life to be the first to do it,' he said. He indicated that if everything went well his first attempt at the barrier would probably be as soon as the August of 1938.

The question of the four-minute mile had been hotly debated on both sides of the Atlantic since the American college miler Glenn Cunningham had run 4:04.4. That remarkable time was achieved in an indoor arena on wood with no wind resistance, but it did demonstrate the possibilities of a four-minute mile.

Whilst some said that Cunningham's effort probably represented the limit of human achievement, Wooderson disagreed. 'Given ideal conditions I do not see why Cunningham's time should not be beaten outdoors,' he said. Ideal conditions were the problem. The most elaborate preparations for a record attempt could be knocked sideways by a bit of a breeze or a track made heavy by rain. Even with track and weather perfect, the attempt could be ruined by bad pacemaking. Accurate pacing is absolutely essential, and where, the press wondered in 1938, were the runners to be found to take Wooderson round a lap apiece at a level 60 seconds? Indoor times were not recognised by the International Federation, and Wooderson was still the accepted world record holder at 4:06.4. In that race he had done two laps in around 58 seconds each, so it was widely believed the four-minute mile might not be beyond him if he could keep to a uniform 60 seconds a lap.

The *Daily Mail* doubted whether human pacemakers could be relied on for such a task. One ingenious solution advocated by the paper was the use of 'a mechanical athlete'. What, they asked, if the White City were to make use of the technology of the greyhound track and mount a dummy athlete to be sent round at 60 seconds a lap under the direction of the control tower? Wooderson himself indicated that he would rather see an all-star field including the Americans Cunningham and San Romani assembled for the August Bank Holiday meeting at the White City. 'That's the way most track records are recorded,' he observed.

Sadly, as so often with Wooderson, he was to be robbed of the opportunity of running the perfect mile. World war was to intervene, and it would be years before he would be able to train and race properly again.

This extraordinary record-breaking champion, the 'Mighty Atom' of the European athletic tracks in the 1930s and 1940s, was first cheated of Olympic honour at the Berlin Games of 1936. A broken bone in his foot robbed him of what many believed would have been a certain medal in the 1,500 metres and the watching world of what would have been a sensational race between Wooderson and the great Jack Lovelock.

War then cheated him of what should have been his finest athletic hours when the Olympic Games of 1940 and 1944 were cancelled. By the time the Games were restarted in London in 1948, Wooderson had hung up his spikes. The lost years between 1938 and his re-emergence in international competition in 1945 should have been Wooderson's greatest.

Sydney Wooderson might never have been an athlete at all except for a longing to emulate his older brother Alfred, who was the best runner at Sutton Valence School in Kent in 1930. In 1931 the 16-year-old Sydney ran in the Public School mile for the first time. He was hardly noticed as he finished sixth. Two years later he won this mile in 4.29.8, the first time an 18-year-old had ducked under 4½ minutes.

In late June 1934 Wooderson made his first senior appearance at a major championship, at the Southern Counties Mile in Guildford. On the starting line were some formidable competitors, including Jack Lovelock, the former world record holder and favourite for the Empire Games in London two months later, Jerry Cornes, silver medallist in the 1932 Olympic Games, and Aubrey Reeve of the Polytechnic Harriers, keen to improve on his best time of 4:20.

Wooderson had left school to become an articled solicitor's clerk and was being coached by Albert Hill, Britain's double Olympic champion in the 800 and 1,500 metres at the 1920 Games. His first big senior mile was a rough-and-tumble race in a field of 25 on a bumpy grass track. A furlong from home Reeve unleashed a winning sprint to knock six seconds off his best time. Lying second with just a few yards to go, and confident despite a niggling knee injury that he was safe, was Jack Lovelock, but Wooderson suddenly unleashed a powerful finishing burst to pass him and finish in 4:15.2.

Following this breakthrough, Wooderson and Lovelock met again that year in the Empire Games mile, where Lovelock saw off the field to win comfortably in 4:12.8. Wooderson took the silver, again with his last stride, sweeping past Jerry Cornes in 4:13.4.

Wooderson's next meeting with Lovelock came in the 1935 AAA Championships. The New Zealander had just returned from Princeton, where he had won another much-publicised Mile of the Century, so when he was beaten by Wooderson it was seen by the press as a sensation. 'I believe', said Guy Butler, an Olympic medallist reporting for the *Morning Post*, "that Lovelock's domination is at an end." Three weeks later the two met again in Glasgow in front of a crowd of 50,000. Again Wooderson won, this time in 4:12.7 for his first United Kingdom record. With his confidence high, Wooderson enthusiastically returned to Blackheath Harriers to tune up for the 1936 Olympic Games.

The preparations went well. In the 1936 Southern Championships Wooderson's winning time of 4:10.8 was another big improvement on his British record, and in the AAA Championships he again out-kicked Lovelock. The scene was set for a mouth-watering clash between the smooth-striding New Zealander and the fiery-finishing Englishman on the Olympic track in Berlin.

But Wooderson's hopes were wrecked in training. When out for one of his regular long Sunday walks with his brother Stanley, Sydney turned his ankle in a rabbit hole. He tried everything – massage, rest, hot and cold bandages – hoping against hope that the ankle would heal and that he would be fit for the Games.

Wooderson kept the injury secret, but when he went to the line of his 1,500 metres heat in Berlin it was only too obvious that something was seriously wrong. As soon as he ran he began to limp badly. The official Olympic British report was bleak: 'From the start all was not well with Wooderson. He was limping appreciably and was obviously at sixes and sevens as to what course it was best to pursue. In the final stretch he tried to drive his unwilling body along faster, but he failed to qualify for the final.'

In that final Jack Lovelock dominated the field and took the gold in 3:47.8, a world record. Wooderson made no attempt to make excuses and claim that he might have won the race. 'Lovelock', he said, 'was more experienced at running in major races than I was. He had been running in international events since the Olympics of 1932 and he was determined to win. I think honestly that I would not have won. I think the ordeal of a big occasion would have affected me and that my nerves would have got the better of me.'

The following season, with his ankle healed, Sydney Wooderson returned to the quest for ever-faster mile times. In August he went to Motspur Park, for a meeting organised by his club, determined to attack the British mile record. The track was in excellent condition, the weather fine, and among the large crowd was old Walter George, who had run 4:12¾ back in August 1886.

The race was a specially arranged handicap, with Wooderson starting off scratch. Reg Thomas, the chief pacemaker, lined up ten yards ahead of him and did an excellent job, towing Wooderson through the half-mile in 2:02.6, before dropping out. The pace was much faster than Wooderson's own British record, and by the last lap his fellow club athletes were screaming at him to sprint for the tape.

He finished in 4:06.4 – just shaving Glenn Cunningham's world record of 4:06.8 set three years before. Four AAA timekeepers held the watches and the track was painstakingly re-measured. Quaintly, for a record attempt, the quarter-mile circuit was found to be two inches and a fraction short of 440 yards, making a difference of 8⅔ inches over the four laps. But this had been anticipated by the officials, and to allow for it they had arranged for Wooderson to start from a mark ten inches behind the usual starting line.

At the announcement of the result Wooderson was carried shoulder high by his admirers. His father and mother were there, along with his coach Albert Hill, and one of the first to congratulate him and speculate about the prospect of a four-minute mile was the 'Wiltshire Wonder', Walter George. Wooderson himself said he was in a state of shock at the record: 'I was amazed and couldn't sleep undisturbed for some days after.' When he could sleep, he dreamed of more records and an even more perfect mile.

The following season, although he was running better than ever, Wooderson could not spare the time for the long sea trip to the Empire Games in Australia because he was taking his law finals. But in training he and his coach were preparing for an assault on the world half-mile record.

On 1 August 1938, at the White City, Wooderson stepped down to the half-mile and won in 1:50.9, an amazing time for a novice. Three weeks later on 20 August, again in a specially arranged handicap race at Motspur Park, he attacked the world records for 800 metres and 880 yards (804.68m) both held by Elroy Robinson of the United States.

The conditions were excellent. The track was hard, and there was no wind. Six other athletes were spread out around the track, all given various starts so that they could set a record-breaking pace. Wooderson passed the quarter-mile mark in 52.7, and by the home straight he had overtaken all the supporting runners except his brother Stanley.

Again Sydney Wooderson had broken barriers and both records. His 800 metres time of 1:48.4 was a world record which lasted only a year until Rudolf Harbig of Germany shattered it quite phenomenally with 1:46.6. But his half-mile time was not matched until the double Olympic 800 metres champion (1948 and 1952), Mal Whitfield of the United States, equalled it in 1950. It was not broken until 1955 when Lon Spurrier, also an American, ran 1:47.5.

Wooderson competed only sporadically through the war years, racing wherever he could and whenever he was asked. He would be ready to travel overnight from London to Glasgow and back, standing in the corridor in the blackout throughout the journey, to draw crowds and raise morale and money for the war effort. The tracks were usually poor and his times were not great.

In neutral Sweden, by contrast, middle-distance athletes led by Gunder Haegg and Arne Andersson were taking huge chunks out of the world mile record. In 1942 Wooderson lost his mile record to Haegg, and by the end of the war Haegg and Andersson had run inside 4:02 and were threatening to break four minutes every time they raced the distance.

With the war in Europe over, British athletics spectators got a first and last chance to see the legendary Swedes in action before they were banned for professionalism. Athletics fans had been treated to flickering, tantalising glimpses of the sensational record breakers in the cinemas. They would stride across the screens in the Pathé newsreels, coming on at the end after news of invasions, victories and defeats. But the chance to see them race on a London track produced a fever of excitement in a city still weary from the Blitz.

So when Haegg and Andersson were invited to take part in the Bank Holiday meeting at the White City stadium on 6 August 1945, a crowd of 54,000, starved for too long of top-class athletics, packed the old place out. The event that had the crowd buzzing was the mile. Sydney Wooderson, at the age of 30, was to take on Arne Andersson.

Despite his age, and everything he had been through, the unlikely-looking Wooderson was still the British hero – and many believed he was still unbeatable. After all, they said, between 1935 and 1940 he had held the world records for the 800 metres, the 880 yards and the mile. But for all his records no man looked less like a champion athlete.

Wooderson had not had the greatest of wars. At first he went into fire-fighting during the Blitz on London, working with a crew just south of Croydon. Then he was conscripted into the army. They put him in the Pioneer Corps because, he said, 'my eyesight was so bad'. Even armed with the best of spectacles Wooderson lacked the brawn for digging ditches. They transferred him to the Royal Electrical and Mechanical Engineers and set him to mending broken wirelesses, but, he said, 'I was never very good at that either.'

What he was very good at was running the mile, and his supporters were certain that if it had not been for the war, he would have broken through the four-minute barrier. He ran when he could as a soldier, but in 1944 rheumatic fever put a stop even to that. He got himself up, though, defied the doctors, who feared he would never run again, and only six months after his discharge from hospital was trotted out to carry the hopes of Britain against Sweden's Andersson.

On paper it seemed the most ill-made of matches, with Wooderson's personal best set eight years before and some five seconds slower than the Swede had recently run. The much taller Andersson looked a picture of health and physical fitness after six years of good living and hard racing against his coun-tryman Gunder Haegg. Wooderson, on the other hand, looked what he was – a 30-year-old soldier who had been living on sub-standard food for six years, and was not long out of his sick bed. But this was the race that the crowd had come to see. Haegg, the world record holder for the mile, was there too. But he had opted to run in the two miles, and there were those who thought he might stand on the infield and watch his own mile record fall.

The meeting was more than a sell-out. Long before the first starting gun, stewards shut the gates and the police tried hopelessly to turn back the crushing crowds who still wanted to get in. Among them were Ralph Bannister and his 16-year-old son Roger, eager to get his first glimpse of international athletics.

The boy had never watched anything grander than a school sports, but he knew his father had an interest in running. In his day Ralph Bannister had won his school mile, collapsing at the tape in an apparent faint as so many runners did in those days after an all-out effort. Ralph Bannister knew too that his thin, gangly son shared this interest in running. Using a cocktail of schoolboy fear and nervous energy, Roger had found that he could earn some respect at school by winning cross-country races, and he often took himself off for a solitary run or long, lonely cycle rides.

For a while it seemed to both father and son that they might see nothing at all that day. The stadium was full, the gates were shut, but the human tide swelled against the barriers. The police cordon broke and thousands more flooded into the stadium, laughing and scrambling their way to the terraces. For the next four hours the teenage Roger Bannister stood and watched with wonder.

The showpiece mile race was a ding-dong battle. Andersson forced the pace from the start, but Wooderson clung to his heels, somehow refusing to be shaken off. At the bell Wooderson's legs became a blur as he edged past the long-striding Swede and the crowd went berserk. The two runners fought every step, and Wooderson held the lead until the last bend. Then Andersson, oozing Scandinavian fitness, fought back and won on the run-in. The watches stopped at 4:08.8. Sydney clocked 4:09.2 – it was his fastest mile since 1939.

With just a month's extra training poured into those pale wartime legs, Wooderson flew to Gothenburg to attack the giant in his own lair. On that occasion he ran so fast that he went through 1,500 metres in the British record time of 3:48.4, but still he could not shake off Andersson. Wooderson was still ahead with 50 metres to go, but in the end Andersson's superior strength pulled him through to victory. Wooderson's time was a tantalising 4:04.2, his best ever. Andersson did 4:03.4. It was Wooderson's last major mile and his last chance to fulfil the dream he had harboured back before the war of running a mile in four minutes.

Wooderson's swansong track season was in 1946, when he moved up in distance. Within twenty-four days he took the AAA three-mile title in record time, won against the French, and then, in Oslo, running the 5,000 metres distance for the first time, triumphed in the European 5,000-metre championship in the second fastest time ever recorded. Behind him were Reiff, Zatopek and Slijkhuis, the men who would take the gold, silver and bronze medals at the 1948 Olympics. Early in 1948, to round off an amazing career, Wooderson won the National Cross-Country Championships over a distance of nine miles.

But Sydney Wooderson's first love had always been the mile. 'Obviously I would have liked to have broken four minutes for the mile and to have won an Olympic title,' he said, 'but that's life. When the war came we didn't know if anything at all would be left of the world as we knew it. Athletic records were hardly important. When it was all over, my time had gone.

'Sport closed up once the bombing started and I went into

the army and was mainly based in Scotland,' he said in the 1980s. 'Around 1944 and '45 I started training again but I've no regrets about the lost years. I think we realised that we had to win the war so we accepted it. Quite frankly you wondered if you were going to be alive by the end, and even though I lost two Olympic Games and had retired when the 1948 Games came along, I can't really regret it. I had a fine time from 1934 to 1939. I wouldn't have wanted all that goes on today. I like it the way it was. There's too much fuss these days.'

But if Wooderson had been robbed of the four-minute mile by the war, he had still proved to be a vital link in the chain that would lead to the barrier being broken. He was coached to his phenomenal performances by Albert Hill, who had learned his trade from Sam Mussabini and Walter George. In Wooderson, the achievement of even-paced running and the secrets of decades of mental and physical training were coming together, and as a role model at international and club level his legacy was enormous.

'He inspired so many because he looked so ordinary,' said Chris Brasher. 'We looked at him and thought, "If he can do that, why can't I?"'

Above all, the flame lit by his August Bank Holiday race against Andersson was to burn for years. As a demonstration of what the wartime British called 'grit', Wooderson's battle with Andersson was unforgettable – the underdog amateur, like a patched-up Spitfire, daring to defy the might of the professionally prepared Swedish running machine. 'As boys we all have our sports heroes,' wrote Bannister a decade later, 'and Wooderson from that day became mine. I admired him as much for his attitude to running as for the feats he achieved. Seeing Wooderson's run that day inspired me with a new interest that has continued ever since.'

Half a century on, Bannister still talks of the race as if it were yesterday. 'Sydney had written a little book, no more than a pamphlet really,' he remembers. 'I read it, re-read it and that was it – I was hooked on miling.'

10

The Kings of Fartlek

If ever Gunder Haegg and I would get together and help each other, the four-minute mile would be ours for the asking.

Arne Andersson

The war blew British athletics apart. There were haphazard meetings organised by the services, some school events continued, and a devoted band of veteran officials, too old to fight, soldiered on with what survived of the athletic club structure. But there were no big championships, and no international matches to inspire a man to dream of battering barriers. For those who kept out of the conflict, however, sport continued, and where they could the crowds, weary of war news, flocked to watch any sort of competition.

Neutral Sweden was where the mile action was. And Gunder Haegg was the big action man – when he could keep himself out of trouble. He must have believed his worries were over as he checked into the Atlantic Hotel in Gothenburg on Monday 29 June 1942. Gunder stepped lightly – like a prisoner about to gulp the air of freedom. He signed his name in the hotel register and picked up the key to room 409. He knew that very soon he would be free at last to do what he did best – to step on a cinder track and race.

For 10 months Haegg had been banned from his sport, under

suspension by the Swedish Athletics Federation. Ten months is a long time to be barred from racing when you're 22 years old, a world record holder and an idol in your homeland. It had happened back in August, when for a moment, as the spectators went wild at the Swedish championships, life for Gunder had seemed too good to be true.

There, on the old Stockholm track where Strode-Jackson had surged to victory in the 1912 Olympics and Paavo Nurmi had set minds and hearts racing at the prospect of the four-minute mile, Haegg had romped away from his great rival Arne Andersson and his boyhood hero Henry Jonsson-Kalarne, to win the 1,500 metres with the watches showing 3:47.5. Even when the officials, sticking strictly to the rules of the day, insisted on rounding it down to 3:47.6, it was still a world record – Gunder's first.

Okay, said his fans, it was only two-tenths of a second faster than Jack Lovelock's old record, but look at the way he did it. He didn't bother with pacing or tactics, he simply hit the front just after halfway and began a rhythmic glide that didn't ease up until he floated through the tape. The new world record holder was a picture of effortlessness. His arms, hands, even his fingers were relaxed, and as he glanced down at the badly churned-up cinder track it looked for a moment as if he was sleep-walking across the line – as if he could break world records with his eyes shut.

But hidden among the headlines that screamed Sweden's track triumph the next day was a short and sinister report that was to trip up the new world record holder and threaten to leave his career in ruins. The Monday edition of the *Eskilstuna-Kuriren* reported that representatives of the Sports Union Club of Eskilstuna had 'after great efforts' succeeded in signing up Haegg to race in their meeting the following Friday.

Even before his world record the young and handsome Gunder had become a target for race promoters. They knew that he could set the turnstiles spinning. The public loved the way he ran. Haegg meant money, he could fill the tills. The truth was that the so-called 'great efforts' made by the over-eager officials of the Eskilstuna meeting turned out to be an undercover payment, said to be 68 kronor – almost as much as one of the Stockholm office workers who would queue to watch Haegg run could hope to earn in a month. In the world of athletics, where any hint of professionalism meant death, Sweden's new world record holder was in deep trouble.

The old amateur code still bent for no one. The horror of professionalism had ended the amateur careers of Walter George, Lon Myers, Jules Ladoumègue and even the greatest of them all – Paavo Nurmi. And in September 1941 the top guns of Swedish athletics pronounced that Haegg's career too was dead. It was not a popular verdict. The press attacked it fiercely. Gunder was a Swedish hero – and the country needed heroes like never before.

The Swedes feared that at any time they could be dragged into a war that was reducing much of Europe to rubble. Despite their declared neutrality they were haunted by the threat of German invasion. The young and charismatic Haegg was much more than an athlete; he was a symbol. He had done his National Service, trained as a soldier, and was held up as a role model, 'a hero of unbridled strength'. There he was in Sweden's best-selling magazine, hailed under the headline of 'Will for Battle' as the ideal Swedish soldier, ready to give his last ounce of strength and stamina for his country.

Some Swedish officials scrabbled around desperately for a way to save Haegg's athletic career. They remembered that when Nurmi was banned for life in 1932 for taking appearance money the Finns flatly refused to accept it, defiantly reinstating him to race again in his homeland and spitting out their hatred of the Swedes, whom they blamed for the disqualification, by cancelling the annual Sweden v. Finland athletic match every year until 1939. Now the Swedes wondered if they could pull the same trick with Haegg.

They knew, too, that the eyes of the athletic world could hardly focus on a payment of 400 kronor through the thick and serious smoke of war. Back in London, Paris and Oxford they had better things to worry about and greater battles to fight. Behind the scenes the Swedes moved quickly to defuse their little bomb. Haegg paid back the money, protesting his innocence and saying that he didn't understand the rules covering amateur status. It was agreed that the heads of four officials – two from Haegg's running club and two from the Eskilstuna club – should roll to show that action had been taken.

After endless committee meetings they got Gunder on the telephone. You are suspended, they told him, for accepting the payment. You are banned from racing. But the ban will expire after 10 months. You'll be allowed to race again from 1 July. Do you understand? Yes, said Haegg, I understand, and I am grateful, very grateful.

So he wasn't finished after all, and his first thoughts were how he would train for his comeback. Outside, the ground was iron hard with the first deep frosts of winter. Gosta Olander, Haegg's coach and guru, had warned him that running on that cruel surface would ruin his legs. But in a few weeks the deep, soft snow would come, and Gunder would mark out a path of 5,000 metres and start the varied-paced work-outs that would build him up through the long, dark Scandinavian winter.

(*Above*) Gentlemen at play: The Oxford-Cambridge mile at Lillie Bridge, in 1869. E. Royds (Cambridge) won from R.V. Somers-Smith (Oxford) in 4:35.0.

The barrier breakers: Walter George (*left*) and (*right*) Roger Bannister, the great record-setters of the nineteenth and twentieth centuries, pose for the camera. (*Below*) The duel of the century: Walter George and William Cummings race as professionals at Lillie Bridge, in the rivalry that pushed George to 4:12 for the mile in 1886.

(*Above*) Jackers, the role model: Winning the Oxford University Sports mile at Iffley Road, in 1913, Arnold Nugent Strode-Jackson was already Olympic champion at 1500 metres. (*Below*) Bound for America: Albert Hill, 800 and 1500 metre Olympic champion in 1920, with his wife and two daughters, at Waterloo Station as he sets off for New York.

(*Above*) Bound for America: A trio of champion milers, Joe Binks (*right*) Sydney Wooderson, and his coach Albert Hill (*left*), leave Victoria in June 1939 for the 'Mile of the Century' in Princeton. (*Below*) Harold 'Chariots of Fire' Abrahams: Winning the AAA Championships 100 yards in 1924 with the Mussabini dip-finish. Abrahams was 100 metre Olympic Champion, 1924.

(*Left*) The time machine: Paavo Nurmi at Stamford Bridge, in 1931, checks his pace on the watch carried in the palm of his hand. Some believed it was a picture of his mother.

(*Below*) The pride of France Jules Ladoumegue, first miler under 4:10. Banned as a professional, he carried on in the circus ring.

eamwork, Oxford-style: Jack Lovelock (no. 22) and Jerry Cornes, in the strip of Oxford Blues, hit the tape together in the Oxford-Cambridge mile, March 1932.

(*Left*) All-weather outfits: Warming up for the 1935 Hospitals Championships, Jack Lovelock (*left*) and his St Mary's team-mate J.N. Gosse, at the Duke of York's track, Chelsea.

(*Below*) Boaters and hand-held stopwatches in the golden age of miling: Jack Lovelock runs world record 4:07.6 at Palmer Stadium, Princeton, 15 July, 1933

The hand of greatness: Walter George, greatest miler of the nineteenth century, congratulates Sydney Wooderson on his world record mile at Motspur Park in 1937.

In July he would compete again. He had already agreed to take part in a race in Gothenburg as soon as the suspension ran out. The organisers told him that Arne Andersson would be there too. And the comeback race would be over 'one English mile'.

Haegg made his way to Gothenburg from his training camp in Valadalen. There he had taken out the frustration of not being free to race by training more fiercely than ever along the forest paths. He hadn't set foot on a cinder running track for the best part of a year and he was brimming over with health, fitness and an overwhelming need to race and to show his friends and the world what he was made of.

With the sentence of suspension hanging over him, he had taken himself off to lick his wounds under the guidance of Sweden's most remarkable coach, Gosta Olander. Half trainer, half spiritual guide, Olander had set up an idyllic camp at Valadalen, where amid the pine forests and the lakeside paths Haegg and some of the finest of Sweden's athletes found fitness and inspiration.

At a time when many of the world's leading middle and long distance runners were being seduced into having their every run timed on the confines of a monotonous cinder track, the Swedish coaches were evangelists of freedom, of training in the most beautiful of natural surroundings. They preached the joy of running. They called their system 'fartlek' – which translates into English as 'speed-play'. It was to inspire generations of runners worldwide. In far-off Australia an eccentric coach called Percy Cerutty used it as the foundation for his own system of training. He set up his training camp in the sand dunes of Portsea, and it was there that in time he preached the joys of fartlek to a young miler called John Landy.

Olander had his men training not over sand hills but through forests and beside lakes over undulating pine and spruce needles. They ran fast and fluently. When it came to middle-distance training, Olander preached quality above quantity – and relaxation above all.

In Gothenburg Haegg relaxed as best he could in the sauna and stretched out on the bed in his hotel room. But when he worked out gently in the Castle Forest, the day before the race, he was virtually pawing the ground, having to hold himself back from exploding and blunting his racing edge. He felt great, but after a long period with no racing could he be sure? There was a part of him that was uncertain, and uncertainty meant fear. Would Andersson fly by at the finish and make him look stupid? Anderson, Haegg knew, was strong. He feared his ability to sprint.

Olander had put Haegg on a schedule of plenty of speed work – though Gunder was no sprinter. But the forest work had put a snap in his running, given him the ability to change pace quickly, to have it in him to push hard on the third lap – when others were harbouring their strength for the finish. Training, though, is not racing. Too many athletes, Gunder knew, could churn it out in training but buckled in the heat of the race.

Racing against the clock is very different to racing against men. There's a terrific nervous strain in a first-class race that begins long before the athletes toe the start line. Unless you can stand the strain, unless you can get your nerves under control, you and your performance can suffer. Gunder found it almost frightening that he wasn't frightened by the trial ahead. He ought to be nervous about this first public demonstration of his fitness. But he wasn't.

A top Swedish sports writer, Nils Engdahl, himself an

Olympic medallist at 400 metres in 1920 and 1924, watched in awe the vibrancy coiled in Haegg's sinewy legs. As the athlete worked out, Engdahl had no doubts. 'There's only one way tomorrow's race is going to go,' he said. 'Gunder is unbeatable.'

Haegg's hotel room was full of letters, cards and telegrams. As well as all those welcoming the exile back to the track there were dozens more congratulating him on getting engaged to his girlfriend Daisy. He was furious at these. He reckoned that part of his life was private and the press had no right running stories about it. 'I'll sue the bastard who wrote that story,' he said. But already Haegg was a celebrity, and he'd have to get used to the crowds that would follow his every move on and off the track.

Half a century later, women who were girls when Gunder was a god still remembered how they used to hang about the haberdashery shop in Malmo where he took a job as a salesman. They would pretend they wanted to buy a necktie for their brothers or their fathers – but what they really wanted was a chance to smile at their hero, perhaps even snatch a few words with him. They would boast to their friends and giggle. They were not happy when Daisy snapped him up.

Gunder was dozing on his bed the next day when Engdahl knocked on the door of room 409 to take him to the meeting. Haegg picked up the soft white leather 'Finish' running spikes lying on his sports bag and swung downstairs to the waiting car. As they drove through the crowds already snaking towards the stadium, he noted drily that there seemed to be a sudden interest in athletics in a town that was normally hooked on football.

Outside the stadium the crowds were going mad. They cheered, they chanted and waved flags wildly. Inside Gunder stood for a few moments in the peace of the dressing room, inhaling the familiar smells of sweat and liniment. It was good to be back. There in a corner sat Bror Hellstrom, 27 years old, strong as an elk, a fireman from Stockholm. Arne Andersson, the real danger, paced restlessly around the dressing room and the corridors under the stand. He was muttering like a boxer before the bell. Gunder, by contrast, seemed more quiet and reserved than usual. He was not sure why, but he felt as if his passion to race had suddenly deserted him. A few in the dressing room wondered if perhaps he was human after all.

One of the athletes, Rune Gustafsson, a champion 800 and 1,500-metre man, sat on a bench kneading his calf muscle, teasing out the tendon with practised fingers. From outside Gunder could hear the public address system, the waves of applause and cheers from the crowd. The stadium gates were already closed. Police on horses were blocking the main entrance, hemmed in by the crowd. Several thousand couldn't get in but still milled around outside. Inside the stadium men with megaphones and blue and yellow flags were urging the crowd to chant '*Heja* Arne, *heja* Gunder – let us see the world's great wonder.'

As he stepped out on to the track, Gunder noticed that the flags were stirring in the evening breeze, and from the speakers of the public address system came military music. Some of the athletes were out on the grass of the infield, already warming up. On the straight the starter raised his gun for a hurdle race. There was the familiar flash, the floating smoke, the thump of the blank cartridge. Gunder took deep breaths and blew the air through his lips. He could sense his heartbeat already getting faster. All around him were the sights, the sounds and smells that reminded him that he was back in business.

Gunder always said about the track that you should regard

yourself as a guest there, a visitor. You go there, he said, as if you were going to a party. But you don't go to parties every day. He knew that this comeback party had to be special. As he warmed up, he ran through the mental ritual that always got him through his races. Run relaxed, run really relaxed; that was his advice to himself or any would-be miler. Run loose, you must never tighten up. Run the first two laps as if you are out on your own, don't get involved in shoving, in the clashes of elbows. Simply run your own race. It gets serious only in the third lap – then you go into top gear, that's when you increase the pace without tightening up.

Gunder was still playing these thoughts endlessly in his head as the booming amplified voice of the announcer hushed the crowd and called the athletes to the line. All over Sweden they huddled around their wireless sets. The live broadcast of Gunder's comeback race against Arne over the English mile was not one to be missed.

If Haegg had any real doubts about his racing fitness they vanished round the first turn as his spikes bit into the track and the strength and confidence poured back into his legs. As the crackling commentary rose to a climax the race unfolded in a repeat of the Stockholm duel ten months before. Arne Andersson was famed for his fast finish, but once more Haegg ran the sting out of him.

The man who had been starved of racing devoured the track and glided across the line in 4:06.1, with Arne Andersson second in 4:06.4. Under the rules then in effect, the time was rounded up to 4:06.2. Gunder smiled. Once again he had knocked just two-tenths off the world record – Sydney Wooderson's record – but he knew there was plenty more to come and that Arne Andersson would be out to get his revenge.

Gunder had already experienced many moments of triumph

in his short athletic life, but none as sweet as this. He was back
– light-footed and light-hearted – and the world would know
it. Unwinding back at the Atlantic Hotel, he pulled a crum-
pled envelope from his pocket. 'Welcome back to the racing
track' read the note inside. It was signed 'from your companions in Eskilstuna.' Haegg put it back in his pocket without a
word. The memory of how their payment had so nearly cost
him his running career was still too raw. He'd have to look
out for potholes like that in future, he vowed, for promoters
too eager to pay him to toe the line, and for journalists too
ready to splash the story. After all, he and Andersson had races
to run and records to set.

By the time this pair had finished battering the mile record
they would have brought it to within a flicker of the four-
minute dream, and their training, their tactics and their very
lives would be combed for the clues that might solve the mystery
of how to run the four-minute mile.

Perhaps you should start when you're six years old. That was
when Gunder's father gave him his first pair of skis. When
the snows of winter came all the boys would use skis to make
the cross-country journey to school. Gunder soon found that
he could start later than the others, catch them up and still be
first to warm his hands around the big wood-burning stove
crackling with pine logs in the schoolroom. Later, when he
tried running without skis, Gunder found that he could run
well too, far faster than his friends of the same age. It was
nothing to boast about, it was just fun, and he and his play-
mates took his ability for granted.

But sometimes Gunder dreamed a little and wondered just
how fast he might run. He knew running could make you a
hero, and a local hero at that. In the Berlin Olympics of 1936

a Swede, Henry Jonsson-Kalarne, had taken the bronze medal in the 5,000 metres, and had gone on to break the world record at 3,000 metres in 1940.

Kalarne came from a farm not far from the Haegg home, Albacken, in the province of Jaemtland. And when the young Gunder wanted some labouring and lumberjack work, he took a job with the very farmer, Fridolf Westman, who had discovered Kalarne and given him his first coaching advice. Westman had been a runner himself, and he gave Haegg free board and lodging in the room that Kalarne had occupied – in the annexe above the bakery.

Gunder was aching to learn and eager to compete. At the age of 17 he had shown that he was ready to have a go at anything in the local Albacken championships. He won the high jump with 4 foot 10 inches; the pole vault with 7 foot 2 inches; and the 1,500 metres in 4 minutes 54 seconds. He even took his chances in the sprints, coming second in both the 100 and 400 metres. Soon he was winning local races at 1,500 and 5,000 metres.

Gunder's father, Nils, was as excited by the early results as his son. He sent 13 Swedish kronor off to Åhlen & Holm, a mail order company, for a pair of track spikes for him. The spikes went with them that summer when Haegg and his father trekked deep into forest country as part of a lumberjacking gang. It was tough work and Gunder loved it. 'It's a job where you learn how to use your muscles,' he said. 'It gives you a very strong back and you get lots of fresh air.'

Even after all the felling and lifting, Haegg would pull on his spikes and run in the cool of the evening on the pine-needled forest paths. His father measured out a 1,500-metre course, starting from the wooden hut they were living in and taking in a stretch of rough track used for carting timber. In later years the tale of Gunder's first time trial over this course would be re-run and re-spun into athletic legend. Nils Haegg, it was said, squatted on the doorstep of the lumberjack's hut armed with a large alarm clock. He started Gunder with a shout and clocked him as he finished.

The time of 4 minutes and 45 seconds, he announced, was first class for the rough, undulating loop and a 17-year-old running alone. In the afterglow, father and son talked long into the night, plotting a glorious future. It was not until years later, so the story goes, that Haegg senior confessed he had deducted 30 seconds from the time – not wishing to pour cold water on the enthusiastic dreams of his would-be-champion son.

It was another interested father who set Arne Andersson, Haegg's greatest rival, on the path to running. He pushed Arne into sport, particularly swimming and athletics, where the family had a fine tradition as competitors. By the time he was 18 the young Andersson was already Swedish 1,500 metres college champion, and by 21 he was breaking four minutes for the 1,500 metres. With the encouragement of his father, Arne shone at a whole range of sports. He ran and swam like a champion, and was in demand as a player of indoor handball and bandy – the local version of ice hockey. Whatever the sport, if he tried it Arne looked like a winner.

The young Andersson's training was more sophisticated than the rough farm and forest running of Gunder Haegg. Andersson went to college to train as a teacher, and with the help of the finest coaching to be had he soon broke through to international level. He became the first Swede to break 3 minutes 50 seconds for the 1,500 metres, in July 1939, when he out-kicked Finland's finest to record 3:48.8.

To Arne it was a hard-earned pay-off for all the hours of

training he had packed in. He clocked up the miles on and off the track – sometimes training for as long as four hours at a stretch – and he backed up the running with regular bouts of strengthening work in the gym. It was not until he was qualified as a teacher and got a job in the suburbs outside Stockholm that he began to modify his training and make it more like that of Haegg.

The change was forced on him by the demands of the job. Unable to find the time for his four-hour sessions, Arne discovered that 'quality' training could achieve as much and more than 'quantity'. He began to concentrate on shorter and tougher periods of running, and, like Haegg, he took to the forest paths. There he measured up a loop of around 3,000 metres which he'd cover once or twice in a session, charging up the hills, jogging to recover and sprinting in bursts to hone his finish.

When these two runners stepped out of the forest loops and on to Sweden's running tracks the records fell as never before. In the 82 days that followed his comeback world record in Gothenburg, Gunder Haegg went on the greatest middle-distance record-shattering binge that the world had ever seen. By 20 September that year he had set 10 new world records between 1,500 and 5,000 metres and brought the mile time down to 4:04.6. In that 1942 season he raced in 33 races at distances from 800 to 5,000 metres. He won the lot.

But there was even more to come, and in 1943 while Haegg took a cargo ship, the Saturnus, to America to race there undefeated, Arne Andersson struck back in Gothenburg on 1 July with a mile record of his own of 4:02.6.

Over the next two seasons Haegg and Andersson slugged it out on the track like prizefighters. Their every meeting was a sell-out and their every appearance had the crowds baying for records. Twice at Malmo it seemed the magic mile must be run and the four-minute barrier must fall.

The first time was on 18 July 1944, on a perfect Scandinavian evening, with the novel addition of spotlights so that the race could be filmed. The cameramen could hardly believe what they were seeing. The closely packed field of five runners covered the first lap in 57.1 seconds. They passed through the half-mile in 1:56.7 and the three-quarters in 2:59.6. This was dream miling indeed, and with the stylish Haegg in the lead the four-minute mile seemed within reach. Andersson was still trailing at the 1,500 metres mark, but the early pace sapped even Haegg's stamina, and Arne came past him before the tape with a devastating burst. He had run an amazing 4:01.6.

When the pair met again on the same Malmo track a year later, on 17 July 1945, there were plenty predicting that this time the four-minute barrier must be smashed. Once more the evening and the track were perfect. Both Haegg and Andersson knew that every detail would have to be right for the dream mile. They were both in great shape, they had both run within a few strides of the magic time, but both knew well that the slightest problem – a pothole in the track, a clash of clattering spikes – could ruin a record run.

The first lap of 56.7 was even faster than in the record mile of the previous year. But Andersson, defending his world record, was running with the niggling realisation that all was not well for him on the night when everything had to be perfect. Bizarrely, an empty cartridge case from the starter's gun had somehow got on to the track. It was caught between Arne's needle-sharp spikes and wedged itself beneath his shoe. The crushed cartridge, its brass tip twisted, was like an instant callus under his foot. He tried to stamp or shake it free, but every step fixed it more firmly. He tried not to break stride despite the unwelcome distraction. It wouldn't stop him, but it threw him a little. He was not happy.

The half-mile was passed in 1:59.4, almost perfect pace for an attempt on four minutes. Haegg went into the lead on the third lap as he loved to do; he went through the three-quarters in 3:01.4. Andersson, still battling with his cartridge case, closed up behind Gunder but couldn't get up on his toes for his trademark sprint and had to settle for second place. Haegg was timed in a new world record of 4:01.4. Once again the four-minute barrier had narrowly survived.

Arne walked away from the finish, his head down. His wife Karin scrambled from the stands to reach him. He peeled off his spike and showed her the cartridge case, shaking his head in anger and frustration. He was left wondering ruefully if he, or anyone else, would ever get everything perfect for an attack on the dream mile.

But speculation over whether the four-minute mile was possible had never been stronger. And if the barrier was going to be broken, it was generally believed, it would fall to one of the two great Swedes. Their battles stimulated plenty of crystal ball gazing. In early 1944, before Haegg or Andersson had ducked below 4:02, Arnold Strode-Jackson, whose Olympic victory had prompted some to dream of four minutes back in 1912, gave his views on the quest for the dream mile time.

'There are experts, men of science and sports followers, who maintain that the mile will never be run in four minutes flat,' he wrote in *Collier's Magazine*. 'I say it is not only possible but inevitable. It will not require a special sort of oxygen mask or a new form of elixir; it will not necessarily be done by a superman or on an electrically charged track. It will probably be done by men now actively engaged in the sport.

'Why am I so confident that this is true? Because races just short of a mile are being run today on what is practically a four-minute-mile basis.' Strode-Jackson predicted confidently that 'the four-minute mile, when it comes, can be run at a rate of 58 seconds for the first quarter; 62 seconds for the second quarter; 61 seconds for the third quarter; and 59 seconds for the last quarter. A mile in four minutes! And about time, too.

'When we stop this nonsense of running like a metronome and with the watch always in mind, we will get back to real racing, the triumph of one runner over another. That is what racing was meant to be and what it will be when we get the four-minute myth out of the way.'

The well-matched rivalry of Haegg and Andersson had driven them to carve chunks off the mile record in a way that had not been seen since the days of Walter George 60 years before. By the time he had finished with it, Haegg had lowered Wooderson's old mile record from 4:06.4 to 4:01.4, an improvement of five seconds. Undoubtedly, the running of Andersson had pushed Haegg to his records.

Finding someone to set the pace or push you to the limit is always a problem for the would-be record breaker. When a worthy opponent emerges, records will usually fall. It took a Cummings to push Walter George, Wide and Peltzer to wind up Nurmi, the Americans to threaten Lovelock. Without an equal, the feat is far more difficult. Ladoumègue and Wooderson had been forced to use pacemakers – and many believed only pacemakers could ever tow a man to the dream mile in four minutes.

With so little to choose between them, Haegg and Andersson revolutionised middle-distance running. They appeared neither to anticipate nor fear any barrier to their record breaking; but for them the race was always what mattered – the joy of being first at the tape. They competed wherever and whenever they could, at meetings great and small all over Sweden. The closer their rivalry, and the closer they edged to the four-minute mile, the greater the crowds that could be enticed through the turn-stiles.

The promoters revelled in their rivalry and were prepared to bend the old amateur code to breaking point to get them on the track. The payments that were whispered about as the meetings were arranged made the 400 kronor that got Haegg banned at the start of his career seem like pocket money. Eventually even Svenska Idrottsforbund, the rulers of Sweden's athletics, ran out of blind eyes to turn.

By the time they last raced each other, on 21 September 1945, Haegg and Andersson knew that they were being chased by rumours of professionalism. That meeting, like so many others, was a complete sell-out. Their rival Lennart Strand stole their thunder in the mile that day, winning in 4:04.8, but off the track their more dangerous opponents in the Swedish Athletic Federation were ready to run them down. Early in 1946 the authorities concluded that there had been too many breaches of the amateur code, and Gunder Haegg and Arne Andersson, along with their old friend and inspiration Henry Jonsson-Kalarne, were banned for life.

Andersson was heart-broken, Haegg philosophical. And for a while the four-minute mile was safe as the men who had run to its very brink realised there was no appeal, no way back from the life ban that had ended their careers. Andersson in particular believed that another full season of competition would have brought either or both of them under the magic four-minute barrier. Sport and competition were so important a part of his life that anger and frustration gave way to depression as he tried vainly to fight the ruling.

Arne believed that he had only just begun to gain the strength that would allow him to run more relaxed and give him the edge over Haegg. He was bitter – convinced in his heart that the times they had set could be bettered. He kept training hard, and eventually took to cycling to try to find an outlet for his competitive juices. He was even tempted into a professional running comeback against the American miler the Reverend Gil Dodds at a trade fair in 1949. But there was no way back to the amateur ranks, and the 'Magic Mile' time, which so many believed belonged to Andersson and Haegg, looked as elusive as ever.

Gunder Haegg took it all more calmly. He had had his time. He had run his races and set his records. He enjoyed his popularity and celebrity and made the best of his sporting legacy. Always in demand for interviews, he became a commentator and showed up at the 1948 Winter Olympics looking as fit as ever at 29 and reporting for the Stockholm sports paper *Idrottsbladet*.

'Is four minutes a barrier?' they would ask him. 'No, I don't think so,' he'd reply.

'Could Arne and I have run the four-minute mile? Probably. Yes, probably.'

11

The Olympic Dream

After all those dark days of the war, the bombing, the killing,
the starvation, the revival of the Olympics was as if the sun had
come out ... I went into the Olympic village and suddenly there
were no more frontiers, no more barriers ... Men and women
who had just lost five years of life were back again.

Emil Zatopek, on the London Games of 1948

When the war ended in 1945, plans were made to pick up the
threads of the Olympic Games, which had not been held since
Hitler's notorious Nazi Olympics of 1936. The 1940 games
should have gone to Tokyo, but following the outbreak of war
between Japan and China in 1938 the International Olympic
Committee withdrew the invitation and asked Helsinki to step
in and take over the 1940 Games. The IOC also planned, at a
meeting in 1939, to nominate London as the venue for the 1944
Olympics. All this forward planning was blown to pieces when
war broke out on 3 September 1939.

Experts can only guess what might have happened to middle-
distance running and the mile record if there had been no war.
Certainly you could have expected fine Olympic performances
from some great middle-distance giants whose careers were
cut short or ruined. Rudolf Harbig of Germany, for example,
had pioneered a new method of conditioning, interval training,

under the supervision of Dr Woldemar Gerschler. In 1939 Harbig set world records of 46 seconds for 400 metres and 1:46.6 for 800 metres – an astonishing time that was not bettered for 16 years. Tragically, he was killed on the Eastern Front in March 1944.

Straight after the war, in 1946, the IOC awarded the Games to London. With only two years to get themselves ready, the organising committee, chaired by the 1928 400-metre hurdle champion, Lord Burghley, faced a formidable task, particularly in view of the austerity of post-war Britain, where people were poor, cold and often hungry. In the winter of 1946/47, while the Games committee were scrabbling together the best facilities Britain could offer, the country shivered in temperatures that fell to –26° Centigrade.

Rationing was even worse than at the height of the war. Many people were out of work, while others were on strike, and factories were shutting down because of a national shortage of coal. Through that harsh winter, homes, businesses, even doctors' surgeries were frequently reduced to candlelight. One of the worst winters in memory brought transport to a standstill, with even boats unable to put to sea.

That summer, the Chancellor of the Exchequer, Hugh Dalton, had warned that even less food would be available than the year before, and tougher austerity measures were brought in, backed up by slogans declaring: 'Work or Want'. It was a bleak background for the athletes, and for the men and women who were preparing to welcome the youth of the world to celebrate the Olympic Games.

Sport, though, was still popular, so much so that midweek horse-racing and football fixtures were banned because it was feared they would encourage too many to stay away from work. In 1948, with the war almost three years behind them, the government at last lifted bread rationing, and thousands of hospitals and doctors' surgeries were brought into the newly formed National Health Service.

Times were still tough enough, though, for the 1948 Olympics to be labelled 'The Austerity Games'. London had emerged from the war battered, torn and bloody but unbowed. The austerity, however, was all-pervading. The committee who cobbled together the 1948 Olympics were faced with some very big problems – not least how to feed, house and equip teams from all over the world. The budget for Wembley's Games was £761,000. There weren't too many frills. The male competitors were housed in military camps and the women in colleges.

There was no special transport. Fanny Blankers-Koen, who won four gold medals in London, said, 'We walked to the station and went by underground to the Olympic stadium.' By way of a concession, those British competitors taking part in the 1948 Olympics were given increased rations for two weeks leading up to the Games. An athletics training camp for Olympic possibles was set up at Butlins in Clacton. According to Stan Cox, the 10,000 metres runner, the real value of the training camp was not the exercise sessions, but the extra food available while the rest of the nation was still on rationing. There was considerable animosity in the country from some who thought the Olympics a waste of money. But the Games were a huge success.

Massive crowds, often in excess of 80,000, made their way to Wembley each day. They had been starved of sporting spectacles for too long. Not surprisingly, Germany and Japan were not invited, and the Soviet Union declined to make its Olympic debut until 1952. Nonetheless, a record 59 nations, 52 of them taking part in athletics, turned up for the London Games.

The opening ceremony, on 29 July, at the Empire Stadium, Wembley, was held in a heatwave. The crowd basked in summer dresses and shirtsleeves to witness Lord Burghley invite King George VI to open the first Games for 12 years. The King's words echoed around Wembley's giant concrete stands, and were heard by millions of wireless listeners and a handful of those in the London area who huddled around tiny black-and-white television screens: 'I proclaim open the Olympic Games of London, celebrating the fourteenth Olympiad of the modern era.'

The crowd were spellbound by the pageantry, dazzled by the scarlet and gold of the trumpeters of the Household Cavalry, delighted by the massed bands of the Brigade of Guards. The teams were led in by Greece, with Britain, the host nation, bringing up the rear of the parade. A fanfare declared the Games open. The Olympic flag was hoisted. Seven thousand pigeons were released, and the last runner in the torch relay which had started in Olympia circled the track to kindle the Olympic flame.

There were plenty, including the Queen, who felt that the honour of running with the torch into London's Olympic stadium should have gone to Sydney Wooderson, who had done so much to keep the flame of athletics flickering through the years of wartime. However, Wooderson was apparently considered too puny-looking for the job, and instead the flame was carried by a tall, blond runner, clad completely in white. He was a former Cambridge 440 and 880 yards runner – John Mark – who had been president of the Cambridge University Athletic Club in 1947 when Roger Bannister first competed for Oxford. Ironically, this Adonis-like athlete had received food parcels through the war from New Zealand, partly fixed up by Jack Lovelock.

With the symbolic flame reborn, the bands and the choir all dressed in white were conducted in the Olympic hymn by Sir Malcolm Sargent, and Wing Commander Donald Finlay, the veteran hurdler, took the Olympic oath. The track events began in glorious weather the following day.

On the fifth day of the Games they lined up for the heats of the metric mile, the 1,500 metres, where many confidently predicted there would be a new world record. The field of 40 entrants was loaded with middle-distance class, particularly from Sweden. There was Lennart Strand, reckoned by those who knew the form to be the favourite. He jointly held the world record of 3:43 with his countryman Gunder Haegg. Haegg was still the holder of the world mile record, while the other Swedish competitors – Gosta Bergkvist and Henry Eriksson – had both bettered the old Olympic record of 3:47.8 set by Jack Lovelock in 1936.

Of the British runners, Doug Wilson and Dick Morris were eliminated in the heats, but Bill Nankeville, the 1948 AAA mile champion, qualified for the final. Also in the field was young Josy Barthel, from Luxembourg, who was to go on to win this event in the next Olympics in 1952. Twelve lined up for the final on the seventh day of the Games. There was a cloudburst and lashing rain just before the start and the runners stepped out on to a track made soft and sludgy by the downpour, the cinder lanes punctuated by puddles. Rain and wind had spoiled any hopes of a world record.

Nothing, though, could dampen the excitement of the Swedish supporters, who kept up a chant of '*Heja, heja*' as their runners dominated the race. Eriksson won easily in 3:49.8 from his more fancied countryman Strand, with Bill Nankeville back in sixth in 3:52.6.

Emil Zatopek became a great favourite with the crowd as

he ran away with the 10,000 metres, averaging 72 seconds for each of his 25 laps to give Czechoslovakia her first ever Olympic title. The British runner Jim Peters, who finished a disappointing eighth in the race, a whole lap behind Zatopek, would go on to become a barrier breaker at marathon running.

Bob Mathias of the USA was the boy wonder of the Games, winning the decathlon at the age of 17, and Fanny Blankers-Koen of Holland the wonder woman. She became the first woman to win four gold medals in a single Olympics. Harrison Dillard found fame as the man who won the wrong event. Nicknamed 'Bones' because he was so skinny, Dillard, from the USA, failed to qualify in his best event, the hurdles, but won gold in the 100 metres anyway.

Bill Nankeville, Britain's 1,500-metre finalist, had secured his place in the Games by winning the mile at the 1948 AAA Championships on 3 July. Beaten into fifth place that afternoon was a young and relatively unknown runner from Oxford University – Roger Bannister. Nankeville continued to be Britain's best miler until he was eventually beaten in these same championships by Bannister in 1951.

Nankeville had emerged as an athlete during the war years, but his approach to training and racing was wonderfully grounded in the past. His training was light and owed much to patterns set in the 1930s. World-record-breaking distance runner Gordon Pirie always said that Nankeville was born half a dozen years too soon. If he had been subjected to the training of the generation of runners who followed him, Pirie said, 'I'm sure he would have been the first four-minute miler.'

Nankeville trained under the guidance of Bill Thomas, Jack Lovelock's old coach. When he asked Thomas if he would coach him he added that he couldn't afford to pay him much. 'Nankeville, my boy,' Thomas replied, 'I'm not interested in money. You will pay me in results.' Thomas's first piece of coaching advice to Nankeville was that he would have to learn to run properly. What mattered above all, said Thomas, was style. In time the press would describe Nankeville as the most stylish of all milers.

By the autumn of 1947, Nankeville was training regularly under Thomas at the old Herne Hill track in London. Hour after hour the coach had him jogging and sprinting around the track, and always it was the same cry – 'Style, style, style!' At 73 years of age, Thomas was still working with the RAF athletic team, and before the war he had been coach to Oxford University. He had produced such great athletes as Jack Lovelock, Jerry Cornes, Sam Ferris, who won the AAA marathon seven years in a row and was second in the 1932 Los Angeles Olympics, and Don Finlay, the hurdler, who won bronze and silver in the Games of 1932 and 1936.

Bill Thomas always insisted that his athletes take a cold shower after training, and even in his seventies he practised what he preached. Once a week he would trot off for a five-mile run and finish off by dousing himself in ice-cold water. His coaching style reeked of a vanished era. He would usually stand at the side of the track in a double-breasted suit, his tie neatly knotted, always wearing a trilby hat. He would silently observe his charges circle the track while he peered constantly at his stopwatch.

On the eve of the 1948 Olympics, Bill Thomas was still using coaching techniques common a century before. Just a fortnight before the Games Nankeville was badly beaten in a slow 1,500 metres in Manchester. On the train back to London he collapsed and once home took to his sick bed. With his crucial race just 14 days away, Nankeville was lying in bed ill, having lost almost a stone in weight.

Bill Thomas was sent for. He promptly prescribed sherry and egg for the athlete, and told him to turn up at the Herne Hill track, where he made him lap slowly on the grass. Nankeville doubted that the treatment would work, but to his delight and surprise, when Thomas demanded that he should test his fitness in a time trial, he ran faster than he had ever done before.

The end came for Bill Thomas in 1953, on the very eve of the four-minute mile, when he was 80. During a heavy storm a thunderbolt hit his house and killed him. After the funeral Bill Nankeville was presented with the old coach's stopwatch.

By 1951 Bill Nankeville, firmly established as Britain's champion miler, hoped to win the AAA championship mile for the fourth year in a row. The pre-race forecasts had narrowed the likely winners down to three: John Parlett, who had moved up from the half mile; Bill Nankeville; and the young Roger Bannister. Parlett was considered the great danger, with Bannister very much the outsider. Consequently Nankeville watched Parlett, and just as he thought he had the beating of him, Bannister streaked away, leaving the other two flat-footed, to win the AAA title in 4:07.8.

A new generation had arrived, and Nankeville's reign as Britain's top miler was over. While Nankeville had been swallowing his egg and sherry potions before the '48 Games, there had been a lively debate about whether Bannister should have been included in the team. In November 1947 he had received an invitation to become a 'possible' for the Olympic Games the following summer. These possibles were to receive assistance that ranged from special coaching to food parcels, sent by the Dominions to supplement the meagre food rations currently available in Britain. Bannister said that he felt he was not ready at the time for the cauldron of the Olympics, and feared it might prejudice his chances for the 1952 Games. He turned the invitation down.

Other athletes at the time, like Sylvia Cheeseman and John Disley, believed that Bannister might have benefited by being blooded at the London Games, and that he would have performed better subsequently in Helsinki in 1952. Bannister himself saw nothing strange in his decision and seemed surprised that it received considerable publicity. 'Bannister says he's too young,' said one headline. However, his old friend and training partner Chris Brasher said that the publicity was entirely predictable and that it was 'an early example of Roger backing into the limelight'.

Even without the lure of the Games, Bannister kept training, and in the early Olympic summer of 1948 he won the mile in the match against Cambridge and in the British University Championships in the identical time of 4:23.4. On 19 June, in a crowded field in the Kinnaird Trophy, he finished a strong fourth in 4:18.7.

With his running going so well, he began to wonder if he should have tried for Olympic selection after all. 'I wavered in my decision,' he said. Certainly his contemporaries believed that he entered the AAA mile championships with the firm hope that he might still win selection for the Games. In the event, although Bannister improved his time to 4:17.2 and was the third Briton home, he was not picked for the team.

Instead, he was given a job as assistant to Colonel Evan Hunter, the commandant of the British Olympic team. His duties ranged from delivering messages and letters to ferrying visitors around the Olympic village in Uxbridge. More significantly, the job allowed the young miler into the Olympic stadium, where what he witnessed was to influence his outlook on athletics for ever.

His first taste of his Olympic duties on the day of the opening ceremony, however, brought panic. It was discovered that the only team without a national flag for the opening parade was Britain's. 'Fortunately I had brought along an old spare flag to Wembley,' said Bannister. 'I had to smash open a window on a locked car in front of a policeman, who wanted to arrest me, grasp the flag and then use it as a battering ram through the crowd, to reach the British team just before they marched into the stadium.'

From inside the stadium over the two weeks of the Games, Bannister was able to see some extraordinary performances on track and field, and was swept along by the ideals that lay behind the Olympics. Before the Games he had seen his running as a very personal affair. It was a way of achieving mastery over himself, control over his body and mind, and a useful tool for building status among his school fellows. But being part of the Olympic movement – even if not as a competitor – gave him a glimpse of sport's greater significance.

'Many of the principles that I had learned in Oxford, and thought to be Oxford's special contribution to sport, I now discovered had existed for over 2,000 years,' said Bannister. 'The debt of loyalty that I had reserved for Oxford I now found I owed to a whole world of sport that was born with the Olympic movement and that was rejuvenated with each Olympic Games.'

The Greek ideal of sport was that its true value was as a preparation for life in general. The Greeks loved the idea of competition, whether it was in sport, drama, art or poetry. The aim of their Games was the improvement of the whole man. The Greek Olympic ideal had become debased only when the idea of the all-rounder with a sound mind in a sound body was lost. Then the professional athlete emerged to dominate sport, devoting all his time to his training without any other occupation. It was this development that proved fatal to the amateur spirit, and to the ancient Greek Olympic Games.

In reviving the Olympic Games in 1896, the French aristocrat Baron de Coubertin had defined his sporting ideal by proclaiming, 'The important thing in the Olympic Games is not winning but taking part. The essential thing in life is not conquering but fighting well.'

By the closing ceremony of the 1948 Games, Roger Bannister was aching to take part himself. He had seen the magnificence of Emil Zatopek's runaway victory in the 10,000 metres. He had seen the strength of European runners in his chosen event, the 1,500 metres. He knew they would be running even faster by the time of the next Olympics and that he would have to do so too.

But what he had seen on the track at Wembley had inspired him and strengthened his ambition. Like Jack Lovelock before him, Roger Bannister now knew exactly what he would be aiming at for the next four years.

12

The Young Bannister

Fear is the strongest driving force in competition. Not fear of
one's opponent but of the skill and high standard which he
represents. Fear, too, of not acquitting oneself well in the
achievement of greater performances or beating formidable
rivals. The athlete defeats fear and conquers himself.

Franz Stampfl

At the time Bill Nankeville was linking up and forging a relationship with Bill Thomas, Roger Bannister was walking into
the quadrangles of Exeter College, Oxford.

Fifteen years earlier, Jack Lovelock, like Bannister a medical
student who found release and fulfilment in his running, was
also a student at Exeter. When Bannister arrived there at the
beginning of the Michaelmas Term in 1946, it was as a 17-
year-old boy among men. Most of the undergraduates were
ex-servicemen, back from the war, older, more mature, and,
above all, more confident than the uncertain school-leaver.

He was proud enough to be a member of this ancient and
famous university but he was intimidated as well as excited by
its possibilities. He was up at Oxford to study medicine, having
long set his heart on a career as a doctor, but he was determined, too, to be a runner.

Already, Roger Bannister's analytical mind had deduced

that he did not have the build or the weight to be a rower or a rugby player, nor the eye for ball games. What he could do was run. The haste with which he took himself off on a lone pilgrimage to the Iffley Road track, and his eagerness to sign up for his college athletics club – which could trace its roots back to 1850 – betrayed a passion for the sport that he was determined to pursue.

'I had found a new source of power and beauty,' he wrote. 'A source I never dreamt existed.' Running, he said, brought him joy, freedom and a challenge that could not be found elsewhere. As a boy he ran everywhere. He remembers the sheer exhilaration of charging up flights of steps on Lansdowne Hill, Bath, his school satchel bouncing on his back. He ran everywhere, he said, because he found it easier than walking.

He remembers, too, how as a boy fear of school bullies or falling bombs could produce a rush of adrenalin that enabled him to tap hidden reservoirs of speed. Winning the school cross-country race at the City of Bath Boys' School did wonders for his self-respect. 'In the peculiar convention of English schools, it now seemed that I would be allowed by my school fellows to work hard because I also won races,' he said. It was apparently 'the magic formula' for being accepted by those who never bothered to work at all.

Bannister had won sprint races while still at his primary school in Harrow before moving to Bath. 'It was something I was good at and it was a pleasure,' he said. This ability to outrun his schoolmates freed him up to enjoy other school activities such as acting, music and archaeology.

He also learned that with a little training, a lot of self-belief and a willingness to drive himself to complete exhaustion, he could beat his fellow pupils in the annual cross-country run. He won the school race three times in a row and says that he fondly dreamt that the teachers would have to give him the trophy outright. 'When the staff heard what was in my mind, which was clearly impossible, they subscribed to a little replica cup, made out of real silver, which is down there with my trophies in Pembroke College. That was my first cup. It's a bit battered but it's a significant cup.'

Bannister's father, Ralph, wore a small gold medallion on his watch chain throughout his life. Ralph, the youngest of eleven children, ran or walked the couple of miles to the Colne Day Secondary School in Lancashire every day. Once a year the school held a mile race. When he was about 14, Bannister's father won it and was presented with the medal, inscribed *First, Mile*. 'I didn't get the medallion until my father died,' says Bannister, 'but it is now with my trophies, which I thought was the right place for it.'

Ralph gave Roger a book on racing and training by Alfred Shrubb, who dominated distance running during the early years of the twentieth century. It was his father, too, who took the schoolboy Bannister to see Sydney Wooderson battle with Arne Andersson at the White City in 1946. Bannister still remembers it vividly. 'Wooderson was four or five inches shorter than Andersson and yet he dared to challenge him. It seemed almost a gross impertinence. And from that day Wooderson was my hero.'

Bannister was brought up reading Arthur Mee's encyclopaedia – eight volumes full of British imperial history and stirring deeds of heroes. 'Arthur Mee was an idealist,' he said. 'He believed in presenting genuine men and women as heroes with a degree of patriotism now unfavourable, so I knew all about Scott and the Pole and glorious failure and early people trying to climb mountains. But up until the time my father took me to see Wooderson I wasn't much interested in sport.'

What Bannister was interested in was exploring the Somerset countryside and living very much in a world of his own. He went on expeditions with a rucksack and a bicycle that was built in the days when weight was a selling point. It gave him an enjoyable sense of independence, and he loved to explore the county from the spectacular delights of Cheddar George to the wide coastal vistas of Weston-super-Mare.

The mixed feelings of pleasure, terror and achievement that had driven him initially as a schoolboy at Bath stayed with Bannister when the family returned to London and he became a pupil at University College School. In Somerset the London boys called the locals 'Bath onions'. At University College School Bannister suddenly felt like a country bumpkin himself. Life, he remembered painfully, was one long blush.

The headmaster came from Rugby School, and Bannister was more or less forced into being an unwilling scrum-half, trampled under enormous forwards. Somehow he was made captain of the second fifteen which was, he says, the least successful team in the history of the school. 'I can remember that once we were beaten by Mill Hill. At half-time the score was over 50–0. The referee, who, rather unfairly, was from Mill Hill, asked, "Who is the captain? Can I have a word with you?" Then he said, "Look here, if you had a talk to your chaps over half-time I'm sure they could play better than this." It was rather humiliating.'

Bannister's headmaster tried to bolster confidence by appointing him a house captain, but even that seemed to have the reverse effect and he retreated further into himself. The school had high academic standards and a fine reputation, but nonetheless Bannister could hardly wait to leave. He took entrance examinations for both Oxford and Cambridge and was offered a place at both universities to read medicine.

His main reason for choosing Oxford was that he could take up his place in the coming October instead of having to wait another year, as was the case for Cambridge. The senior classics tutor at St John's, Cambridge, who told Bannister he was too young and that he should wait for a year turned out, coincidentally, to be the senior treasurer of the Cambridge University Athletic Club. It was an opinion that he was to live to regret.

Bannister's father suggested Exeter College. 'He went to the public library and he looked up Oxford colleges and saw that Exeter College had a West Country link and, as I had been to Bath, he thought that might be good for me. Once up at Oxford I was determined to work and play as hard as I could and experience everything,' said Bannister.

Almost immediately after arriving at Exeter, he set off to inspect the Iffley Road running track. If he expected to see it humming with athletic activity he was to be disappointed. Apart from a groundsman, it was quiet and deserted. He was, though, able to savour the atmosphere of the place where Olympic champions like Arnold Strode-Jackson and Jack Lovelock had run their miles. He didn't dare set foot on the track, but back at Exeter College, he made enthusiastic attempts to sign up for the athletic club and a few days later persuaded a heavily built oarsman to join him for a run.

Bannister turned out in plimsolls and the oil-stained kit he had used for running at school. After he and the rower had been trotting around at the track for nearly half an hour, the groundsman who had been watching them came over to say that he had been there in the time of Lovelock and that he thought the oarsman's powerful stride showed promise. 'But,' he said, turning to Bannister, 'I'm afraid you'll never be any good. You just haven't got the strength or build for it.'

It was a judgement that hurt Bannister very deeply, but he was not going to let a groundsman's criticism knock him off his stride. Two weeks later he ran in the freshman's sports mile, where he was beaten by one second by an ex-serviceman, Peter Curry, in 4:53. Curry was a fine cross-country runner who competed in the 1948 Olympic steeplechase. It was the first time Bannister had raced a mile and the first time he had worn spikes. Sandy Duncan, who was doing some coaching at Oxford, told him after the race that he could knock 20 seconds off his time if he stopped bouncing.

In the months that followed, Bannister tried cross-country running. His first appearance in Oxford colours was on Saturday 23 November 1946, when he ran in a seven-mile race against Blackheath Harriers at Hayes in Kent. It was a traditional, muddy English course and in the field was Sydney Wooderson. It was the only time they ever raced against each other. Bannister finished fifth and Wooderson third.

The winter of 1946/47 was particularly severe, with much of the country brought to a standstill by the great freeze. The old running track at Iffley Road (three laps to the mile and run clockwise) remained snowbound throughout the entire term, and it was not even possible to run trials to select the Varsity Match team. Track training was snowed off, and for a week or two Roger Bannister joined others wobbling on clattering skates on the ice-bound playground at Port Meadow. When he tired of this he tramped to Iffley Road, where day after day he helped shovel snow in an attempt to clear the track.

The president of OUAC cobbled together his team for the match against Cambridge on 22 March. Anyone still around from the previous year was automatically selected, but there was a gap in the team for a third-string miler. Roger Bannister got it. Some say the president had spotted him training, others that he was picked for the team because of his enthusiastic snow-shovelling.

A sizeable crowd braved the weather that March for the annual meeting between the athletes of Oxford and Cambridge at the neutral venue in London. They huddled, wrapped in college scarves and overcoats. The winter snow had given way to rain, which fell steadily, and large pools of water built up, churning the White City cinder track to porridge.

Bannister was excited and nervous, delighted to be in the team but made anxious by all the talk of the older Blues of the need to beat the 'Tabs' – as the Oxford men called their opponents. There were token handshakes at the start line as the six runners shivered slightly in their baggy blue-trimmed shorts. At the gun it was the three Cambridge runners who led the field. Bannister stayed well back, content to be towed around faster than he had ever run before.

At the bell he was still hanging on, weary with fatigue. But halfway down the back straight, the excitement of the occasion kicked in. Here he was, after just a couple of terms at Oxford, running in the Blues team in the mile on the very track where he had seen his hero Sydney Wooderson two years before.

'I felt a crazy desire to overtake the whole field,' Bannister remembered. His body responded at once. The explosion of energy was dramatic. The press said of him at the time that 'he tore along with a long raking stride' and that as he won the race, in 4:30.8 by twenty yards, 'Bannister looked a definite Olympic possible.'

He hardly heard the wild cheering because his victory had brought him near to exhaustion. He slumped, his head down, panting, his hands on his knees. But there was a glow of enormous satisfaction too. The race had shown him two things that would shape his future – he had the will to win, and a great gift for the sport. 'My confidence was quite restored,' he said. 'I could almost have stopped running at that moment.'

13

Blue Heaven

Big occasions and races which have been eagerly anticipated
almost to the point of dread are where great deeds can be
accomplished.

Jack Lovelock

Showered and dressed, Roger Bannister was introduced that
evening to Harold Abrahams. Then he was asked to shake the
hand of Jack Lovelock, the 1936 Olympic champion, who had
spent much of his life in the quest for the four-minute mile.
He remembers the affable smile, the crinkly fair hair, and
being so overawed that he clumsily caused Lovelock to spill
his drink.

The 'long raking stride' that the press had noted during
Bannister's run led some old Blues to recall the style of Arnold
Strode-Jackson. For the boy who had the day before been an
unknown third-string miler, the talk of joining the 'Olympic
possibles' was heady stuff. He returned to Oxford vowing that
while medicine would still come first, he would make time for
his running and enjoy the status of being a Blue.

Even by Bannister's day, being a Blue was beginning to lose
some of its lustre and distinction. Sport could no longer elbow
academic work into second place. 'The picture of a noisy crowd
of Blues parading crested sweaters almost invisible beneath

yards of coloured scarfing as they wander from Vincent's to Iffley Road is now out of date,' declared Bannister in 1955. 'Old Blues say Oxford is not what it was. It never is.

'In the late 1940s, grammar schools had not been abolished and there were more state school students then than there have been since. I think we saw ourselves as a meritocratic elite, selected by examination on intellectual grounds, but we were there to experiment with all kinds of possible careers and have fun whether it was acting, the Union or sport.

'There was no resentment then in society of the presence of Oxford and Cambridge. The country was proud of them both. They were something wonderful, giving a quality of education that led to careers in public life and the professions. No one then tried to pour scorn on Oxford life.'

The tradition was that you should serve your apprenticeship as an athlete through the university athletic club. Senior runners would pass their experience on to the next generation. Many boys had already received coaching at public schools and there was much emphasis placed on the value of the smooth and perfect running action. 'The university method', Bannister noted, 'has had great success yet is apparently casual. Undergraduates are, without exception, haunted by the fear of being thought to take anything seriously. I know that I developed a pose of apparent indifference to hide the tremendous enthusiasm which I felt for running from the day I set foot in Oxford. Behind this general façade I found I could quickly learn a great deal about training. Nothing is sacred in Oxford and every training programme was attacked and analysed.'

You could learn just about every trick of the athletic trade at Vincent's Club. There in the armchaired bar, crowded with Blues and long sporting memories, Arnold Strode-Jackson, hero of the Great War and winner of the Olympic 1,500 metres in 1912, would hold court.

Stoopingly tall, in a Sherlock Holmes cloak, with a limp that screamed shrapnel, he carried, even in old age, the rangy look of a top-class miler. One of his pet theories, seductive in its simplicity, was that the secret of the success of Oxford's middle-distance runners lay in the way they ran round the track. Quite simply, they went round it the wrong way. While the rest of the sporting world ran anti-clockwise round their cinder tracks, Oxford men traditionally ran in the opposite direction.

'Old Jackers', as he was known to the boys in the Blues team, reckoned that if you ran clockwise round the track you would strengthen the left leg more than the right. 'Most people, as anyone will tell you,' he would drawl, 'are right footed, so their right leg is naturally stronger. Race and train running the other way and you will even things up with a perfectly balanced stride.' Generations of Oxford milers had heard the quaint theory and some of them swore by it.

There was another aspect of the Iffley Road track that made it one of the strangest in England. It was three, not the customary four, laps to the mile and there was a dip on the back straight so severe they used to say runners would disappear and re-emerge running uphill to the finish. Somehow, though, the middle-distance magician Jack Lovelock had managed 4:12 there, skipping nonchalantly over the stretch on the inside lane where the roots of an elm had shoved their way up through the cinder cover.

In April 1948 Roger Bannister, only just 19, was elected President of the Oxford University Athletic Club. His opening address to the club in the hall of Worcester College got off to an appalling false start. He was hesitant and uncomfortable, with an over-prepared and over-serious speech. When he realised how badly things were going, he cut his losses. He tore up his notes and threw them aside. To his delight he discovered that if he just had the courage to say what he meant, to speak from the heart, the words would flow as fluently as his legs moved on the track.

He wanted to make the club bigger and better – with more members, professional coaching and fine facilities. He wanted, too, to revive the tradition of taking teams from Oxford and Cambridge to tour America. That went down well. But his final suggestion cut to the very soul of the Oxford University tradition. Bannister declared he wanted to see the old track ripped up and replaced by one of four laps to the mile. He knew it was heresy, and that it would meet with fierce opposition, but he knew, too, that nobody was going to set a world mile record on it in its current state.

Cinder tracks, pioneered by the professionals, had been around in England since the 1850s. Their appearance predated the revival of the modern Olympic Games staged in Athens. They were laid at the high tide of Victorian sporting confidence, by the gentlemen who gave the world lawn tennis, cricket and two shapes of football.

They knew that for serious sport they needed tracks that were level, accurate in measurement, with surfaces that were firm and fast. Too firm and the clattering spikes would not be able to stab and withdraw with the grace of a stiletto; too loose and the spikes would slip and scar the surface into ugly uselessness; too wet and the cinders would be sticky and dragging; too dry and the powdery hardness would wreck the best of legs.

Cinder track-making was skilled and expensive work, and maintenance was everything. A good groundsman, armed with hose, rake and roller, was worth two seconds a lap at least, they said at Oxford.

The entire surface area had to be excavated to a depth of 12 inches, then the inside edging of timber would be fixed. Inch-accurate measurement was vital, so that the distance round at exactly a foot from the edging measured precisely 440 yards. The excavation would be lined with lime to kill off all plant life, before being filled with layer upon layer of cinder clinkers, the spent fuel of railways and factories.

The top three inches, the final surface, was what mattered most. This was of fine ash mixed with soil to bind it. The old groundsmen kept their secrets to themselves but it was reckoned that a medium-heavy loam soil tending towards the texture of clay, well dried and finely screened, should be mixed in the proportion of one part of soil to 15 parts of ash.

In the summer of 1949, as the bulldozers moved in to Iffley Road, Roger Bannister looked out at the sun-dried turf and the sticky heaps of clay and vowed that when the track was ready he would choose it for some of his biggest races. It was two years before the digging and rolling was done. At the opening meeting of the re-laid track, Bannister ran the mile in 4:15.2.

In March 1949, in his third annual Oxford–Cambridge match, Bannister got his name in the record books, replacing the time of 4:17.8 by C. C. Henderson-Hamilton, Trinity, Oxford, set in 1905. Over the years this time had defied attacks by Arnold Strode-Jackson, Jerry Cornes and even Jack Lovelock. Bannister managed 4:16.2, showing extremely good pace judgement for someone still not 20 years of age.

This was also the year during which Bannister developed the famous finishing burst that was to become his trademark. He cut an awesome figure as he strode away from strong fields with blazing final laps. He visited the United States, where he recorded 4:11.9 against Princeton and Cornell, followed, a few days later, with 4:11.1 against Harvard and Yale. Both races were won with last laps that took less than a minute.

There was much talk already of the fabled four-minute mile and who might be the first to run it. In England Bill Nankeville was being touted as a possibility. In Ireland John Joe Barry said he was the boy to do it, and in America every college track coach was on the lookout. In Britain's *Athletics Weekly*, Jimmy Green tipped Roger Bannister.

Using the 'Oxford method', Bannister was certainly getting the results. He had settled into a pattern of training, running for half an hour three or four times a week. He reckoned he could learn more from other athletes about how to train than from any professional coach who had never been a runner himself. He knew that the runner had to make his own decisions on the track.

'If a man coaches himself then he has only himself to blame when he is beaten,' he said, though he did concede that 'All this may be wrong.' But the Oxford method had already produced 12 Olympic champions – 'men whose personality and determination were sufficient to enable them to plan successful athletic careers and at the same time to achieve balanced lives'.

Bannister achieved excellent results on his very light training schedule because he was able to make the best possible use of his nervous energy. He suffered for it afterwards though. 'The night after my races I was too tired physically and too excited mentally to sleep,' he noted. 'The muscles of my legs would ache. Large quantities of salt are lost through excessive perspiration and if I did not eat salt immediately after the race I was racked with cramp.'

Jim Alford, a AAA coach, lent him a report on the training methods of Gunder Haegg, who trained almost entirely away from the track using the fartlek system, which alternated very fast bursts with stretches of gentle running or walking. It had produced devastatingly fast times for the Swede, and Bannister began to use fartlek in his own training.

All through his career Roger Bannister was criticised by the press and athletics administrators for not putting himself under the control of a coach. When he went to America in 1951 to run in the Benjamin Franklin Mile, one newspaper wrote, 'No manager, no trainer, no masseur, no friends! He's nuts – or he's good!' Bannister won without a coach, before a crowd of 40,000, in 4:08.3. This race raised him to twentieth on the all-time mile list. The American press said that his victory had been achieved in the 'classic English manner'.

There had been a touch of national triumph in Bannister's victory over his American opponents. It was the third in a series of British wins. The Cambridge Boat Race crew had beaten Harvard, boxer Randolph Turpin had beaten Sugar Ray Robinson, and now the American sports reporters wondered would this English boy beat them to the four-minute mile.

In England Harold Abrahams reflected, 'What he needs now is confidence in his own ability. Modesty – a characteristic of Wooderson – in Bannister amounts to an almost complete reluctance to acknowledge his greatness. He has the brains to plan and dominate the Olympic final as Lovelock did in 1936. To beat the world – and I believe he can – he must cultivate a purposeful aggression.'

At one stage, while at Oxford, Bannister said he tried hard to find a coach. Most of the ones who were around in the first half of the twentieth century were hangovers from the old

masseur-trainers of the previous century. They were the
changing room attendants, ever ready to slap powerful-smelling
liniments on to aching muscles or injuries. Many of them had
gradually picked up their experience from the athletes around
them. Some of them had also been runners themselves in their
day.

Bill Thomas belonged to this tradition and had been coach
for many years to Oxford University. Jack Lovelock had great
faith in him, and in the 1940s he was still coaching a number
of top athletes, including Bill Nankeville. 'I went along to see
him,' said Bannister, 'and he stood by the track, bowler-hatted,
watching me run round. He grunted continuously but said
little. Though the comments he made were probably extremely
shrewd, he seemed upset when I asked him why he said this
or that. I think he worked intuitively and I needed reasons for
things I did.

'I was always baffled by Lovelock's absolute reliance on him.
I just couldn't communicate with a man like Bill Thomas, and
although he would have been fifteen years younger in
Lovelock's day, I could never understand why Lovelock had
to take Thomas with him to America when he went there to
take part in the Mile of the Century.'

In the British winter of 1950, Roger Bannister – without
the benefit of a coach – took himself off to the homeland of
Jack Lovelock to take part in the Centennial Games cele-
brating a hundred years of British settlement in New Zealand.
There, in Christchurch, on a grass track, he ran 4:09.9 – a new
Australasian record – followed home by Don MacMillan, the
Australian mile champion, in 4:12.8.

MacMillan, who in time was to play the role of pacemaker
in the most controversial attack of all on the four-minute-mile
barrier, was something of a giant among middle-distance

runners. Standing 6 foot 3 inches and weighing close to 14 stone, he was an early pupil of the colourful coach Percy Cerutty. Cerutty, who was to play a part in the shaping of the young John Landy, regarded MacMillan as the first of Australia's really great milers. A willing guinea pig for Cerutty's eccentric theories on tough conditioning and galloping movements, MacMillan was the first Australian to better 4:10 for the mile.

As training methods became apparently more sophisticated, many athletes and coaches wondered whether it would be art or science that would unlock the secrets of perfect performance. Would the ideal athlete be an animal or a robot? Should you be training in the forest or on the treadmill?

In 1950, with two years to go before the Olympic Games in Helsinki, such questions ran tantalisingly through the mind of Roger Bannister as he made the transition from undergraduate to research worker. He had worked out a plan that he hoped would bring his running to a peak for his 'perfect race' at the Games. He wanted to line up for as many first-class events as his still fragile young body could handle, and like Jack Lovelock, he wanted to compete abroad, not just for the youthful joy of discovery but to accustom his body to changes of climate, to the food of strangers, to the disruption of time zones.

Only by racing in other lands could you observe your opponents, those athletes who would line up against you in Helsinki. Race them now, out of the spotlight of the Olympics, and you might check their tactics, assess their abilities, test their strengths and tease out their weakness.

Already the young, enquiring, medically analytical mind of Bannister wanted to take the mystery out of everything connected to his sport. He had long had a lyrical passion for running; what, he wondered, might scientific enquiry uncover about his body, his mind, his training and racing? Even as he plotted his two-year master plan for the Olympics, medicine was still at the core of his life, his first love and his career. But his passion was for running, and if he could uncover a way of exploring both through his research work, it would be a job made in heaven.

That was what had lured him into accepting a research fellowship at Merton College. There, armed with a motorised treadmill, gas masks, blood guns and an array of what looked like torture chamber equipment, he and his colleague Dr Cunningham set themselves to explore whether pure oxygen or a mixture of air and oxygen was better for the body under stress. It was strictly academic research, insisted Bannister, but with the final 1,000 feet of Everest yet to be climbed and the four-minute mile still an elusive dream, who knew where such experiments might lead.

The research involved getting athletes on the treadmill and pumping various cocktails of air and oxygen into them while running them into a paralysis of exhaustion. The University Athletic Club provided a ready supply of volunteers – though the mixture of blood, sweat and lactic acid meant that many were not that keen to return.

Poring over the results long into the night, Bannister began to take an increasing interest in the physiology and potential of athletes. What, he wondered, made one athlete better than another? Training, he instinctively believed, was only ever part of the puzzle. In any case, could man ever devise the perfect training method? Was there any scientific way of assessing athletic power, and was there a perfect running build?

Sprinters, they say, are born, not made. Usually they are big, strong men boasting well-sculpted torsos and powerfully developed legs. They need to be able to use the explosive packed in their muscles, never needing to force their lungs to smuggle in extra supplies. They can gallop the straight without drawing breath. They swagger in their strength and blast off from their blocks.

The distance man is leaner than the sprinter, looks hungry and haunted and is often a touch taller. He is a miser, hoarding his breath and his fitness, built to spend his effort wisely over the minutes – or in the case of marathon runners sparingly over the hours. The distance man's controlled breathing holds the breakdown of his tissues at bay, and recruits stores of energy to replace what has been spent along the way.

The sprinter, forced to run long distance, does so with a groan, his steps laboured and slow. His pathetic oxygen conversion rates will always make it painful work. Similarly, the distance man can never truly sprint. He has not been blessed at birth with enough fast-twitch fibres in his leg muscles. No matter how much agony they spend on training, neither man can buy the other's body. There are men, as well as horses, for courses. Some sprint, some can run for ever.

Not that you can always tell by looking at them. A suit, a college scarf, an overcoat can make an athlete disappear. But strip him off and make him move and the champion is no longer in disguise. The loose-limbed ease of movement, the balance of poise and power will give him away whatever his shape and size.

Norris McWhirter, pocket-sized, pale but deceptively powerful, was a sprinter. In later years he became editor of *The Guinness Book of Records* and he and Bannister became godparents to each other's children. They were fellow athletes, fellow Blues, fellow members of the elite Vincent's Club. When

Roger wanted an athletic guinea pig there was none more willing than Norris.

Half a century on, McWhirter shakes his head at the memory of the treadmill. It was remorseless. Some said they could adjust the speed and incline to make it the equivalent of running up Everest in six hours. You had to breathe through a mask linked up to great gas bags. Every couple of minutes the motor would growl with menace and the speed would increase, then the treadmill would jolt and you went thrashing up an ever-steeper hill. You kept wondering if your knees would smack your chin. Then the scientists would grab your hand. They had a blood gun that sprang a scalpel-sharp blade into your finger. They needed the blood samples to measure the levels of lactic acid – the by-product of effort that could poison and cramp the strongest of legs. The experience would break anyone.

When you did break, you catapulted off the back of the treadmill to collapse in a pool of blood-streaked sweat on a mattress on the floor. A few minutes on that running machine felt longer than a marathon, and McWhirter recalls with wonder that Bannister exhausted himself on the contraption a dozen times or so. 'After that,' he says with a twinkle, 'the four-minute mile must have seemed like a day off.'

One day in 1951, McWhirter came off the treadmill on to the mattress with a train to catch to London. He had almost left it too late – certainly too late to change. They bundled him into a car, from car to platform, from platform to carriage. He drew breath on his seat and wondered for a moment why the other passengers looked so alarmed. And then he realised they were looking at his shirt smeared heavily with blood where his fingers had checked on his own heartbeat.

Three years later he would take that train the other way. It would take him back to Oxford and to Iffley Road, back to a meeting with Roger Bannister, to a place beyond the sweat and the blood – at the other end of the treadmill.

An April evening in 1951 at Motspur Park saw the beginning of the partnership between Bannister and Chris Chataway which was to bring the four-minute record ever closer. One month earlier, Chataway had taken over Bannister's mantle as winner of the Oxford–Cambridge mile, in 4:16.4 – a time for the event beaten twice by Bannister but by no one else.

On 17 April, Imperial College London and Walton AC were taking part in an inter-club meeting, and Bannister was invited to compete as a guest in the three-quarter-mile event. In a field of five runners, Chataway set the pace. The half-mile was reached in 1:59.7 and Chataway then pulled off the track to leave Bannister on his own to finish the race and record a time of 2:56.8 for the full distance. This was a new English native record, displacing the old record of 2:59.6 held by Sydney Wooderson.

At the end of the run Bannister looked surprisingly relaxed and untroubled and he went on to cover another lap just to limber down. The Chataway–Bannister partnership had got off to a good start.

By the spring of 1952 Bannister's Olympic preparations were provoking plenty of criticism. To avoid the nervous strain of competition, he had cut back savagely on the number of races he entered to concentrate on building up to his peak. When he did run fast, it was usually in private and at secret time trials. The time needed for training and competition meant that he had to juggle his priorities. He had moved on from Oxford to continue his studies to become a doctor at St Mary's in London, and he was spending long hours attending lectures or working on the hospital wards.

He had trained alone through the previous winter, snatching time when he could on the grass playing fields at Harrow School near his home. Usually it was for half an hour or so in the dark using the Swedish fartlek system.

The unlit playing fields could be dangerous. One night he smacked his shin on the concrete edge of a bridge and had to miss a month's training while the gash healed. He was frequently attacked in the press for spurning the help of coaches, for 'training in secret' and for refusing to put his fitness to the test in top-class races. Bannister considered he was saving himself for Helsinki; the press reckoned he was dodging the opposition.

'Roger took it all terribly to heart,' said Chris Brasher, the training companion who was to act as pacemaker in later record attempts. 'The newspapers went on and on about him being a "lone wolf" and got very steamed up when he said he wouldn't run in the mile in the AAA championships before the Games. They thought he should do. They thought he was arrogant, just expecting to get picked for the team because of his previous record. They thought he was selfish not putting enough back into the sport. They didn't understand how Roger liked to do things.'

Bannister himself said, 'I did not expect people to understand my scheme of training. I only hoped that they would be patient with me and trust that I was doing my best to prepare for the Olympic race. I had no coach or adviser and hence no alibi if things went wrong. I decided that it was my duty to train as I thought best for the Olympic final whatever that might involve. It was a goal so high as to be worth every sacrifice. If others thought my methods madness, then I must go on alone.

'I was now cornered. Victory at Helsinki was the only way out.'

Bannister thought it was probable that the 1952 Games would be his only Olympics. Running was not his sole interest and he certainly believed that he could not afford to spend another four years jeopardising his future in medicine. 'Success or failure at one throw,' he wrote. 'This seemed right.'

In fact, his training, particularly against the stopwatch, was going exceptionally well. He was helped enormously in his time trials by Chris Chataway, who had followed him as Oxford University's leading miler but who was bound for the Helsinki Olympics as a 5,000-metre runner.

Chataway had shown a blazing natural ability as an athelete right from the time he started running as a schoolboy. There were just two books about running in the library at Sherborne School and Chataway had studied both eagerly. Athletics was not a major activity in a school where rugby was the bench-mark of sporting status and track and field games were squeezed into a couple of weeks at the end of the summer term.

But if the opportunities to run were limited, the sturdy red-haired boy who could play a passable game of rugby and was tough enough to captain the school at boxing loved reading about it. One of the library books recounted the epic series of races between Gunder Haegg and Arne Andersson and spoke lyrically of the Swedish fartlek method.

The other well-thumbed volume in the school library was *Athletics* by members of Achilles – an elite club formed in 1920 and made up entirely of athletes from Oxford and Cambridge. The foreword was by Lord Burghley and the chapter read again and again by the schoolboy Chataway was the one on miling by Jack Lovelock.

By the time Achilles revised their publication in 1955, Chataway had a chapter of his own devoted to distance running,

Chris Brasher had a section on the steeplechase and cross-country running, and, of course, the chapter on the mile saw Jack Lovelock giving way to Dr Roger Bannister. The original Achilles book reeked of the Oxbridge ethos and approach to running, with much emphasis on style and rest, and with dire warnings about the dangers of over-training and staleness.

'Although that was the first coaching book I read,' says Chataway, 'I didn't really follow that system of training. I wrote to the AAA and said I would like to have a coach and they gave me one with whom I corresponded. I have long since forgotten his name but he must have been pretty old, or at least his methods were like something out of history. He recommended I carry corks in my hands to get the position of my fingers right, and he said I shouldn't run too much. Instead, I should go for long walks. Even after I left school and was in the army, I used to walk around the lanes of Shropshire in the dark rather than run.'

After setting a new school record at the half-mile at the age of 16, in 2:13 with a first lap of 60 seconds, Chataway entered himself in the Public School mile and was delighted to finish third in 4:45. "I thought this is it. I gave up boxing and took *Athletics Weekly* instead."

His improvement was rapid. In 1949 he broke 4:30 for the first time, and the following year, as an officer cadet in the army, he broke the inter-services mile record with 4:15.6. 'When I got to Oxford I found that all the training was really derived from Jack Lovelock, and although Bannister was still there doing research, he was really quite a distant figure halfway towards being a don and I hardly saw him during my first year.'

Despite the most casual approach to training, Chataway

equalled Jack Lovelock's Iffley Road record of 4:12 just four months after his twentieth birthday. He said, 'I was enormously impressed by the effortless superiority thing at Oxford. Whereas when I was in the army I thought a great deal about training and so on, once I got to Oxford I was most anxious not to be seen as a boring hard trainer. Whenever I saw Roger he gave me the impression that he did very little training, if any. He said he did none at all in the vacations.

'"I'm going to America," Roger once said to me. "I shall go because I like going to America and I shall have to run some race out there, but I haven't done any training." Well, when he raced he actually did 4:08 so he must have been consistently misleading me as well as everybody else about what he did do for training. Of course, we all pretended we didn't need to train. We all lied about it. I was busy doing the same to my competitors.

'My impression then of Roger was that Lovelock was his model. Roger's plan was to do exactly what Jack Lovelock had done, which was to win the Olympic 1,500 metres and then give up. And if he had won there is no question that is what would have happened. He'd have got his gold medal and only a few athletic enthusiasts would still remember his name.'

Just ten days before the final of the 1,500 metres in the Helsinki Games, Bannister and Chataway arranged to run a time trial at Motspur Park. Chataway took the first lap and a half, and Bannister went on to complete a three-quarter-mile in 2:52.9. The time was sensational, with each lap faster than the previous one – 58.5, 57.5 and 56.9. It was almost four seconds better than the official world record of 2:56.6 set by Arne Andersson in 1944. Bannister's own English Native record was 2:56.8, set at Motspur Park in April 1951.

Just like Lovelock, Bannister wanted the result of this time

trial hushed up. Those who had witnessed it were sworn to
secrecy. 'But those in the know', said Chris Brasher, 'realised
Roger was the best in the world, and that there and then the
four-minute mile was certain. He would only have needed to
jog around another lap in 66 or 67 seconds and he'd have done
it. That was the run that set it all up. It was one of the most
important runs of his life.'

Bannister went to bed that night a very happy man. 'I had
never run at such speed before,' he said, 'and it did not take
much out of me. I ranked it as equal to, if not better than, a
four-minute mile. I felt joyously full of the running that I had
restrained for so long.'

The next day brought a painful awakening. There in the
morning newspapers was a headline announcing 'Semi-finals
for the Olympic 1,500 metres'. The announcement gripped
him like cramp. Owing to the large number of entries there
were to be races on three consecutive days – heats, semi-finals
and then the final.

All of Bannister's training had been geared to competing in
just two races. Physically and psychologically he believed he
was unready to run in three. He felt the change in the
programme would hit him harder than his rivals who spent
more hours at their training.

Bannister had dreamed, like Jack Lovelock before him, of
preparing himself for one supreme effort at the Olympics and
then stepping from the track to pursue his life in medicine.
Now it seemed an extra race might rob him of the gold medal
– and of his dream.

14

Another Land, Another Hero

You could hitch Roger Bannister to the rear of Twentieth Century Limited [a US Express Train] and I would still outrun him.

Wes Santee

If Jack Lovelock was a model for Roger Bannister to follow, the man who chased him home in Berlin and took the silver medal was to be the role model for another of the principal players in the drama leading to the perfect mile.

They like their sports heroes big in America, and they didn't come any bigger than Glenn Cunningham – the man the American press dubbed 'the Iron Horse of Kansas'. Cunningham was the archetype of the great American miler. When he raced Lovelock in that Olympic 1,500 metres in 1936, both men broke the previous world record.

Two years earlier, Cunningham, running against two of his biggest rivals, Bill Bonthron of Princeton, and the University of Pennsylvania's Gene Venske, broke the world record for the mile. It was on 16 June 1934, on the same cinder track where Jack Lovelock had set his world record just a year before, that Cunningham defeated Bonthron. He finished 40 yards ahead to set the new world record at 4:06.8. When the race was over, Cunningham's fans were quick to point out that this great miler had now run seven of the 13 fastest miles ever covered in competition – and they believed the coveted four-minute mile was his for the taking.

The American sporting press went wild for their record-shattering miler. They called him 'Galloping Glenn' and 'the Kansas Locomotive'. It was not surprising that the legend of Cunningham was one of the most enduring of American sports stories and one that was guaranteed to inspire a young Kansas boy like Wes Santee. By the time Santee was himself established as America's leading miler, in the mid-1950s, he was being trotted out everywhere to give inspirational and motivating talks, particularly to groups of young people.

Whenever he did so, Wes Santee would hold up the example of Cunningham. Like Cunningham, he would say, 'You should never give up, no matter what happens, no matter how overwhelming the difficulties. You should always try to win through.'

Santee, who looked the part of the cowboy, was 6 foot 1 inch tall with crew-cut hair. When he wasn't wearing track spikes he wore his trademark cowboy boots, and usually sported a Stetson hat. When he spoke publicly he would invariably enthuse over how Cunningham had fought back from a near fatal childhood accident to become quite simply the greatest miler in the world.

It was a story repeated often, and, like all legends, it was sometimes embellished. But the truth of how Cunningham had become a runner at all was truly fantastic. As a child he would run with his older brother Floyd from the farm where they lived to their one-room schoolhouse in western Kansas. They were always the first to arrive, and every morning Floyd would get the paraffin stove going to warm up the schoolroom. One wintry day, when Glenn was eight years old, a delivery truck inadvertently delivered petrol rather than paraffin to the school building, and when Floyd lit the stove it exploded into flame, killing the older brother instantly and leaving the younger close to death for nearly six weeks. So badly burned were the young boy's legs that the doctors considered amputating them, and they feared he would never walk normally again. Glenn spent more than six months in hospital while they grafted skin on to his ruined limbs.

In the years that followed, through stubborn determination, Glenn forced himself to exercise. First he learned to walk and then he tried running, in an attempt to build up his withered leg muscles. So hard did he work at his exercises that in time his legs grew stronger and more flexible than they might normally have been. It was even said the boy found it far less painful to run than to walk.

By the age of 12 Glenn Cunningham had built himself up to the point where he was able to take on, and beat, his schoolmates in a race. Years later, as an adult, he would say that even though he had run the Olympics, 'no race was more important than that race I ran when I was twelve years old'.

By the time he arrived at the University of Kansas, Cunningham was already making headlines because of the records he had set as a schoolboy. Stripped to his running kit, he had 'the torso of a wrestler and the legs of a will-o'-the-wisp'. It was also said that the scar tissue on his legs was so bad that it took him an hour to loosen up for a race.

Cunningham's athletics career stretched from 1931 until the outbreak of World War II, and he ducked under 4:10 for the mile no fewer than 20 times. Here was an American hero who had fought back from disaster and who never smoked, never drank. His fitness was legendary. Jack Lovelock said that for consistency 'there was no runner in the world who could match

Cunningham', and that this was the man who ran 'in high gear every minute'.

To the sports-loving Americans in the 1930s Glenn Cunningham was the most colourful and exciting of competitors. He attracted vast crowds wherever he appeared. In a land where indoor athletics could pull in big-spending audiences and generous sponsorship, Cunningham beat the world indoor record for the 1,500 metres three times. His 3:48.4 set in 1938 stood for 17 years until Wes Santee broke it.

Cunningham also broke the United States mile record three times and ran in the Olympic Games of 1932 and 1936. But it was his indoor mile record that sent reporters into a frenzy about the prospect of a four-minute mile. In March 1938, on an oversized wooden track in Hanover, New Hampshire, he ran 4:04.4.

By the late 1940s there was one particular boy in Kansas who both hero-worshipped Glenn Cunningham and sought to emulate him, declaring that one day he too was going to be one of the world's great milers. Wes Santee had grown up with tales of Cunningham's personal perseverance and his performances on the track echoing in his head. He had also grown up tough, with all the strength of a boy made to work every waking hour on a farm, allied to the youthful lilt of a natural athlete.

Santee's father was an uneducated farm hand, whose schooling, Wes later said, was at best 'helter-skelter'. Times were tough for the Santee family and everyone was expected to pitch in as they tried to scrape together enough money to buy their 2,000-acre ranch. The family thought they were to have been left the property as an inheritance, but somehow Santee's father had mucked up the paperwork. So they borrowed money and vowed to work to buy the land.

Wes, as the oldest boy in the family, was expected to pull

his weight doing the hard physical work of a rancher. His father resented every minute that his son had to spend in the classroom, and certainly did not want to see precious time and energy wasted on running. So the young high school boy found it difficult, and often impossible, to carve out any time to train or compete. When he did so it was usually in secret – and he would often have to beg lifts from neighbours to local track races.

In time, the more his father tried to drag him away from running, the more Wes seized upon it as a way to rebel. He was also determined to get the education his father had never enjoyed.

Santee would run everywhere on the farm – from barn to barn, and wherever there was a far-away fence to be fixed or cattle to be rounded up. 'I didn't hit it off with my father too well,' he said, 'and while he took the truck, I would run whenever I could on the property. I preferred it to travelling in the truck with him. He did his best but he was from a very different world.'

In later years newspaper reports used to delight in repeating the story of how the young Wes Santee had learned his characteristic running style, his powerful, choppy stride, by modelling his action on the horses at the farm. One day, when he was only seven years old it was said, he was in the corral of the ranch playing with one of the colts. When the colt started to run, the young boy tried to keep up with it.

'Keep your feet under you like a colt does,' shouted a grizzled old cowpoke, a three-quarters Osage Indian, who was sitting on the corral fence. 'If you want to be a good runner, run like a horse. White man runs like a squaw, turning his feet in all directions. Keep your feet under you.'

Wherever he learned his secret, Wes Santee grew up with

a powerful short stride which was tremendously effective at the middle distances. 'When I was young,' he says, 'and starting to run well in grade school, I was constantly reminded of how well Cunningham used to run and I was urged to try to break his records. Then as I started to grow up I did break all of his high school and then college records. Glenn Cunningham used to come to visit the University of Kansas campus during the Kansas relays so eventually we got to know each other very well.'

In Kansas, where the local population still idolised Cunningham, the press were quick to pick up on the exploits of a new potential top-class miler. By the time he was leaving for college, unlike the young Roger Bannister, who saw his running as a recreation – a necessary escape from the tread-mill of his studies – Wes Santee regarded his raw talent as the ticket that could win him an education.

The University of Kansas was the stamping ground of his hero Glenn Cunningham. It also had a track coach, Bill Easton, who was highly respected and got results. By the time Santee met Easton, the brash young high school boy had already run 4:26.4 for the mile – a state record and better than Cunningham had done at the same age back in 1930. Easton, sometimes known as 'Wild Bill', was a short, stout, bespectacled middle-aged man. He had been appointed track and cross-country coach at the university in the autumn of 1947, and already his reputation was impressive.

In the culture of American colleges, the power of the sports coach is formidable. The prestige and the authority wielded is quite unlike anything seen in the British university tradition. Bill Easton had an honesty and straightforwardness that appealed to the young Santee. His instinct told him that he'd get along with Easton, but although pupil and teacher hit it off immediately, the demands that would be placed on the young runner by the University of Kansas' track programme were spelled out quite clearly.

The year would begin with the indoor track season. This would be followed by the tough inter-college relay circuit beginning in April, with big meetings like the Drake Relays, the Texas Relays and the Kansas Relays. Most importantly, teamwork and team demands, Easton said, had to take priority over individual ambitions. Of course there would also be the academic work, but above all, Easton explained to Santee, he would be there on an athletic scholarship. This was the American way – in complete contrast to the Oxford of the 1940s and '50s where Bannister and Chataway ran a little at a time and place of their own choosing, happy to pretend both to their fellows and to their tutors that they ran even less than they admitted to.

There could be no question of the young Santee holding himself back for one or two great races a season, or attempting to build himself up to a peak. Bill Easton and the athletic scholarship system expected their athletes to run when and where required – and that was often. Nonetheless, athletics, in the United States and everywhere else, remained a strictly amateur sport. You could win yourself a scholarship, run your way through college to secure an excellent education – but athletics was not a career, it was not a way to make money.

Unlike Bannister in Britain, Santee had to run to order, whenever he was told to do so and over distances chosen by Bill Easton, his coach. It seemed to do him no harm. His running improved dramatically under Easton's shrewd coaching, and while still a freshman, aged only 18, he was selected to run for the United States in Japan.

Santee was delighted to be chosen to represent his country,

but he was also amazed and annoyed to discover how many officials had been dispatched by the Amateur Athletic Union to accompany the athletes. These officials were not coaches. They had been sent along apparently as a reward for their services to athletics. Santee considered they were little more than freeloaders, there for the ride and for a free holiday in Japan, and he would say so to anyone who would listen.

Santee's early success meant that he started getting invitations galore from the AAU to race at big meetings where he would meet top-class competition. But this also meant there would be conflict with his college commitments.

At the big indoor events like those in New York's Madison Square Gardens, the mile was one of the top attractions – and Wes Santee was much in demand. He loved the hype, he loved being in the limelight and he loved the publicity. He was running well and oozed a self-confidence that some found brash and arrogant. 'Some people say I was cocky,' Santee remembers. 'Was I cocky? I don't know. I was certainly outspoken. If I knew I could run faster than the guy I was due to race, then I said so. That was confidence.'

The young Santee was sure enough of his own ability to know he could pack stadiums, get those turnstiles spinning. That was why the promoters who stood to make the money were so keen to invite him. The crew-cut cowboy runner, in his check shirt and high-heeled boots, was loved by the press. 'I used to keep scrapbooks of all the publicity I was getting,' he remembers. 'It was enormous. The coverage I got makes Tiger Woods look like small time. Every weekend for years the sports pages of every major newspaper in the country carried stories about me and my mile.'

Bill Easton, whose livelihood depended on the successful performances of his college track team, certainly did not want his star miler run ragged to fill the pockets of the promoters. He wanted Santee to win valuable points for his college team, and he also wanted to get him fit and ready for the trials that would be used to select the US Olympic squad for the Helsinki Games.

The 1,500 metres (the metric mile) was Santee's best event. But Wes and his coach decided that, to be sure of the ticket for Helsinki, the young runner should try to qualify in the tough US trials for both the 1,500 and the 5,000 metres.

Their Olympic campaign started well. Wes won the AAU championships at 1,500 metres, which qualified him for the Olympic trials, and as the top college athlete at 5,000 metres he was invited to compete in that event too. So he now had two chances of making the Olympic team. He and Easton saw no reason why he shouldn't qualify for both and then make a decision. They reckoned they would probably opt for the 1,500 metres, which Easton believed to be Santee's best bet. But they reckoned without officialdom.

Wes ran a fine race to come second in the 5,000 metres to Curtis Stone and book a place in the Olympic team. The next day he turned up for the 1,500 metres. He warmed up, confident as usual, then stripped off his tracksuit.

'I was already standing on the line,' he remembers, 'when two guys pulled me out.' He was angry and baffled. He was told that the criteria for entries had been changed at the last minute by the AAU. They said they had decided to pick the athletes qualified to contest the trials on their times alone, and not on the races they had won. Santee and his coach had previously been told that his win in the AAU championships had qualified him for the trials, and were understandably furious.

It would not be the last run-in that Santee was to have with officialdom. But there was no arguing with the officials of the

AAU, and Santee had to settle for going to Helsinki in the 5,000 metres rather than his favourite event.

Both Easton and Santee knew that he was already America's best miler in a land where coaches had for years been tipping their finest athletes to break the four-minute barrier. In 1941 America's best 1,500 metres man, Walter Mehl, had promised to do it. 'Because it has been thought physiologically impossible no one has laid out a plan for it. I think I can do it this season or next. It is only a question of knocking four seconds off Glenn Cunningham's time set on an indoor track.'

In 1938, when the American Louis Zamperini ran 4:08.3, his coach Dean Cromwell predicted that he would be the man to run the mile in under four minutes. Zamperini laughed it off, commenting that everyone knew such a time was impossible. Zamperini had run the 5,000 metres in the 1936 Olympics, aged 19, and was remembered fondly by his United States team-mates as the man who stole the swastika from Hitler's Chancellery in Berlin.

As an army air force captain during the Second World War, he crashed in the Pacific in 1943 while on a search and rescue mission. He spent 47 days adrift and alone in a small rubber life raft. He was officially declared dead, but was captured and spent two and a half years as a Japanese prisoner of war.

As a propaganda stunt, the Japanese forced Zamperini, suffering badly from near starvation, to compete against Japanese runners who were well fed and in good condition. 'They found out I had run in the Olympics,' he said, 'and wanted to show their runners could defeat me. I had absolutely no desire to compete, but I was given to understand that if I did not run, not only I, but the whole camp, would suffer. My pride was not worth that. And once I started round that little oval, I felt that this was my game, even my business, and pride returned.'

Zamperini managed to overtake the Japanese shortly before the finish, and his captors desperately kept the race going hoping he would eventually tire. But the American did not give up so easily, and as the Japanese fell further and further behind, they eventually had to call off the race. There were no big cheques, no headlines or ballyhoo as a reward for this victory. Just a beating from his guards.

Now the mantle of the man most likely to claim the four-minute mile for America had fallen on the well-muscled shoulders of Wes Santee. 'I don't know when it will be,' he said, 'but I'll run it, you can be sure of that. I am as certain I can run the four-minute mile as you are that you can drive your car home.'

But for Wes Santee, the mile would have to wait.

15

The Passion of Perce

The Mile is like Life. You can never let up, never stop thinking
and you can be beaten at any point. I want to master it.

John Landy

They were beginning to shout about breaking the four-minute
barrier on the other side of the world too. When Roger
Bannister won the Centennial Mile in the New Zealand Games
of 1950, the man who came second was the giant Australian
middle-distance champion Don MacMillan. He was coached
by a man who could shout louder than anyone, and whose
ideas on conditioning the body and the mind were revolutionary.

Percy Wells Cerutty sprang on to the athletics scene in his
fifties like some demented white-haired prophet from the Old
Testament, his leathered skin, scorched nut-brown by the
Australian sun, contrasting vividly with the tiny pair of white
shorts which was all he usually wore.

'I am not interested in athletics,' he would proclaim, 'I am
only interested in achievement.' Cerutty, born in a working-
class Melbourne suburb in 1895, had achieved much for a
sickly child who, at the age of six, had suffered from a bout
of double pneumonia. This left him with a damaged left lung
that gave him pain and discomfort when walking or running.

But rather than give in to it he began to experiment with less painful patterns of movement.

He sensed that animals moved more naturally and efficiently than humans. He spent hours watching horses run and used to say he had learned far more from them than from any athlete. He studied gazelles, antelopes and even apes in his search for the secrets of effortless movement. Apes, he said, ran with an easy shuffle, skimming across the ground with no high knee lift – their arms and shoulders were loose, their elbows unlocked. Run like the animals, he would urge. Or take yourself off into the Australian Outback and note how the Aborigines move without the negative inhibitions of so-called civilised man.

At the age of 18, Cerutty had his first taste of athletic competition, when he entered and won a local mile race. In the colours of Malvern Harriers he ran well, though he did practically no training, and chalked up a big win over Malcolm Boyd, an Australian international runner of the time, in 4:32. But the young Cerutty was still frequently sick, particularly after races, and, unable to prepare for the 1920 Olympics, he retired from the sport.

In 1939, at the age of 43, he suffered a complete nervous and physical breakdown and was laid off from his work as a civil servant. He lost a vast amount of weight, became hopelessly weak and suffered constant migraines to the point where doctors feared for his life.

Mobilising his exceptional willpower, he fought his way back to health and fitness by returning to the sport of his youth, and at the age of 47 he began a second career as a marathon runner, setting Australian national records at distances of up to 60 miles. He ran over 100 miles in 24 hours, and his experiences in re-building his body also re-shaped his philosophy of life.

(*Right*) The Mighty Atom: Sydney Wooderson, the unlikely hero who inspired Bannister. 'If Wooderson could do it, we thought anyone could,' said Chris Brasher.

(*Left*) Robbed at gunpoint: Sweden's Arne Andersson shows the cartridge case jammed in his spikes that some believe cost him the 4 minute mile on 17 July, 1945.

(*Right*) Gunder the Wonder: Sweden's Gunder Haegg, who with Arne Andersson blazed the trail to the 4 minute mile. Haegg brought the record to 4:01.4 in July 1945.

(*Below*) Still anyone's race: Final bend of the 1500 metres in the 1952 Olympics. The winner, Josy Barthel (no 406), is still two yards down. Bannister finished fourth.

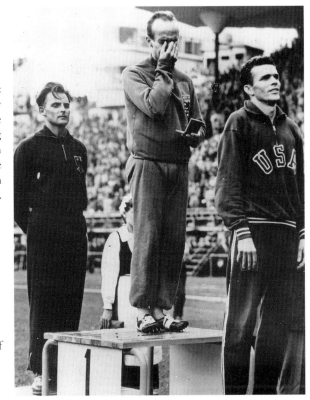

(*Right*) Tears of triumph: Luxembourg's Josy Barthel, 1500 metre champion, weeps during his national anthem as he stands on the victory rostrum in Helsinki, 1952.

(*Below*) Down and out: Chris Chataway crashes to the track after hitting the curb on the last lap of the 1952 Olympic 5,000 metres, while Emil Zatopek heads for gold.

Good timing: Chris Chataway yells the lap time at Bannister during the 4 x one mile relay at the White City, 1 August, 1953. Britain set a world record of 16 min 41 sec.

(*Right*) White City duel: Wes Santee of the USA outkicked by Britain's Gordon Pirie in the Emsley Carr Mile, 8 August, 1953, at the White City.

Below) The Kansas Cowboy: Wes Santee, wearing 118 on a ain-sodden White City track n 9 August, 1952. He won the British Games mile in 4:12.0.

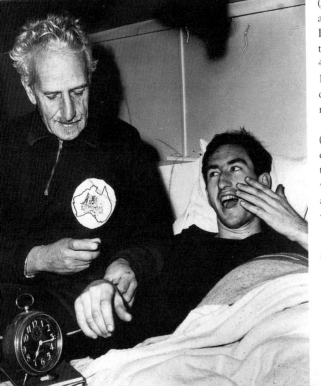

(*Above left*) So near, and yet… Gentleman John Landy, second man through the 4 minute barrier, runs 4:01.6 in Stockholm 8 June, 1954, 13 days before he captured Bannister's record.

(*Above right*) The artist-coach: Franz Stampfl, the duffel-coated motivator, who plotted the pacing and preparation for the 4 minute mile.

(*Left*) Guru to the great: Percy Wells Cerutty, self-styled 'Maker of Champions', takes the pulse of his finest pupil, Herb Elliott, who ran a world record 3:54.5 mile in 1957.

(*Above*) High stepping to glory: Brasher sets the pace, while Bannister and Chataway follow in formation through the opening laps of the Iffley Road mile in 1954.
(*Below*) Like an exploded lightbulb: Bannister, close to collapse, after the Oxford mile, supported by Franz Stampfl, in the flat cap.

Their finest hour: Bannister, Chataway and Brasher meet Britain's Prime Minister, Sir Winston Churchill, four weeks after breaking the 4 minute mile.

Having developed his theories of physical and mental fitness, he couldn't wait to preach them to the world. He set up a training camp close to the ocean at Portsea and began to recruit sporting disciples to follow what he styled his 'Stotan creed'. The word was invented by Cerutty from a combination of 'Stoic' and 'Spartan'. The Stotan creed was a hotchpotch of inspirational poetry, philosophy, and ideas on pain and suffering. 'You've got to woo nature like a sweetheart,' said Cerutty, and his eclectic creed could embrace sporting naked in the surf and running naked on the beach as happily as reciting the poetry of Tennyson or declaiming the Sermon on the Mount.

Above all, Cerutty had a withering contempt for sophisticated modern training methods and the coaches who advocated them. Particularly he despised the regimented running of repeated intervals on the track, with each burst being mechanically timed against the stopwatch.

He reckoned that the distance runner Emil Zatopek was living proof that his theories on human movement were correct – and that Zatopek ran so well not because of his interval training, but because he had simply uncovered the secret of how to do it. Zatopek had evolved his own style, head thrashing, arms rising and falling rhythmically, shoulders rolling as if racked with pain. The way he moved, Cerutty reckoned, unlocked the potential that exists in all humans for complete breathing, using the full lung capacity. 'Tidal breathing' was what Cerutty called it. Like suffering, it wasn't pretty to watch, but it worked.

Any athlete who presented himself to Cerutty had to make a total commitment to his way-out ideas. He must learn to endure extremes of heat and cold, to live rough and to eat only natural, uncooked food. He would have to train his body to endure being pushed day after day to the limit. Cerutty himself, even in his seventies, was famous for leading his athletes in repeated charges up the steep sand dunes of the Portsea training camp, hanging on in front until his body could take no more, and screaming abuse and encouragement as his pupils passed him.

When not engaged in frantic physical activity, Cerutty would preach endlessly and loudly about great philosophers, record holders and champions of the past, urging his followers to emulate them and become record breakers of the future. 'He nearly drives you crazy, saying the same things over and over again, until you get damned sick of it,' said his greatest protégé, the 1960 Olympic 1,500 metre champion, Herb Elliott, 'but when he's not here we miss the old beggar.'

Among Cerutty's early recruits was Don MacMillan, whom he turned into Australia's best miler in the 1950s. MacMillan, whose father had also once been Australia's champion miler, was one of a group of athletes who had spotted the potential of an elegant young runner called John Landy from Geelong Grammar School. MacMillan encouraged Landy to meet Cerutty and sample his style of training.

The Svengali-like personality of the self-styled 'Conditioner of Men' attracted some athletes but drove others to dash off in the opposite direction. There were those who thought the 'Chief Stotan' was a genius; others found him crazy and insufferable. Initially, the shy and wide-eyed boy from Geelong Grammar looked in wonder and disbelief at the silver-haired, wiry old wizard, who seemed to think that nothing was impossible.

There could hardly have been a greater contrast between the wild, overpowering coach and the modest, unassuming athlete. John Landy had been born in Queensland into a very different world to the eccentric, self-educated Cerutty. Landy's father was a well-to-do accountant and a high-ranking member of the Melbourne Cricket Club. As a child John enjoyed the easy comforts and privileges that prosperity in post-war Australia could bring, and he was sent to Geelong Grammar – reckoned by many to be the finest school in the land, renowned both for its high academic standards and for its great sporting tradition.

The young Landy was handsome, slim but well muscled, and fine raw material for sport. Graceful in his movements, with dark curly hair above a high forehead, he had a ready smile and an easy-going charm that made him popular among his schoolmates. He could run, that was obvious to anyone who saw his immaculate style, but he had the all-round talents of a sportsman that made any game look easy. In the rough, tough scrap of an Australian Rules football game, the normally quiet Landy would discard his inhibitions, and when it came to sprinting he could explode with the best of them. He was so good at Australian Rules football that his friends encouraged him to take it up at the highest level with one of the big clubs. And he loved the easy conviviality of the post-match celebrations, with its beer and warm banter.

But by the time he went up to Melbourne University to study agricultural science, Landy knew that if he was going to excel at sport he would have to stop dabbling. He set his eye on the middle distances and planned to see how far the mile might take him.

No one who ran in Australia could be unaware of the existence of Percy Cerutty. He was a great self-publicist and regularly made headlines for tongue-lashing many of the country's leading sportsmen as 'failures'. He had urged the Australian Olympic squad, on their return from the London Olympic

Games in 1948, to take on the Europeans and the Americans, who he reckoned were war-weary and ready to be beaten.

Cerutty was never slow to predict that all existing world records would be torn apart once the world's athletes caught up with his training techniques. He talked blithely of lengthening an athlete's stride — to produce 100 yards in 8 seconds or a half-mile in 1:32. He was already crowing that the four-minute mile could fall any time to his best miler Don MacMillan.

But for Percy Cerutty four minutes was only the start. He said that if his training and racing techniques could be properly developed, he would see a mile run in his lifetime in 3:20. The preparation, he said, would involve prodigious quantities of endurance running and weight-lifting during the conditioning period, and interval running done ultimately at near sprinting speed on sand and grass during a period of race practice.

Above all, stressed Cerutty, it would involve the athlete running with a proper galloping movement, the secret of all great speed for the human animal, which would allow the runner to use his full lung capacity and unleash a ferociously long stride. With the mile world record still standing to the Swede Gunder Haegg at 4:01.4, it was little wonder that so many scoffed at Cerutty.

He spat his contempt at the non-believers, saying anything would be possible once athletes had learned to pass through the pain barrier. The sound barrier had been broken by Chuck Yeager in 1947, an achievement that Cerutty latched on to eagerly. Like the sound barrier, he said, the pain barrier would be just as remarkable, physically and emotionally, and wonderful to experience.

'I've not experienced the phenomenon in the air,' he

conceded, 'but I have heard the thuds and bumps that accompany the feat. When it comes to the pain barrier I have a little more first-hand experience.' To push beyond it, Cerutty believed, a miler would have to run with abandon from the start, burying all thought of conserving energy; then, when he reached the point in the race where he felt so much pain that it was impossible to continue, if he pushed on he would be released suddenly from all physical constriction and run like one possessed. The athlete would have conquered 'not space, or time, but himself' – even if he would 'feel and look close to death'.

One of Landy's hobbies was collecting butterflies and moths – not quite the iron-man approach likely to endear him to Cerutty. But the guru had gathered round him a band of athletes that included Les Perry, Geoff Warren, Ray Weinberg and Don MacMillan, some of the best in Australia. Their glamour and achievements were enough to tempt Landy to find out for himself what the colourful coach had to offer. Crank he might be, but Landy had little to lose by meeting him.

'Landy had no special gifts,' Cerutty was to observe later. 'He made himself into the running machine that he became.' Landy was certainly something of a late developer. He ran his very first mile at the age of 17, while still a pupil at Geelong Grammar School, in 4:58. But, as Cerutty was to note, at 19 years of age, even after plenty of middle-distance races, his best time for the mile was only 4:37. What got Landy to the top, Cerutty claimed, was his dedication and purpose, his refusal to let anything stand in his way. Of course, the coach would add with a grin, 'He had to find someone who could help in the early stages to lead him along the road that ends in a world record.'

After the initial meeting and a few runs with the group around Melbourne's Botanic Gardens, Don MacMillan persuaded Landy that he should visit Cerutty's training camp.

'At Portsea,' said Cerutty, 'we run up sand hills wherever they are found, over sand dunes and on the heavy part of the sandy beaches. We trudge up mountains, too. We work for a couple of hours at least twice a week with the heaviest weights we can handle.

'We go out for non-stop runs of upwards of twenty miles. For a miler we build up to around two hundred miles each month. Then we go into the surf, sometimes during the winter, as part of our toughening. We try to go to the snowfields, too, once each winter. Conditioning, mentally and physically, must go on continuously, in all our spare time away from work or studies.'

It was certainly no holiday camp, and one week was more than enough for Landy. Training with Cerutty's group might have toughened and speeded up the young would-be miler, but he found the coach too cranky, and he wasn't keen on the diet either – oatmeal, raw eggs, raw fish and nuts.

The lessons of Geelong Grammar had made a deep impression on Landy and he was, above all, a gentleman. It showed in the way he carried himself, both on and off the track. Cerutty jibed that he lacked the killer instinct, but it was a quality that a few seasons later was to mark John Landy out as a quite extraordinary sporting hero.

During the 1956 Australian mile championship, a number of athletes collided and fell in the third lap – junior world record holder Ron Clarke among them. Landy, who was behind him when he fell, leapt over Clarke, then went back to make sure that he was all right. Having helped Clarke to his feet, Landy looked up and saw the field about 40 yards away. In panic and desperation he rejoined the race, and as the crowd went wild he caught up again with the leaders and went on to win in a time of 4:04.2.

It was one of the most amazing performances of all time. Even the cynics in the press box stood up and applauded Landy's action, and many eyewitnesses reckoned that they had seen the greatest mile race in history.

The incident became part of Australian folklore and earned Landy for all time the title of 'Gentleman John'. But Cerutty was not so impressed. He considered running to be a far from gentlemanly pursuit. He believed it was a primitive act, basically an act of violence, committed by the runner against himself. When Landy stopped mid-race to pick up Ron Clarke, this merely indicated to Cerutty that he did not possess the vital and ruthless determination to win at all costs.

Though later in his career Landy played down the influence that Cerutty had had in his athletic development, on 10 November 1951, after running a mile in 4:14.6, which was faster than MacMillan's national championship win that year, he presented the coach with a photo of himself crossing the winning line, inscribed with the date and the time. He signed it: 'To Perce, the bloke that made it possible.'

By early 1952, the 21-year-old John Landy was beginning to attract the attention of the Australian Olympic selectors with a number of very promising performances. On 12 January, at Melbourne's Olympic Park, he ran a mile in 4:11 and 3,000 metres in 8:35 – which was just two seconds slower than Don MacMillan's national record. He was beaten by MacMillan, however, in the 1952 Australian mile championships, and was selected for the Helsinki Olympics team only on the condition that he pay his own way to Finland.

The Landy family were proud and delighted and were not

going to let slip the opportunity of having their son run in the Olympic Games. The local community, too, rallied round to help raise the necessary funds.

The Australian team, Landy and MacMillan among them, travelled to Helsinki via Britain. In Europe, Landy was ready to soak up all the experience he could. In his first warm-up race he ran 8:24 for the two miles, a new best for him, and on 14 June he went along with other athletes from the Australian team to take part in the AAA championships.

An enormous crowd of 46,000 turned out to give the British Olympic team a good send-off. There in the royal box was Queen Elizabeth, not yet crowned, her husband Prince Philip, and her sister Princess Margaret. On the infield a bevy of past British champions were presented to the crowd. They included Lord Burghley, Harold Abrahams, and the man who still held the British mile record, Sydney Wooderson. Roger Bannister, the heir apparent to Wooderson, was there too, but he had stirred up considerable criticism by opting not to run the mile, but instead to sharpen his speed in the half-mile.

Some thought Bannister was dodging the competition of Bill Nankeville and that he was arrogant enough to believe himself to be an automatic selection to run the Olympic 1,500 metres. But Bannister believed he should be saving himself for one supreme effort in Helsinki.

Up against Nankeville in the mile were MacMillan and Landy. Their coach was in the stadium too. As the stands were filling up and the athletes for the early events beginning their warm-ups, the crowd were entertained by the sight of a bronzed, wiry, white-haired figure, wearing just a skimpy pair of running shorts, galloping around the track as if in a race of his own. The bemused officials first shouted at him and then tried to bundle him off the track. The more they tried, the faster he ran. And as he dodged and weaved his way past them, the crowd laughed and cheered the impromptu entertainment.

Getting ready to run his own race, John Landy was amused but a little embarrassed. But Cerutty was only following the advice he had given his athletes. 'Let them know we're here,' he said. 'Run like hell and show them the boys from Australia have arrived.'

John Landy completely outpaced his countryman MacMillan, but Bill Nankeville won the race in 4:09.8, if only just. He was pushed all the way by Landy, who improved his personal best to 4:11. It was the first time most of the crowd had seen or heard of Landy, or indeed the colourful coach Percy Cerutty, but they would, in time, hear plenty more of both.

16

The Watershed Games

We should never forget that Britain is the cradle of amateur
sport. The rest of the world looks to us to play our part in
maintaining that high tradition, and this surely is yet another
reason for making a tremendous effort to ensure that we are
adequately represented in Helsinki. It may be that but few of
the firsts will come our way, but at any rate we will put up a
show worthy of our country.

Lord Burghley

The torch relay was an idea dreamed up by Carl Diem, the
organising genius behind the 1936 Berlin Games – the so-called
Nazi Olympics. The flame was kindled at Olympia in Greece,
using a mirror and the rays of the sun. It became a fixture, an
instant tradition that seemed as old as the Games themselves.

In Helsinki, in 1952, as the rain splashed in the cool of the
Scandinavian evening, there was a moment of hushed still-
ness as a balding middle-aged figure wearing the vest of
Finland, white shorts and black leather spikes, padded into
the stadium, torch in hand. The first letter of his name lit up
the scoreboard, and the crowd erupted in a roar of homage
and adulation for the greatest of all Finnish athletic heroes –
Paavo Nurmi.

He was 55 years old and there had been rumours that he

would not be included in the relay because his body was crip-
pled with rheumatism. Others claimed the Olympic Committee
would never let a man who had been banned for alleged
breaches of amateurism carry the Olympic flame.

But there he was, moving with the same rhythmic, smooth
action so that you half expected him to be squinting at a stopwatch in the palm of his left hand.

He ran alone while the crowed screamed their joy, many
with tears running down their faces. Then he lit a flame at
the side of the track before handing the torch to his countryman Hannes Kolehmainen, who represented an even older part
of Finland's glorious athletic past.

Kolehmainen had won gold medals for the 5,000 and 10,000
metres and cross-country in the Stockholm Games of 1912,
and came back as a veteran to win the marathon in the Olympics
of 1920. His running days over, he was working as the
groundsman at the Helsinki stadium. Now the 62-year-old
took a lift to the tower above the track to light a second flame.

As silence fell on the stadium, with the crowd waiting for
the Olympic hymn, a blonde girl, scantily dressed as an ancient
Greek, ran into the arena from an entrance opposite the grandstand. Clad in diaphanous white robes, hair flowing in the
wind, she ran round the track. As she reached the rostrum
and seized the microphone, surprised officials sprang to life
and bundled the intruder away to a police car. These Olympics
were modern indeed, and Barbara Pleyer, a 17-year-old
German student, may have been the Games' first streaker.

The rest of the opening ceremony went smoothly enough,
although many spectators were baffled by the peculiarities of
the Finnish language. Great Britain marched behind a banner
bearing the name 'Iso-Britannia', and it was even more difficult to recognise the United States as 'Yadysvallad'. Another

team entered with the name 'Nevvostoliitto' – it was the USSR in their first Olympic parade.

The Finns had been invited to host the Games of 1940, but as war spread around the globe, Helsinki's opportunity to stage the Olympics was postponed until 1952. There was a political dimension to these watershed Games, too. For the first time since Stockholm in 1912, the Russians were back – but they hardly entered into the spirit of old de Coubertin's dream of bringing the world together.

Amazingly, the Russians, at the Games as the Soviet Union, were allowed to set up their own Olympic village some five miles outside the city. There in the pine forests at Otaniemi, they were joined by teams from Bulgaria, Czechoslovakia, Hungary, Poland and Romania. To underline the separateness of this Eastern Bloc camp, the Russians hung a huge portrait of Stalin on the front of the technical college that served as their headquarters. To trumpet the superiority of their system they erected a giant scoreboard showing who was leading each day in the unofficial overall medal table.

This was all very well while the Russians looked like dominating, but late in the Games, the USA fought back with a vengeance. Five gold medals in the boxing saw them suddenly overhaul the Russians, who immediately, to the amusement of visiting journalists, started to tear down the scoreboard.

But up in the stands during the opening ceremony, politics were forgotten. There, transfixed by the sight of Paavo Nurmi, were the coaches and athletes who had learned so much from the master. Among them were three young men – Roger Bannister, John Landy and Wes Santee – all getting their first exhilarating taste of Olympic competition.

Britain had high hopes for their team, particularly for Roger Bannister. 'It is hard all these years later to realise how great the weight of expectation was,' said Chris Brasher. 'You've got to remember what conditions were like in 1952. There was all the rationing and the austerity. The country didn't seem able to pick itself up after all the effort of the war and there was almost a complete lack of sporting success abroad.

'Typically British, we wondered if the war had drained all our ambition and will. But there was, particularly if you were a reader of the sports pages, one big hope – a tall, pale Oxford medical student who seemed to have perfect control of himself. After all, hadn't he refused an invitation to take part in the 1948 Olympic Games at Wembley because he thought he was too young? Hadn't he always mapped out his racing to bring himself to a peak on the most important days? Wasn't he another Jack Lovelock, like him an Oxford medical student? Wasn't he like the Lovelock who had won the 1,500 metres title at the 1936 Olympics?'

The appearance of a youthful Queen Elizabeth at the English AAA championships before the Games had captured perfectly the mixture of euphoria and longing of a nation eager to get up and running after the weary years of war. Wartime rationing was easing at last, although it was not to be completely ended until 1954. So sugar, butter, cheese, margarine, cooking fat, bacon, meats and tea were still hard to come by. But diets were healthy enough for a hungry runner, who could boost his depleted muscles with plenty of bread, vegetables and milk.

Performance-enhancing food supplements and the scourge of drugs had yet to cast their shadow over this simple sport. Hard-training athletes drank Horlicks or Lucozade. Sports magazines advertised Crookes Halibut Oil – 25 capsules for half a crown (12 ½ p).

There were no big pay-days and no big prizes. A miler who knew how to out-fox the handicappers and win might carry

home toasters, kettles, cutlery sets, watches, clocks and barome-
ters galore, but if he took 'expenses' he had better beware. The
amateur rules were rigidly enforced. Competitors were expected
to buy all their own kit and equipment, including running shoes.
Most of the track spikes worn by the best British athletes were
hand-made by G.T. Law & Son of Wimbledon, whose shoes
encased the feet of Jack Lovelock, or J.W. Foster and Sons of
Bolton. They cost between £2 and £5 a pair, and were usually
made to measure, of leather and crocodile skin. Off the track
there were no fancy 'trainers', just canvas plimsolls.

The British press and public took it for granted that their
finest athletes would step from this cosy cinder-tracked world
into the competitive crucible of the Olympic Games and bring
home the medals. If Roger Bannister couldn't win the 1,500
metres, maybe Bill Nankeville could. He had won the AAA
mile in 4:09.8, taking the title for the fourth time, so perhaps
he could do the same in Helsinki.

Other distance runners who were reckoned to have a chance
in the Games were Chris Chataway and Gordon Pirie in the
5,000 metres. Chataway, much more outgoing and relaxed
than Bannister, would happily give an interview to any reporter
who asked. Pirie took everything more seriously. He was
churning out seven miles a day in preparation for his battles
on the track and was, they said, tucked up safely in bed by
8.30 every night.

If you couldn't quite make it in the mile, if you didn't have
the God-given ability to match strides with the Bannisters, the
Nankevilles or the Chataways, the usual advice was to have a
go at the steeplechase. Here a man might make up in effort
what he lacked in natural speed. Two who tried for Britain in
Helsinki were John Disley and Chris Brasher.

The elegant Disley had a strange race at the Games. He

appeared to drift around in seventh place, seemingly in a trance, until galvanised into action by Britain's chief athletics coach Geoff Dyson. 'I woke up and began to chase the leaders,' he said. He floated past four rivals, finishing in 8:51.8 to take the bronze medal.

Disley's was a lone success. Chris Brasher would finish eleventh out of twelve in the steeplechase. Chris Chataway would run his heart out, only to trip in exhaustion on the last lap of the 5,000 metres and finish fifth. Gordon Pirie finished out of the medals in fourth. But at least they made the final. Two who didn't, experiencing the trauma of elimination in the heats of the 5,000 metres, were John Landy and Wes Santee.

But while many athletes were to find the Games tough going, there were others in Helsinki who had been exploring new ways to train, new ways to win. Men like Josy Barthel, winner of the 1,500 metres, who was using German interval training. And above all there was the man who was to show that this new method could produce the most extraordinary results. This man, the greatest hero of the Games, was the natural successor to Paavo Nurmi. The Czech Emil Zatopek conquered, like some reincarnated Nurmi, both the 5,000 and the 10,000 metres. Then he finished his week by winning the marathon, a distance at which he had never before competed.

Bannister himself was going through turmoil. Just prior to the Games, five of the world's athletic authorities were asked to forecast the probable results. Three of the predictions – those by Dr Roberto Quercetani of Italy, Fulvio Regli of Switzerland and the McWhirter twins of Britain – put Bannister in first place for the 1,500 metres. A fourth prediction, from Dr Donald Potts of the USA, had him in second. 'That', said Bannister, 'is the burden that was on me. That was what I was facing.'

The 1,500 metres began on Thursday 24 July, with six heats – the first four in each heat qualifying for the semi-finals the following day. In Bannister's heat his opponents included Andrija Otenhajmer of Yugoslavia, Patrick El Mabrouk of France, John Landy of Australia and Bob McMillen of the USA. It was a slow and scrambling first three laps, with no one wanting to take the lead, followed by a furious sprint. El Mabrouk won in 3:55.8 with Bannister third in 3:56. John Landy was eliminated in fifth place. 'This did not exhaust me unduly, but I had not been sleeping much all week and I got no sleep afterwards,' Bannister remembered.

The sleep problem is something recalled well by Chris Chataway, and it was, he said, 'terribly self-defeating. I shared a room with Roger and, looking back now, I think that he was defeated purely in his own mind, that he could have won that final easily.

'He'd done a fantastic time trial over three-quarters of a mile at Motspur Park ten days before. I paced him for the first half and he did 2:52.9 and there was absolutely no question that he was just the best in the world. He had far more natural ability than anyone else and in my opinion it was a very thin year. There was nobody much else around. People like Josy Barthel weren't that good, and even though it was a horrible shock to have to do heats and a semi-final, the heats were pretty slow.

'But Roger was absolutely devastated by the thought of the extra race and I can remember him lying on that bed. The buildings we were in were to become public housing after the Games and it was just a square box of a room with iron bedsteads. We'd strung a blanket up across the window to try to keep out the perpetual Scandinavian daylight. With us was Nick Stacey who was very funny. He maintained an absolutely non-stop cabaret act throughout. He was quite a good sprinter. In fact he would tell everybody that he was the fastest white man on earth. He said it so often that one dismissed it as a joke, but I think it proved to be so, at least in the 200 metres.

'Nick had this wooden box in the corner of the room on which he would practise the victory ceremony. Some days Avery Brundage, the Olympic President, would be approaching his "rostrum" and Nick would say, "Well, it was nothing, sir, really. Pure luck, sir, pure luck." Then other days he would be punching the air saying, "By God, that showed them."

'Nick kept us very amused. He got this Coca-Cola bottle and he reckoned that the best way to stop himself having wet dreams and wasting precious energy was to tie the Coca-Cola bottle to the back of his pyjamas. We would like to believe that we were all as funny and light-hearted as Nick but we weren't – and Roger least of all. Roger was lying on his bed moaning the entire time and there was talk that he might be ill in some way, but I don't think he was. I think it was all psychological.'

In Bannister's semi-final Josy Barthel galloped home first in 3:50.4, with a last lap under 60 seconds. Bannister looked uncomfortable in fifth, with the first six to qualify for the final. 'The following night was one of the most unpleasant I have ever spent,' he said. 'My legs ached and I was unable to sleep. I felt I hated running. I thought of the stadium to be filled next day with 70,000 people all waiting and watching. I thought, too, of the moment when victory was in the balance and I must galvanise my tired limbs to fresh effort. In my sleepless nights I had run the race a thousand times.'

By the time he lined up for the final, anxiety had given way to fear, and fear had been elbowed aside by panic. Bannister had defied advice, gone his own way, trained by his own

methods, raced his own races – a victory would justify everything. But he knew that if he failed, the press and the public
would turn on him.

The opposition in the 1,500 metres was impressive. Werner
Lueg, the big-striding West German and current world record
holder at the distance, had to begin as one of the favourites.
Others tipped El Mabrouk of France. Josy Barthel had looked
surprisingly good in the heats but none of the real experts rated
his chances. At a dinner just before the Games, a German
athletics official had pronounced, 'We all know that Luxembourg does not expect to win any gold medals at Helsinki.
Even Monsieur Barthel will be no Olympic champion. But as
you know, the important thing in the Olympic Games is not
so much winning as taking part.'

Bannister was nourished by the knowledge that with his
three-quarter-mile time trial behind him, he could certainly
run at world record speed. But he feared he would not prove
strong enough to run three races back to back.

'I hardly had the strength to warm up,' he said. 'My step
had no spring, my face no colour, the ruthless fighting of the
semi-final, the worry and lack of sleep had exhausted me.'

As expected, the Germans set the pace. Rolf Lamers led for
much of the first 800 metres, reached in 2:01.4, then Lueg took
over at a speed that was going to drop any but the best. By the
time the bell signalled the last lap, Lueg still held the lead,
hoping to draw the sting from the fast finishers.

Bannister moved up to make his customary killer burst 300
metres from the finish, but he could not sustain it. 'What
happened was I got to the ideal position at the beginning of
the final straight and gave the order to sprint, but I couldn't,'
he said. 'My legs simply failed to respond. Of course I now
know – and it's taken 50 years of physiology with biopsies of

muscles and so on to give us the science – that the muscle fibres were depleted of glycogen. You need a supply of glycogen for your anaerobic work, your sprinting. Years on, the problem I had is perfectly clear, but at the crucial moment I had no strength left to force my aching legs to go faster.'

Barthel and McMillen swept by Bannister and both ran down Lueg before the tape. The race was over. Bannister was defeated and fourth. Josy Barthel, running 3:45.2, had won Luxembourg's only medal of the Games. The pain that gripped Bannister was much more than the usual exhaustion that followed at the end of a race. Lactic acid mixed with despair, disappointment and anger is the most bitter of athletic cocktails. He had broken the Olympic record and set a new British record with 3:46 – but he had failed to win a medal.

'Roger knew then that it was going to be four years before the next Olympics and that he was going to be too busy working as a doctor,' said Chris Brasher. 'He knew he would never find the time to commit himself to go for an Olympic victory again.'

The press were not happy either. One headline read: 'No – Roger wasn't nearly tough enough' and the writer ended his report with the stinging comment: 'I feel like suing British athletes for breach of promise.'

A letter in *The Times* on 13 August read: 'Staff writers were almost unanimous that the 1,500 metres final showed this athlete's [Bannister's] training methods to be wrong; an error to which many of them had drawn attention earlier in the summer, only to find it condoned by British athletic officials to the point of Bannister's abstention from competitive running over the distance.'

Other writers were kinder and noted that coming fourth in

a race at the Games and breaking the Olympic record could hardly be described as 'failure'.

The Times of 4 August reported: 'Bannister and Nankeville, but mainly the former, provided another example of the splendid British best which still was not quite good enough. Both had to run two stiff and most uncomfortable races in the heats and Nankeville, because surprisingly enough he allowed himself to be boxed at the very moment he ought to have been free, failed to reach the final. Bannister had to be content with fourth. Yet his own time of 3:46 was nearly two seconds inside Lovelock's record in Berlin – a classic effort if ever there was one – and represented a mile in approximately 4:04.8. That of itself was a rare achievement.'

For John Landy the lack of international racing experience was only too apparent. He was eliminated in the heats of both the 5,000 and the 1,500 metres. Landy had been selected for Helsinki as the third string in the metric mile. His fares had been raised by charity and the efforts of his friends and family back in Geelong. Percy Cerutty was quick to remind him of this, contemptuously adding that, by flopping badly in the Olympic heats, he had wasted all that generosity.

And Wes Santee, for all his swagger, found himself out of his depth in the 5,000 metres, lined up against experienced veterans like the Czech Zatopek, Anufryev of Russia and Albertsson of Sweden. The best he could manage was thirteenth in the qualifying heat. In the first half of the race he ran himself ragged, recklessly trying to match strides with Herbert Schade, the German.

If that hurt, so did being a spectator for the 1,500 metres. There Santee had to watch his countryman Bob McMillen, a miler he had often beaten back in America, take the silver medal, just a stride behind the winner. Santee had run the wrong race – both he and his coach Bill Easton knew it. They could hardly wait to get back to Kansas to the mile and to the records that they knew were waiting to be broken.

The press, which had torn into Roger Bannister for his failure, were kinder to Chataway. He was seen as the man who ran till he dropped. 'Chataway's failure in the 5,000 metres perhaps did as much to restore British credit as a virile country – if anyone persisted in doubting it after 1939–45 – as any victory would have done,' reported *The Times* on 4 August, in an article headlined 'The True Spirit'. 'Chataway's courage and determination in rising and running on after a bad tumble at the final bend won for him both a good place and the admiration of all who witnessed the race. There surely was the true Olympic – and one hopes still the British – spirit at its best.

'One may think that wiser counsels may have spared Chataway at this stage of his athletic career the acid test of a battle with Zatopek, sending him instead perhaps into the 1,500 metres, though such a move would have been difficult. But that, after all, is a study in team tactics rather than sport. Chataway, shaken and exhausted though he was, yet reached fifth place, passed by his fellow Briton Pirie – another young runner of the highest promise – almost on the tape.'

Roger Bannister could take little comfort in the headlines he had attracted. 'But,' said his friend Brasher, 'I believe that it was the headlines that screamed his failure that set Roger on the quest for the first four-minute mile. I believe it all started during those Olympic Games in 1952 in Helsinki. Roger knew that by the time of the next Olympics he would have qualified as a doctor and would be working all the hours of the day and night in a hospital.

'But 1954 was the year of the Empire Games and European Championships. They could be his last in international athletics.

Roger knew, too, that neither an Empire Games title nor a European title could quite make up for a lost Olympic title. But the four-minute mile – there was a target to go for. It was an ambition that would surely be unique in history.'

'Luck and history certainly come into it,' said Chataway. 'I suppose that the late introduction of the extra race for the 1,500 metres would have been seen as terribly bad luck by Roger. But what he took to be the worst luck actually turned out to be the best of luck. It just goes to show that you never know in life what is good news and what is bad news, or what is bad luck and what is good luck at the time.'

17

The New Way to Train

Why should I practise running slow? I already know how to run
slow. I want to learn to run fast. Everyone said: Emil, you are a
fool! But when I first won the European Championship, they
said: Emil, you are a genius!

Emil Zatopek

There were too many planes shuttling in and out of Helsinki's
airport once the Games were over. Flights were held up by the
overcrowding, and there was plenty of time for athletes and
coaches to mingle in the airport lounge.

As he waited for his delayed plane to London, Gordon Pirie
came across a huddle of British runners who had cornered the
German coach Woldemar Gerschler. Chris Brasher, Chris
Chataway and Roger Bannister were all firing questions at the
German, taking in everything he was saying – and even scrib-
bling notes.

Pirie had never met Gerschler, but he knew he was the
coach who had trained Josy Barthel. Gerschler seemed quite
happy to tell the British athletes exactly how he had turned
the little-known middle-distance runner from Luxembourg
into an Olympic champion. The lightly trained university
athletes were amazed to learn how strenuously Barthel had
prepared. Brasher and Chataway even asked the German if he

would take on coaching and advising them too. Gerschler replied that he would be happy to do so, but only if they were prepared to visit him in Freiburg to undergo scientific assessment of their condition and potential.

For Gordon Pirie the invitation was irresistible. Here was the coach who had pioneered the interval training that had made Emil Zatopek seemingly unbeatable. Here was the man who had the secrets of the new way to train. Pirie could hardly wait to scrape together the fare to Freiburg.

There were letters, too, exchanged later between Chris Brasher and Gerschler. 'Anyone who'd seen Zatopek run had to know how he did it,' Brasher said. 'We had to learn what made it possible. We had to wonder what this sort of training might do for our own running.'

By winning three gold medals in Helsinki in 1952, Emil Zatopek, the 'human locomotive', became a folk hero for runners the world over. His appetite for mileage and hard work shattered all previous theories about what strain the human body could absorb. He, more than any other man since Paavo Nurmi, kicked open the door that led to modern distance running.

Born in the Czechoslovakian town of Zlin to peasant parents in 1922, Zatopek grew up to speak seven languages. He left school at 15 to work in a shoe factory, but took no part in sport until he was 19, when there was a local race sponsored by the factory where he worked. Zatopek was press-ganged into running. Legend has it that to get out of competing he even told his boss that he was sick and had a bad knee. But the factory doctor said he looked healthy enough and he was instructed to participate.

Once up and running, he set out to win. In fact, he ended up in second place, but it was a good enough performance to get him spotted by an older runner, who invited him to join a running club. His first track event in Czechoslovakia was a 3,000 metres, in which he ran 9:12, and again came second. A local newspaper report was headlined: 'A good performance by Zatopek'. It was said that Emil kept the clipping folded neatly in his wallet for years.

Zatopek observed that for distance racing he needed both speed and stamina. So for speed he would run a short distance, 100 or 200 metres, and to build up stamina he would repeat it many times, with just a brief rest of 200 metres jogging in between. There were plenty who questioned his brutally simple approach, but he soon began to get the results he wanted. He took ideas from Paavo Nurmi and decided that whatever Nurmi had done he would multiply. Zatopek's first important international race was the 5,000 metres in the European Championships in Oslo, Norway, in 1946. It was won by Sydney Wooderson, the former mile world record holder – with the young Zatopek in fifth place.

During the winter of 1946/47, with Europe gripped by sub-zero temperatures, Zatopek trained by bounding through deep snow, leaping with giant, exaggerated strides while wearing his Czech army boots. He reckoned the boots gave plenty of protection to the feet, stopping his ankles from turning. Their weight added extra resistance to his workout.

At the 1948 Olympics in London, Zatopek was not reck-oned to have much chance in the 10,000 metres against Viljo Heino, the world record holder from Finland. The race was on the first day of the Games and it was suggested that Zatopek planned to hit the right pace by having a friend in the stands with two coloured shirts – one red and one white. If the 400 metre split time was faster than world record pace, a white shirt would be held up; if it was slower, the shirt would be red. Whether or not he was receiving a signal from the stand, on the ninth lap he made a move through the field and on the tenth lap he took the lead from Heino. The world record holder pulled out of the race with seven laps to go, unable to handle Zatopek's aggressive front-running. Zatopek finished unchallenged in a new Olympic record of 29:59.6 – 47 seconds ahead of Alain Mimoun, an Algerian competing for France. It was the first gold medal ever for Czechoslovakia.

The next day he ran in the heats of the 5,000 metres, and two days later in the final. There he narrowly failed to catch Gaston Reiff on the line and had to settle for the silver. Nevertheless, he returned to Prague a national hero and married Dana Ingrova, who had finished seventh in the javelin in London.

By the following year the 10,000 metre world record was his, and the stories about him were spreading fast. When his wife Dana wanted help with the laundry, apparently Emil ran for two hours in a tub of water, pummelling the washing with his feet. He frequently held his breath for as long as he could simply to get his body used to the idea of being starved of oxygen.

According to Gordon Pirie, Emil and Dana would romp like children, turning hard training into play. 'Once in fun', said Pirie, 'he threw her into a stream. Unfortunately her foot hit a rock and she broke an ankle. While she had her leg in plaster Emil ran with her on his back through deep snow for training.'

Just before the 1950 European Championships in Brussels, Zatopek was hospitalised with food poisoning and was unable to train for two weeks. Despite medical advice that he should not run, he won both the 10,000 and the 5,000 metres in the second fastest times ever recorded for those distances. The truth was he had probably benefited from the rest after all that hard training.

By 1951, in one workout he was running 20 x 200 metres, followed by 40 x 400 metres and then another 20 x 200 metres, all with just 200-metre jog intervals between the hard efforts. His theory was that if the training were rigorous enough, the race would seem easy.

At the 1952 Olympics, on the newly laid red cinder track, Zatopek hit the front in the 10,000 metres after eight laps and won in a record time 15 seconds ahead of Mimoun, his nearest rival.

He did not have things quite so easy in the 5,000 metres. There he came up against the young Chris Chataway, Gaston Reiff, the Olympic champion from London in 1948, and also Schade, who was the holder of the world best time for the distance in 1952. When Zatopek tried to sprint away on the last lap he found the other runners could match him, and Chataway, Schade and Mimoun were all in front of him. But somehow, in the final 200 metres, Zatopek dug deep and found an amazing sprint to force himself past his tiring rivals. Chataway hit the inside kerb and stumbled, and Zatopek, with a last lap of 57.9 and a final 200 metres of 28.3, snatched victory.

Three days later Zatopek turned out for the marathon. It was his first attempt on the distance, against the fastest marathon runner in the world, Britain's Jim Peters. The prospect of a Zatopek treble drew a crowd of over 68,000 to the Helsinki stadium that Sunday afternoon. Zatopek's strategy for the race was simple. 'Jim Peters of England was the favourite and I just decided to run close to him. I didn't know him at all, only that his number was 187.'

Peters led the race for the first 10 miles, with Zatopek tracking him about 50 yards behind. Shortly after 10 miles

Zatopek drew alongside Peters. 'I asked him if the pace was fast enough and he said yes. I think he was a little annoyed by my questions, so he began to run on the other side of the road. But I thought he looked a little tired.' Peters fell back, and dropped out of the race at 21 miles, complaining of pain in his left side.

Zatopek stepped on the accelerator and the crowd in the stadium saw the scoreboard record his ever-increasing lead. A deafening chant of *Za-to-pek, Za-to-pek* greeted him as he entered the arena. He crossed the line in 2:23:03.2, nearly two and a half minutes ahead of the next man. He raised his arms in triumph and grinned.

Zatopek had made Olympic history and changed the course of distance running by taking a new method of training and pushing it to limits that no other athlete had dared to attempt. He won because he was unwilling to acknowledge boundaries.

'When a person trains once nothing happens,' he said. 'When a person forces himself to do a thing a hundred or a thousand times then he certainly develops in ways more than physical. Is it raining? That doesn't matter. Am I tired? That doesn't matter either. Willpower becomes no longer a problem.'

Like so much else in the world of running, Zatopek's favoured system of interval training could be traced back to Paavo Nurmi. The world's coaches had spent years poring over the training of the Finns – and in particular Nurmi. The Finnish athletes were the Kenyans of their day, dominating distance running, and everyone wanted to emulate them and share their secrets. Copycat versions of their training soon spread to other countries, where it was adapted and modified both by national temperament and by scientific research. Two schools of training emerged.

In Sweden the Finnish method was changed very little.

During the 1930s, Gosta Olander took the hard, varied-paced system of running into the stimulating environment of the forests and lakes and produced fartlek – which helped Haegg and Andersson get within ten strides of the four-minute mile and was the method used in the early careers of both Landy and Bannister.

The Germans, too, had studied Nurmi's Finnish training and concluded that there was an important gap – not enough speed work. In the 1930s, their coach Woldemar Gerschler took as his guinea pig the talented 400-metre runner Rudolph Harbig. The results were revolutionary, and ushered in an era during which the record books were rewritten as never before.

At the outbreak of the Second World War, Gerschler was working at the University of Freiburg in the Black Forest, where he was one of the first coaches in athletics history to attempt to base his methods on sound physiological and psychological principles. He, and the athletes he coached, worked closely with Dr Hans Reindell, a physiologist, and with a number of sports psychologists. Gerschler and Reindell pioneered interval training, which has changed for ever the conditioning of athletes in endurance events – not just running, but also swimming, rowing and Nordic skiing.

Gerschler's greatest contribution to running was his work on the importance of cardiovascular conditioning and the way in which he devised training schedules to maximise cardiovascular fitness. He pioneered a system that was calculated to increase the stroke volume of the heart, its ability to deliver blood and oxygen to the legs. To do this he used short, fast runs, which were repeated a great number of times.

The name of the system comes from the interval or rest period between the fast runs. Gerschler and Reindell considered the resting interval the most important part of a workout.

Their research suggested that the heart adapted to the effort and grew stronger during the rest interval, and they would never allow their runners to begin the next fast run until their pulse rate had returned to 120 beats per minute. Without this monitored rest interval the heart could be overworked, leading to fatigue and exhaustion.

In November 1938, Rudolph Harbig began the training that was to prove the value of Gerschler's new system. In the early months of his conditioning Harbig trained three times a week, once in the gym, once on the track and then for up to three hours every Sunday morning in the woods, alternating fast and slow running. This was an unheard-of volume of training for a runner whose longest racing distance was 800 metres. As his fitness improved, Harbig began doing fast interval repeats. In May 1939 he ran 5 x 200 metres in around 24 seconds. On 15 July he raced 800 metres in 1:46.6. This knocked a phenomenal 1.6 seconds off the world record and was a time that stood unbeaten for 16 years. Within a month Harbig raced 400 metres in a new world record time of 46 seconds dead.

The new way to train had arrived, and those who knew about it were quite relaxed about sharing their secrets. It was not just Gerschler, with his impromptu seminar on interval training in Helsinki airport. John Disley, who won bronze in the steeplechase at those Games, remembers that Zatopek talked quite openly about the details of the hard training sessions he did, in stark contrast to some of his fellow runners, who played down what they were doing, or were secretive about it. 'Zatopek was open and honest and willing to share his training ideas with anyone,' said Disley.

John Landy, too, spent all the time he could in Helsinki listening to the lessons of Zatopek, eagerly soaking up everything he could learn about how to train and race. He returned to Australia, his notebooks crammed with the details of the new way to train.

Gordon Pirie similarly was amazed by Zatopek's willingness to share the secrets of his success. 'So many runners are secretive, fearing that others may copy them,' said Pirie, 'but Zatopek wanted everybody to know how he did it. He was well aware that only the best would emerge at the top, and if they did so by copying him, nobody would be more pleased than Emil.'

His methods, Pirie added, 'were of course derided by the take-it-easy British school'. Pirie was particular critical of the training approach of Bannister and Chataway. Both, he believed, suffered from the theory that a runner could train to be at his peak for a particular day, so need not be in year-round training. 'It would save a lot of blood, toil, tears and sweat if this theory were true,' said Pirie, 'but there is no shortcut to greatness.'

Bannister's apparently effortless style, Pirie warned, misled a great many young athletes into trying to copy him. 'He always seemed to me to be concealing the suffering of his body.' Pirie reckoned Bannister was exceptionally endowed by nature and could have been far greater if he had trained properly. 'I believe', he said confidently, 'that in 1954 he could have run the mile in 3:50.'

As they flopped sleepless on their beds in the Helsinki Olympic village, Bannister and Chataway wondered what it was that made Zatopek superhuman. 'Here we are, doing a third of the running he's doing,' said Chataway. 'While he goes for a 20-mile training run on his only free day, we lie here, panting with exhaustion, moaning that the gods are unkind to us and that we're too intelligent to train hard.'

Fifty years on, Chataway says: 'The answers were obvious

really. We trained ridiculously. We ought to have applied more intelligence and we ought to have done more training. The price we paid was that our races were very painful.

'If we succeeded, I suppose, it was because we had been blessed with quite a lot of natural ability, but we had a good deal of intellectual arrogance too. The way we saw it was that there were these hacks, runners with nothing to think about and nothing better to do – so they plodded around hour after hour. But not us, we didn't need to do that. It was misplaced intellectual arrogance. I suspect that Zatopek, who was doing all this training that we disdained so much, was a great deal more intelligent than we were. It took us a long while to wake up to it.'

'I introduced Chataway and Roger Bannister to Gerschler,' said Chris Brasher, 'in the airport on the way back from Finland. Roger was fascinated by the details of the interval training that Josy Barthel had been using. We all realised that we could train a lot harder without any fear of going stale.

'That race in Helsinki gave Bannister a reason to keep running,' continued Brasher, 'and it gave us all a way of training that could make us faster. The real race for the four-minute mile started right there in Helsinki.'

18

The Men Who Lost and Won

The Europeans are almost certain to better four minutes in 1953,
and I'd like to get in before them.

John Landy

In the 1950s Raymond Glendenning was Britain's leading sports
commentator. His gravelly, authoritative voice was known to
millions through his radio broadcasts. A daunting figure, a
little overweight, with a wide, drooping wartime pilot's moustache and Brylcreemed hair, he surveyed the sporting world
through heavy-framed spectacles and a cloud of smoke from
his ever-present cigarette.

But his was the voice of sport. And in 1951, at a Brains Trust
– a round-table conference of a dozen of Britain's sportsmen,
chaired by Glendenning – he asked a young Roger Bannister
the question that already had people speculating in bars and
stadium dressing rooms throughout the land. 'What are the
prospects', boomed Glendenning, 'of a four-minute mile by a
Britisher?'

'I would say that there is a reasonable possibility of our
doing it,' was Roger Bannister's reply. 'If you can find a man
who can run a mile in 4:04 like Wooderson, it is reasonable
that you will find someone who can go below that when he
has someone to run against. He must know what he is aiming

at, and run with people who would do his pacemaking.'

As a potential mission statement it could not have been clearer.

'Immediately after the Helsinki Games,' said Chris Chataway, 'Roger Bannister wrote me a letter saying that he would like to make two attempts on the four-minute mile later that year. He asked if I would pace him, saying that nobody could do it on their own and that he felt extremely comfortable running behind me. "Twice before you've really drawn it out of me," he wrote, "and I feel I could do it with you." Roger added that, of course, he'd do the same for me in the following year.

'But with the Games over,' said Chataway, 'I was absolutely finished. I'd made arrangements to go with a relative in his car across France to stay in Switzerland. I'd never been abroad on holiday, it was a big thing, so I said no. Some years later Roger told me that if he'd done it then, if he'd broken four minutes in 1952, he'd have given up athletics there and then – just as he would have given up', adds Chataway, 'if he'd won the Olympic 1,500 metres.

'I don't think I remember any talk of the four-minute mile between us before those Helsinki Games,' said Chataway, 'but it was clear that Roger immediately saw the breaking of that record as providing a vindication of his athletic career. He said in his letter that nobody could do it alone, and it was quite clear from the letter that he wanted to do it. In the letter he talked not of breaking Haegg's record, but specifically of running the four-minute mile, and it was obvious that he was well aware of how significant such a run would be.'

Bannister was acutely aware that he had reached a moment of decision. His hospital work was becoming more demanding and he came close to stopping running immediately following the Olympic Games. He had to find a new goal, a new reason to run. The European and Empire Games were not due to take place until 1954, the year of his medical finals. He believed his choice lay between stopping running at once and continuing for two more years.

'I believe that the substance of athletics is being able to produce a performance on the appropriate day with adequate notice against opponents who also had equal notice,' said Bannister, 'but quite quickly in 1952 I foresaw that if I wanted to continue to take part in the Empire Games and the European Championships two years later, it was going to be necessary to be able to run a four-minute mile to make sure of winning these. That is why I wrote to Chris Chataway asking if he would help to pace me to run the four-minute mile.'

Bannister needed to prove his attitude towards training had been the right one. 'I could accept being beaten in the Olympics,' he said. 'That had happened to many stronger favourites than me. What I objected to was that my defeat was taken by so many as proof that my way of training was wrong. I could not bear the thought that some other athlete might want to train along the lines that I had used, and that I might be held up as a bad example to dissuade him.

'My running had become something of a crusade. It was as if I were preaching about a special attitude towards running that I felt was right. It was a combination of the university attitude that Oxford had taught me, coupled with my own love of running as one of the most perfect forms of physical expression.

'The Olympic Games were in July, and in August or September there were meetings where a fast mile might be possible. Having done the 2:52.9 for three-quarters, I felt quite confident that given the right conditions I would be able to break the four-minute mile.'

Even with Chataway temporarily out of the picture as a pacemaker, Bannister wondered if he might break records before the year was out. The memory of the Motspur Park time trial still burned strongly, and even when exhausted by the early rounds of the 1,500 metres in Helsinki, he had run the equivalent of a 4:04 mile. With that sort of fitness and the proper pacing, anything might yet be possible.

So when Bannister discovered that a bright young middle-distance hope called Brian Hewson had been selected to run with him in a match between the AAA and the Combined Services at Uxbridge in mid-August, he decided to enlist his help. 'He wrote to me asking if I would help him in a record attempt at that meeting,' said Hewson in his autobiography. 'He wanted me to pace him for the first two and a half laps of the mile to pull him out.'

Hewson did his best. He went through the first lap in 60 seconds, and the half-mile in 2:04, before dropping out at two and a half laps, leaving Bannister out on his own. In the event, Bannister slowed dramatically, and although he won the race, in 4:13.8, he was almost caught by the chasing pack. Bannister concluded that he had passed his peak for the season, that the speed and fitness he had enjoyed before the Games had vanished and would have to be rebuilt.

If Roger Bannister was smarting from the criticism he had been handed by the British press, his fellow Oxbridge athletes, Chataway and Brasher, had fared little better in Helsinki, while Wes Santee and John Landy had failed at the Games as well. However, all five had learned and experienced much, and in the months to come, each was to play a major role in the unfolding drama that led to attack after attack on the four-minute mile.

The rivalry between Gunder Haegg and Arne Andersson

had brought them to the brink of success in 1945. 'Arne and I ought to have collaborated,' said Haegg. 'We never talked about records, we never trained together, never helped each other. We only wanted to win. If we'd planned it, we'd have done it – beaten four minutes for sure.'

Wanting to win, irrespective of the time, was something that Bannister readily understood. 'I sometimes think that we would be better off without stopwatches, so that no one would know how fast or slow a race was run,' he wrote. 'The important thing would be the struggle of one man against another for supremacy.

'Like odds quoted on horses, times may tell you something of a man's chance of winning, but they can tell you nothing of his style or length of stride, nor can a javelin thrower's distances tell you of his grace of throw. They can give you no conception of the joy there is in watching a champion athlete's supreme integration of movement, his genius at harnessing efficiently power that is partly inborn and partly ingrained by years of training.'

But whatever his views on record times, the four-minute mile had hung around Bannister's heels since Joe Binks, the veteran miler and sports reporter, had singled him out as the man to do it following the Oxford–Cambridge match in 1947. At first, Bannister says, he thought of the four-minute mile merely as a new record. It had no intrinsic merit, it was simply a time like any other. It was merely a strange coincidence that the round figure of four minutes was just below the existing world record for the mile. However, the round figure of four minutes captured the public imagination and turned it into an apparently mysterious barrier that had to be broken.

Bannister, with his medical knowledge, understood well that any miler was limited by lack of oxygen, and that, in order to keep his oxygen requirement to a minimum, he would need to run at precisely 15 miles per hour to achieve the target of a four-minute mile. The ideal pace would be four even laps of 60 seconds each. So if time was the object of the race, if the aim was to run a record, other competitors would have to be ignored, unless they were willing to co-operate in setting and achieving a pre-determined time schedule.

'To say, however, that four minutes is only a time was presumptuous,' said Bannister, 'unless I had an answer for the inevitable follow-up question – well, if it's possible, why don't you do it?'

On 4 August, just a couple of weeks after the Helsinki Games, the traditional British Empire v. USA match took place at the White City in London. For the only time in their careers, the three great milers met in the same race – Wes Santee competing for the United States, and Roger Bannister and John Landy for the British Empire, in the 4 x 1 mile relay. The race was won by the United States. Wes Santee told his teammate Bob McMillen that he enjoyed the event far more than his Olympic experience. McMillen was not surprised. 'The mile is where you belong,' he said, 'it's easily your best event.'

Santee could hardly wait to get back to the tracks of America to start churning out the miles again. He was sure he could break the four-minute barrier, but first he needed to pick up points for his University of Kansas team. Bill Easton, his coach, ran him hard and ran him often.

'Sometimes', said Santee, 'I was running four races in a weekend. Bill Easton had me working to a programme that meant I could run a 4:08 or a 4:10 mile almost any time. Easton and I reckoned I would run under four minutes if the track and weather conditions were right. But doing all those races hurt my chances and, unlike the guys in Europe, we weren't allowed to use a rabbit to set the pace. We always had to race it out.'

Even so, the ever-confident Santee looked a tremendous prospect. His turn of speed was breathtaking, his range of distances awesome. He oozed strength and fitness. He filled the stadiums and dominated the headlines.

'Over in Europe,' said Santee, 'Roger Bannister had the country behind him. There was a feeling of "Let's do it for England". Here it was always school against school. Nobody worried about getting the four-minute mile for America as long as I kept winning the points for the college track team. I knew for sure that in the right race, up against the top guys, I could run the four-minute mile, but as long as I was always running for the college team, some other guy might do it first, somewhere on the other side of the world.'

On the other side of the world, John Landy was contemplating the lessons he had learned from Zatopek and other European runners who had competed in Finland. His arm action, they told him, was all wrong. He was running with too much tension, and even his spiked running shoes were not doing him any favours. Try shorter spikes, was Zatopek's advice, and get shoes with rubber under the heels to absorb the pounding on hard cinder tracks. Landy had been running in Australian spikes that were designed for short sprinting. He needed to be shod like a miler.

The more John Landy lapped up the advice he was given, the more old Percy Cerutty spat his disapproval. Track training, said Cerutty, destroyed the soul. Get back to nature, run like an animal, throw away your shoes, eat nuts and berries and charge up sand hills to glory – that was the Cerutty creed. He despised interval training.

There were reports in the Australian press that Landy had

walked out on his colourful coach. Cerutty, though, maintained that they had merely parted company for a while and that Landy would come running back, that he could never survive without a coach to guide him. But as soon as he got back to Australia, John Landy could hardly wait to make the break.

Because of his trip to Europe, he had fallen well behind with his academic work at Melbourne University, where he was studying agriculture, and he had to put in the hours to catch up. But despite this increased workload, he vowed somehow to carve out enough time to follow his new athletics regime. He began training regularly, sometimes for an hour, sometimes for as much as an hour and a half, often very late at night. He ran on a roughly measured gravel path in a park, churning out repeats over 600 yards, using the rise and fall of the interval method that Zatopek had pioneered.

Gradually Landy began to achieve more economy, combined with a new relaxation. His failure in the Olympic Games had not been treated kindly in the press, though by comparison with the headlines handed out to Bannister back in Britain, he might have felt that he got off lightly. Nevertheless, he realised that he had gone into the Games without sufficient preparation. For all the work with Cerutty's training squad, he had not been fit enough and his confidence had been badly hit.

To restore that confidence he would have to train harder than ever and produce a result that would win back respect for him as an Australian mile runner. The Australian record for the mile stood to another of Cerutty's protégés, Don MacMillan, who had run 4:08.9. It was a target for Landy to shoot at, and he took the first opportunity he could to test his new training methods.

The venue was Melbourne's Olympic Park, the date 13 December 1952, mid-winter back in Europe, but high summer in Australia. The event was a low-key inter-club meeting, and Landy's approach to the race was extraordinary. On his way to the track he stopped off to eat two pies and a chocolate nut sundae about an hour before the race. As a result he arrived so late that he only just made the start, and lined up in the second row of runners.

Landy's most dangerous opponent in the mile was another of Cerutty's sand-hill squad, Les Perry. The track was rough, crushed red cinders that were heavy after weeks of rain and clung to the spikes of the sprinters, who churned it up further in the early races.

Despite the heavy training that he had been putting in (and the pies and chocolate nut sundae), Landy felt surprisingly good. The crowd was small but enthusiastic, but not noisy enough to drown the voice of Percy Cerutty, who was leaping around gesticulating and gabbling as loudly as ever.

Les Perry took off fast at the start, with Landy tucked in close behind him. Both men looked good as the first lap was covered in under a minute. Perry still held the lead as he and Landy went through the half-mile in 2:01, with the rest of the field nowhere. Then, as the reckless early pace sapped the speed from Perry's legs, Landy romped past him and pulled easily away. At the bell, Landy was all on his own in 3 minutes and 3 seconds.

The speed had made the crowd yell so loudly that Landy didn't even hear the time called at three laps. But he knew he was flowing well and he wanted MacMillan's record. 'I hoped to run around 4:08,' he said. The crowd kept screaming as Landy raced through the last lap, again in under the minute, and hit the tape 70 yards or more ahead of Les Perry. For a while Landy was baffled. 'I remember being very upset at the end; nobody would speak to me because at first they couldn't believe the time I'd run.'

Then they rushed to congratulate him, to slap him on the back and lift him shoulder high. The time-keepers showed each other watches but still took a long while before they were ready to announce the result. Landy kept asking anxiously if he'd beaten MacMillan's 4:08.9. They told him he'd shattered it – running 4:02.1. It was the fastest mile of the year in the world and Landy was now the third fastest miler of all time. Only the Swedes, Gunder Haegg and Arne Andersson, had ever run faster.

On the roughest of tracks and without the aid of an opponent pacing him for the second half-mile, Landy had come within half a dozen yards of Haegg's world record. In one mighty leap he had gone from being a mediocre Australian miler with a best time of 4:10 to the man most likely to smash a hole through the four-minute barrier. He seemed slow to grasp the significance of what he had just done, but there were plenty in the crowd, and around the world, who were quick to point out that in better racing conditions the record could have been his.

As the reality of the time set in, Landy announced his next target to the world: 'The Europeans', he said, 'are almost certain to better four minutes in 1953, and I'd like to get in before them.' It was December 1952, and Landy still had plenty of Australian summertime left to play with.

The news of Landy's achievement provoked a frisson of amazement, even disbelief, around the world. 'The headline the next day in the *New York Times*', Landy remembers, 'was "Please Pass the Salt" – in other words the reporter, whose name was Arthur Daley, didn't believe I'd done it. They told their tennis writer to watch my next race a fortnight later. There I ran 4:02.8, so he cabled the States saying it's for real, and that it looked like John Landy could run the four-minute mile.'

19

Coaches of Fire

By the time you'd listened to Franz, you would be in no doubt
that breaking the world record would be as good as painting
the *Mona Lisa*. He just invested the whole thing with glamour
and magic.

Chris Chataway

The athletes of Oxford and Cambridge, with their languid
approach to their sport, were notoriously difficult to coach.
They guarded their running as a pastime, and though they
loved to win they were not too keen on being goaded into
greater efforts by a coach.

There were plenty who reckoned Roger Bannister needed
help – the British press constantly ran stories criticising his
'lone wolf' approach – and there were plenty who thought
Franz Stampfl was the man for the job.

Chris Chataway finally admitted that a coach might be able
to teach a thing or two to even the most self-sufficient athlete.
Writing in 1955, he said that he had 'previously held the arrogant view that really there was nothing useful that a coach
could tell me'. He explained that he liked to decide his own
training sessions, and believed he knew himself and his own
body better than anyone else. However, he added, 'I have
recently realised that a really good coach can be of invaluable

assistance. For the young runner he can be a shortcut to success – saving years of trial and error. Above all,' he said, 'the function of a coach is to encourage and advise at certain important times.' The big problem, said Chataway, was to find the right person – a task, he reckoned, as difficult as finding the right wife. The man who had changed his mind was Franz Stampfl.

The long quest for the four-minute mile is a fascinating example of the thread that passes from coach to coach, and coach to athlete. The coaching lore behind the achievement was handed from mentor to mentor – a baton in an unbroken relay that stretches over decades.

Perhaps the first great coach to dream that a mile in four minutes was possible was the colourful Sam Mussabini. He drew up training and racing schedules for the double Olympic champion Albert Hill in 1920, hoping to bring it within reach. World war robbed Hill of his best years, but he did shatter the British mile record that had stood for 29 years.

When Mussabini hung up his stopwatch and retired, Albert Hill took over his coaching role and passed on his methods, his lore and his secrets. Twelve years after his own record-breaking run, Hill was acting as mentor and coach in his turn to Britain's next great miler, Sydney Wooderson. Under the guidance of Hill, Wooderson broke the world record and brought the best mile time run by a Briton down to 4:04.2 – tantalisingly within kicking distance of the record.

Wooderson, too, lost some of his finest years to world war, but on an August Bank Holiday in 1945, the teenage Roger Bannister saw Wooderson race a mile against the young Swede Arne Andersson. As Bannister watched Wooderson in full flight, the dream of that master mentor Sam Mussabini was at last on track to becoming reality. Old Sam had drummed into Hill that record breaking was just a matter of time, careful training and even-paced running. These were the methods and the message that Hill passed on to Wooderson, and a glimpse of Wooderson in action was enough to awaken in Bannister the dream of breaking barriers.

In fact, for all their talk of 'effortless superiority', there was a tradition, of sorts, of coaching at Oxford and Cambridge. At the turn of the century, Clemmy Jackson – the uncle of the 1,500-metre champion at the 1912 Olympics, Arnold Strode-Jackson – had played a valuable role at Oxford, offering training advice to the young undergraduates tuning up for their battles against Cambridge.

For their part, Cambridge for many years employed Alec Nelson, a fine runner and coach, who groomed undergraduates like Harold Abrahams. In 1915, Oxford hired as their professional coach Alf Shrubb, the greatest distance runner of his generation, and one-time holder of every world record over imperial distances from two to 10 miles.

Though he was a champion runner, Shrubb did not work out well as a coach. The problem was that, even though well past 40, he was far fitter and faster than the part-time amateurs he was supposed to be training. 'Right, gentlemen, we will begin with a few turns around the track,' he would announce. He would then set off trotting at a pace they could hardly handle, and suggest schedules they would never follow.

Shrubb was followed in time by Bill Thomas, who trained and groomed the elegant Jack Lovelock to within smiling distance of the four-minute mile. Despite the reliance of Lovelock on Thomas, Roger Bannister echoed the views of many when he said that Oxford students preferred to make up their own minds about the way they prepared for races, and did not like to take their orders from a coach.

'The university athlete is first and foremost a human being, who runs his sport and does not allow it to run him,' Bannister observed. 'He drinks beer and he listens to coaches, when he feels inclined. It has produced men whose personality and determination were sufficient to enable them to achieve balanced lives and, at the same time, to plan successful athletic careers and stand the strain of first-class competition.'

Even in later years, when he welcomed the appointment by Oxford of John Jeffrey, a physical education lecturer and highly qualified professional coach, Bannister added that 'Never will our universities become so coach-conscious and coach-dominated as are universities in the USA.'

Despite his negative experience with Bill Thomas, Bannister said that he did look around for a coach who might suit his approach to running. He was certainly eager to keep abreast of the latest training regimes and to pick up information where he could. He read the detailed and copious training diaries of Jack Lovelock. 'There are 20 volumes of diaries,' said Bannister. 'Lovelock was obviously obsessive and meticulously recorded his every training session, but I learned little of practical use.' However, when an AAA coach lent him an account of the fartlek used by Gunder Haegg, Bannister eagerly incorporated the system of fast and slow running on soft surfaces into his own regime.

At the 1952 Helsinki Olympics Bannister took on board, too, information about the methods of both Emil Zatopek and Woldemar Gerschler, and was eager to discover details of the interval running that had been used by the surprise winner of the 1,500 metres, Josy Barthel. 'The lessons of Zatopek and Gerschler were there to be learned,' said Bannister.

Franz Stampfl liked to be thought of as the man who put science into British sport. 'The first person to introduce these methods in England in 1938 was me,' he said. 'I introduced biological and physiological approaches to running and mechanics to throwing, and today, they are generally accepted throughout the world.'

It remains a highly debatable claim. Nevertheless, Stampfl was an elegant, charismatic, inspirational figure who established himself as a freelance athletics coach. Every evening he ran training sessions at the Duke of York's Barracks in Chelsea, where he charged a shilling for anyone who turned up. Brasher and Chataway soon became part of his school.

The Austrian's expansive personality appealed particularly to the romantic and emotional Brasher, who became a devotee. Brasher often said that Bannister was reluctant to acknowledge the debt he owed to Stampfl for the part he played in breaking through the four-minute barrier. He believed Bannister was effectively 'coached by remote control' – that Stampfl worked through Bannister's training partners, himself and Chris Chataway.

As well as supervising the training sessions at the Duke of York's Barracks, Stampfl took on the job of coaching at Oxford University two days a week. Although he turned up at Oxford after Bannister had left, coach and athlete saw each other often and Bannister welcomed the opportunity to discuss racing problems with him.

The two men also shared a passionate and dedicated belief in the beneficial effects of athletics. 'We may live artificial twentieth-century lives,' wrote Bannister in a foreword to Stampfl's book on running, 'but we are no less capable than our ancestors of releasing zest for physical activity. Sport, and particularly running, should inspire the whole man, mind and body.' Stampfl, like Bannister, refused to acknowledge any limits to human performance.

Very rapidly, and with no official backing because he had no formal coaching qualifications, Stampfl established himself in Britain.

'Here was this ebullient mid-European,' said Chataway, 'who didn't know a hell of a lot about running, but who had this fantastic ability to inspire and who had extravagant views about everything. That he and Chris Brasher got on immediately wasn't so surprising. Perhaps it was not too surprising that I was enormously impressed by him. But quite how it was that he cast some of his spell and magic over Roger was much more mystifying.

'He had a thick Austrian accent, very well-cut tweed jackets, elegant and well-cut cavalry twill trousers and a tweed cap. And what I remember most', said Chataway, 'is going to a little restaurant behind Peter Jones, where I suppose we would have a bottle of red wine and the conversation would be about pictures, because he was an art student, or about politics. You wouldn't take his views on politics too seriously, they veered around a great deal. They were often extreme, but always fun.

'There would be great arguments, but what I know is that he could touch what we were doing with magic. By the time you'd listened to Franz, you would be in no doubt that breaking the world record would be as good as painting the *Mona Lisa*. He just invested the whole thing with glamour and magic.

'He made you certain that you could do it, and that it would be a disgrace if you didn't. If you missed the chance to break a record, how could you ever forgive yourself? All this made a huge impression on me, and it must, I think, have made an impression on Roger too.'

By November 1953, Chataway, Brasher and Bannister were meeting Franz Stampfl regularly. Chataway and Brasher discussed their training with him in detail and sought his advice on planning their schedules. Their previous light regimes were replaced by interval training, which might in an evening mean 10 x 440 yards with a two-minute jogging 'rest' period in between, or four or five half-miles run, again, with only a short breathing space.

And it wasn't just runners Stampfl was knocking into shape. He was shocked by how little training was done by footballers, boxers and tennis players. Britain's boxing champion, Don Cockell, turned up to see if Stampfl could help prepare him fight Rocky Marciano for the heavyweight title of the world, and Franz worked with enthusiasm on the boxer's pear-shaped body.

For a while after the Helsinki Olympics Chataway had seriously contemplated giving up athletics. He had left Oxford to begin work for Guinness and it became increasingly difficult for him to fit in training. But, he said, 'this negative attitude didn't last five minutes with Franz. He had the knack of making training seem not in the least bit tedious. He saw all sports, and particularly athletics, as an exciting challenge.'

An additional challenge for Chris Brasher, who was, by the winter of 1952, training enthusiastically under the eye of Stampfl, was how to get Franz's ideas on interval training through to his friend Bannister. 'Chris Chataway and I coaxed Roger into coming along with us on Friday nights to the Duke of York's Barracks,' said Brasher, 'and he was soon doing the same track sessions as we were. Franz worked out with us what we'd be doing and Roger joined in.'

Bannister remembers things a little differently, and points out, too, that the fierce loyalty and support for Stampfl from Brasher was no surprise, because Brasher owed so much to the man who turned him from a club runner into an Olympic champion.

'Chris was a bit like Stampfl in his personality,' said Bannister, 'voluble, firm and never in any doubt. Both he and Chataway have said that I was overly generous in praising them for the part they played as pacemakers in the four-minute mile. From my point of view, Franz worked with his protégés and made the world record possible because of the pacemaking. But certainly it was my design that the race would be on 6 May, and that the three-quarters had to be less than three minutes. I didn't concern myself with the arrangements of the two pacemakers.

'Chris Brasher was a person of great passions and you can see why he felt a passionate loyalty towards Franz. I could never share his absolute confidence in Stampfl, because he was a person given to such extravagant talk. When somebody says, "I could take half a dozen men off the King's Road and make them into four-minute milers," which Stampfl did say, I think somebody with my caution starts hearing alarm bells.

'But Franz had total dedication from Chris Brasher, and Chris had, after all, tried to help me when I ran 4:02, so there was no doubt of his willingness or loyalty. Chris Brasher went on working with Franz until the Melbourne Olympics, with weekly exchanges of training schedules by tape recordings and so on, and kept very close to Stampfl.

'Chris Chataway', said Bannister, 'had a very low boredom threshold and thought more or less of giving up after the disappointment of Helsinki. But he found that with Franz and Chris Brasher he could keep his interest going. I joined them later in November and, in my own mind, I was really looking to work with them at getting the pace right for an attempt at the four-minute mile. Franz was part of the package. He was the coach to them and I was very happy to join his group. When it came to the day of the race, I valued having somebody like Franz

Stampfl there. He was different to anybody else I'd met.'

Stampfl himself said in 1955: 'Roger Bannister was given the same attention – and no more – as I gave to the many hundreds of athletes who passed through my hands. He was an ideal subject, although fairly highly strung, and at the time he approached me he had a slight inferiority complex. This was an asset. It gave Bannister and myself something to work on. After a few months of interval running and weight training exercises, he strengthened considerably, and I knew that he would run a faster mile than ever before, once he entered competition early in 1954.'

Stampfl believed that if you were going to coach properly you had to get under the skin and into the personality of each athlete you handled. He believed, too, that anything that passed between athlete and coach was covered by the same confidentiality as that between doctor and patient. He said that a coach should turn no one away, that there was no athlete so useless that he couldn't be improved through the use of intelligent and graduated training.

He was fully aware that not all athletes were in need of full-time coaching and that there were those who preferred to work out their own destinies. Many, he said, were able to do so intelligently and successfully. Later, many such athletes would come to a point where they might need to turn to a coach for some detail of advice, and on such an occasion a coach could be of tremendous value. Then, when the problem was solved, they could return to their solitary methods. 'I have known many such lone wolves, both great and small, whom I've been privileged to advise, often on quite minor matters,' he said. 'The important thing is that the coach should be willing to give of his experience whenever it's required.'

Also, Stampfl stressed, the coach should be as unobtrusive

as possible and never force his opinion upon the athlete. Persuasion, he said, was the best weapon. The coach who could transmit his own ideas to an athlete, without the runner being aware of it, would send his man to the start quietly confident of a plan of which both approved. Confidence was the most important quality in the coach–athlete relationship. Without it little could be achieved. 'With it, the two men pull together in double harness to become a team.'

Coaching, he said, was more than a job. 'It is a vocation, which one follows from the same sort of compulsion as drives some to write, some to paint, some to build bridges.'

Chris Brasher believed that Stampfl's power as a coach derived from his tough experiences of life. He was born in Vienna in 1913, and died in Melbourne in 1995, having spent the last 15 years of his life in a wheelchair after a car accident left him a quadriplegic, although such was his determination that he continued to coach.

In Vienna, the young Stampfl was precocious in many fields – a fine javelin thrower and a trained artist, with an interest in poetry and philosophy. 'In 1936,' he said, 'I went to the Olympic Games in Berlin and I came back terribly worried about what the future held. I saw the militarism and the brutality of it all and I made up my mind not to stay in Austria. I wanted, of course, to stay in England, and I made an application to the Home Office, and they said to me: "I am afraid you can't stay here unless you do a job which no other Englishman can do."

'Well, I thought I would now put into action my ideas about athletics and so I went to the Amateur Athletic Association and asked for an interview. Oddly enough, the person who interviewed me was Harold Abrahams. He said that he would give me a chance. And that's when I started coaching.'

When the Second World War broke out, Stampfl wanted to join the British army, but found himself, along with many refugees from Hitler's Germany, classed as an alien. He was shipped to an internment camp in Canada on board the liner *Andorra Star*. The ship was torpedoed en route and sank with a great loss of life. Of the 2,400 crew and internees aboard, only 400 survived.

Stampfl was one of them, picked up after hours in an icy, oil-filled ocean. From Canada he was shipped to Australia, where he spent the rest of the war. 'It was a miserable experience,' he said. 'I arrived in Australia, I'm quite certain, like the original prisoners and convicts.'

Stampfl's wartime experiences, particularly being torpedoed, gave him a great deal of inner strength. 'I'd been through these experiences,' he would say, 'I don't need somebody to tell me what I should be doing, either in coaching or in anything.'

He believed the mental aspect of coaching was little understood. 'I grew up, of course, in Vienna, and every Viennese believes he is another Freud. So I felt that in any performance, any human act, there is nothing completely physical and nothing completely mental either.' He would say to his athletes: 'Do not worry, it is only pain,' and would ignore complaints about soreness or injury and urge his athletes to concentrate on the ultimate goal. After an hour or two in a teashop or a wine bar with Franz, they would often believe that they could beat anyone in the world.

Stampfl had little time for the emphasis on style that preoccupied so many earlier coaches. He believed running was the most natural of all athletic movement, and that style and efficiency depended more on the fitness of the runner than on any learned pattern of movement. He recognised instinctively that the way a runner held his arms and moved his legs depended largely on his strength and his skeletal structure. That way everybody's style was individual, and attempts to change it were as likely to lead to loss of efficiency as to improvement. Don't copy anybody else, he advised.

He was certainly very modern in pointing out that young children usually embody an almost perfect running style. They have never been told about style, but their natural action can so easily be lost once coaches step in and insist on teaching them what they consider to be copybook movements. Rather than style, Stampfl placed tremendous emphasis on the will to win. The competitive spirit was something that he talked of often. He would speak lyrically of how willpower could always overcome the protests of a failing body and produce deeds of athletic heroism.

Stampfl might not have had technical qualifications as a coach, but he knew enough about running to analyse questions of pacing, front-running and relaxation. He believed that the great difference between front-runners and those who preferred to follow was one of temperament.

When it came to athletes who preferred to follow the pace of others, Stampfl regarded Chataway, Bannister, Derek Johnson and Gunnar Nielsen as among the greatest 'positional' runners in the world. There was much talk about how far a man who was following a front-runner could dare to fall behind before contact was lost – before the front-runner got away. If a man knew he was still in the hunt, he was capable of prodigious efforts, said Franz, but if his confidence in closing the gap faltered, then the inspiration he was gathering from the excitement of the chase would falter too.

Running, Stampfl was fond of saying, was an art, and every runner an artist. Most athletes, he reckoned, suffered from too little training, rather than too much. In this belief, he knew, he was coming up against the preconceived notions of athletes like Chataway and Bannister, who lived in dread of 'staleness'. Stampfl believed that staleness was primarily the result of lack of competition rather than over-training.

Any coach, who was worth his salt, he said, 'will spot the man who is overdoing things. The man who is his own coach, however, must also be his own conscience. If he fools himself there is nobody to drag him back to the path of rectitude.' But, said Franz, 'Nobody, unless he is a complete moron, can eat, drink and sleep athletics without the fun, that ought to be there, giving way to drudgery. Some of the world's greatest runners', he added, 'smoke a little and drink a little, without any apparent lowering in their performances – although, in my opinion, they are better off without.'

Stampfl's style as a coach was certainly very different to that of the men who had coached or influenced his rivals in the race to be the world's first four-minute miler. In Kansas, Bill Easton had built his athlete, Wes Santee, into a miler who could churn out world-class times week after week, relentlessly beating all comers at the distance. Both coach and athlete confidently believed the four-minute mile was theirs for the taking.

Meanwhile, in Melbourne, John Landy was becoming ever fitter, pounding out his vast weekly mileages in training and believing that his superior conditioning would win him the prize.

Back in England, 'Franz was around', said Brasher, 'when Roger needed him most. Before the Oxford mile, during it, and in Vancouver for the Empire Games. The real value of Franz was that he was inspirational, that he helped to get the three of us, Roger, Chris and myself, training regularly together as a group, and, above all, that he did the backroom planning to get the pacing right for the four-minute mile.'

'The core,' said Bannister, 'the real reason for my contact with Franz, was that I needed pacemaking. Chris Chataway had tried to pace me at the same meeting the year before, and I was perfectly happy to go for the four-minute mile, because I knew from the time trial I had done over three-quarters of a mile in 2:52.9 that, if the conditions were right, I could do a four-minute mile. So my whole focus was on how to ensure that the pacemaking would be right. Franz was the person, I think, who was able to prepare the two Chrises for that.

'But to me, Franz was always an adviser, not a coach. An adviser advises you, a coach, most people think, is the chap who says do this and that. Far from there being any ill feeling between us, Franz always welcomed me whenever we met, and asked me to write the foreword to his book on running, which was published the year after the four-minute mile was broken. I was very happy to do so and said there: "He has been with me at the time of critical races and, indeed, in the last year, his counsel has often helped me to defeat formidable opponents on the track."'

Franz Stampfl himself, showing his characteristic shrewd understanding of human nature, defined in that book what he saw as the coach's role. 'Guide, philosopher and friend, counsellor and confessor, a prop at times of mental tension, a coach's job is big enough for any man,' he wrote. 'And, when all the shouting is over, when the senior partner in the firm has broken the record, made the headlines and joined the immortals, the junior partner's reward comes from the satisfaction of a job well done. Who could ask for more?'

20

The New Elizabethans

Chris Brasher, Chris Chataway and I, all of us at Oxford
and Cambridge Universities, seemed more privileged than we
actually were. We were labelled young Elizabethans, possessing
more than a touch of single-mindedness, optimism, and that
now unfashionable quality, patriotism.

Roger Bannister

In 1953 Mount Everest would fall to Edmund Hillary and
Tenzing Norgay, paced and pushed to the peak by very British
teamwork. The news that at last two human beings had stood
at the top of the world was delivered to the public on the eve
of the Coronation of Queen Elizabeth II.

Two million people on the streets of London, and millions
more glued to their flickering black-and-white television sets,
watched as the 27-year-old was carried in a golden coach to
Westminster Abbey, ushering in what the press were heralding
as a 'New Elizabethan Age'.

With sweet rationing ending in Britain in February, and
Stalin breathing his last in Moscow, the long shadow of the
war seemed at last to be lifting. In America a fresh-faced Jack
Kennedy was marrying Jacqueline Bouvier. At Wembley that
old wizard Stanley Matthews, Britain's greatest football hero,
was at last winning an FA Cup final medal, in Blackpool's

THE NEW ELIZABETHANS 241

victory over Bolton. At the Oval, England's cricket team, under the captaincy of Len Hutton, regained the Ashes from Australia for the first time in 19 years. At Buckingham Palace, Gordon Richards, the finest jockey in the sport of kings, was knighted.

And before the new year was three days old, John Landy in Australia was lining up to race again.

In those days, before global television and the internet, sporting news from far-off Australia usually took a while to filter through. In Britain and America fanatical athletics fans waited eagerly for every word from Joe Galli, Australia's leading athletics journalist. He was already tipping Landy to break Haegg's world record. 'I am not plugging Landy because he is an Australian,' he wrote. 'I have no nationalistic tendencies at all but I *know* he is a great runner.'

'It didn't need a fortune teller to realise that something special was in the offing,' said track statistician Stan Greenberg. 'The race was on in earnest.'

To mark Coronation year, Britain's biggest-selling Sunday newspaper, the *News of the World*, came up with an idea that caught the excitement of the battle for the dream mile. It announced that it would sponsor a mile race open to the finest athletes in the world. The race, to be called the Emsley Carr Mile, was announced by Sir William Carr in memory of his father Emsley, who, like him, had been for decades the proprietor of the newspaper and a great follower of athletics. Tremendous interest in the idea had been whipped up by the athletics reporter on the *News of the World*, the veteran mile record holder from back in 1902, Joe Binks.

The Emsley Carr Mile was to be run at the White City stadium in London for the first time on 8 August. The trophy for the winner was a large, leather-bound book containing a history of mile racing. Its foreword began: 'In the Coronation year of 1953 an outstanding ambition of world track athletes is to achieve the four-minute mile. In order to encourage runners from home and overseas in this quest, the *News of the World* has instituted this annual contest.'

The would-be four-minute-milers of the world needed little encouragement in their quest. What they did need was information about their rivals. Roger Bannister was kept informed every time Landy set foot on a track by Norris and Ross McWhirter.

'No other journalists were as well informed about the athletics scene as the McWhirters,' said Chris Brasher. 'Their passion for statistics was legendary. They fed everything to Roger Bannister and to others like Harold Abrahams and Franz Stampfl. They were always trying to wind up Roger to go for the four-minute mile.'

The McWhirters were eager that this little moment in history, this little spot of sporting territory should be annexed by Britain. They knew that Bannister was Britain's best hope. They knew, too, that perfect pacing was one of the great secrets of breaking the barrier and they pored over their statistics and ranking lists, plotting how the puzzle might best be solved.

Back in Australia, Percy Cerutty was not going to pass up the chance of using Landy's amazing breakthrough to get publicity for himself and his Portsea training camp. He was happy to give the Australian press the impression that he was the mastermind behind Landy's achievement and his repeated attempts to run the four-minute mile.

On the first Saturday of 1953, a huge crowd turned out at the Olympic Park in Melbourne to watch Landy run in what the Australian press were trumpeting as an attack on the four-minute barrier. His 4:02.1 mile had set speculation blazing.

Landy confessed that he was suffering from a cold, and as

soon as he stepped on to the track, he knew that running at world record speed was going to be almost impossible. A high and gusting wind made conditions far from ideal, and the track was rough and looked badly maintained. But the crowd had come to see a world-record-breaking performance and were baying for a flat-out race.

Once again Cerutty's boy, Les Perry, stormed off in the lead, this time faster than ever, and at the bell the stopwatches read 3:01. But there was one opponent Landy couldn't beat. He was 100 yards clear of the other runners, but the wind buffeted him mercilessly. Even so, his time at 1,500 metres – 3:44.4 – was a second faster than Josy Barthel's finishing time in the Olympic final the year before, and was the fastest ever 1,500 metres in the course of a mile race. He ran his mile in 4:02.8. Nonetheless, the crowd was disappointed. Three weeks later, on 24 January, Landy ran 4:04.2 on a grass track at Perth, and once again the papers moaned that he had failed.

At the Oxford–Cambridge match in March, the 22-year-old Chris Chataway became Britain's third fastest miler ever, running 4:08.4. His team-mates, Peter Miller and David Law, set up the early pace, showing that the way to produce a fast mile was to tow a man round. Pacemaking was becoming something of an Oxford speciality.

In the 1950s, pacemaking was strictly illegal. No athlete was supposed to enter a race unless he intended to complete it and try to win it. But the rule was difficult to enforce, and was becoming increasingly blurred as athletes strove for records. For Bannister the problem had to be sidestepped as elegantly as possible. What the pacemakers – the hares – had to do was put up a reasonable show of running to finish, and attempting to win. If they weren't stupid enough to actually say they were pacemaking, the officials were likely to turn a blind eye.

Bannister and Chataway lined up together in the mile at Oxford on 2 May 1953, for the annual match between Oxford University and the Amateur Athletic Association. It was the day of that famous Stanley Matthews Cup Final at Wembley, and only a few sports reporters turned up at Iffley Road. Bannister's stated aim was an attack on Sydney Wooderson's British mile record of 4:06.4, which had stood ever since the handicap race at Motspur Park on 28 August 1937. On that occasion Reg Thomas had been given 10 yards' start and paced Wooderson for half a mile. Then other runners with up to 250 yards' start towed him round in the later stages. This was the old handicap system, and it was really the only approach open to Wooderson when no other runner in the land could stretch him over the mile.

On this May day, Chataway, who had taken an afternoon out from the last-minute panic of revising for his final exams, had agreed to run as hard as he could for the first three laps. Then it would be up to Bannister to make his dash for home. Officials at the meeting chose to see no problem and the pace-making went like clockwork.

When the bell clanged at 3:05.2, Bannister strode past his tiring friend, who pulled off the track after only a few more yards. Bannister, with a brilliantly fast final lap of 58.4, hit the tape in 4:03.6 – a new British record. John Disley, the Olympic bronze medallist in the steeplechase, was second in 4:15.4, with Sid Bryant, renowned both for his aggressive use of elbows and for his quirky sense of humour, third.

'That four-minute mile moves ever nearer with Bannister's great new British record,' reported *Athletics Weekly*. But they noted too how Bannister had achieved the record and commented on the prospect of a four-minute mile: 'If and when it is done it is likely to be in a race where Bannister has a fast pacemaker such as Chris Chataway who must take a good deal of the credit for last Saturday's time.'

Bannister was absolutely delighted with the success of what had been virtually a full-scale dress rehearsal for the big show to come on the same track twelve months later. 'We ran the first half-mile too slowly to come near the four-minute mile,' he said, 'but we were delighted to have done so well in a first attempt. This race made me realise that the four-minute mile was not out of reach. It was only a question of time – but would someone else reach the goal first?'

21

Like a Brick Wall

I'm afraid that record attempts are not in my line and this has
strengthened my opposition to such a race.

Jack Lovelock, diary entry after missing a world record attempt

After Bannister's triumph in the Oxford race, the British
athletics public were hungrier than ever for success.

On 6 May, at Leyton, there was an attack on the 4 x 1,500
metres relay world record. The Achilles club, represented by
David Law, Chris Brasher, Chris Chataway and Roger
Bannister, failed to beat it, but their time of 15:49.6 bettered
the best time set by a British quartet, at Cologne in 1931.

On 17 May, at Wimbledon, Bannister made an attempt to
better Arne Andersson's three-quarter-mile world record of
2:56.6. Brasher and Angus Scott, both of Achilles, were there
to set the pace. Strong wind made any hope of a record out of
the question and Bannister ran an exhausting 2:59.8. 'It was
like running into a brick wall on the bends,' he said.

On 23 May, at the White City stadium, Bannister took part
in the invitation mile in the British Games, and again it was
billed by the press as a record attempt. The field included Don
Seaman of the London Athletic Club and Don MacMillan
from Australia, with a squad of milers from the continent. But
in this race no one wanted to act as pacemaker and Bannister,

running easily throughout, took the lead 300 yards from home to win in 4:09.4 with a storming last lap of 56.6. With no hope of a record, part of the 30,000 crowd jeered and slow-hand-clapped Bannister, and the press criticised him for 'holding back'.

Hopes were high among his supporters that Bannister might take another tilt at the four-minute mile at Iffley Road on 30 May, in the match between Oxford and London University. Again the wind ruled it out. He opted for the half-mile instead, and managed a ground record of 1:51.9.

Stepping down in distance to sharpen up your speed is a technique that can work wonders for a middle-distance runner, and after his successful tilt at the half-mile, Bannister decided to hone his speed further by taking part in the quarter-mile at the Middlesex County Championships. It was a sprint too far. He ran a flat-out first 100 yards, but as he went to overtake another runner in an outside lane he felt a twang in his left thigh 'as sharp as a violin string snapping'. His leg seized up and he limped off the track with a pulled muscle for the first time in his career. He had simply been running too fast, demanding a sprinter's performance from his miler's muscles.

The pulled muscle could not have come at a worse moment. For that very day in America Wes Santee lined up in the mile against two of the finest middle-distance runners in the world – Finland's Denis Johansson and Belgium's Gaston Reiff. Speculation about who might be the first through the barrier was reaching fever pitch. The Swedes Gunder Haegg and Arne Andersson were being constantly bombarded with the question. One day they would tip Santee, the next Roger Bannister. In Australia, the track's most avid chronicler, Joe Galli, was tipping John Landy. In America, Wes Santee was tipping Wes Santee.

Denis Johansson, a lean, dark-haired, cavalier, cigarette-smoking Finn, who had won an athletics scholarship to Purdue University in the States, was a master of the pre-race wind-up. Before his mile with Santee, he confidently predicted that four minutes would soon be broken and that he, a Finn from the land of great runners, would be the man to do it. 'Remember Nurmi,' he would say. 'He was from Finland.' Nurmi was from Johansson's own club in Turku, and had notched up a world record for the mile. Johansson vowed he would be part of that tradition and return the world record to Finland.

When reporters asked him about their own local hero, Wes Santee, Johansson would scoff provocatively. 'He's too young, too immature,' he would taunt. 'Physically and psychologically, young Santee has a long way to run before he can be the best at the mile.' Santee was furious, and Bill Easton shrewdly harnessed that fury for the race.

'Sit on him', advised Easton, 'for the first half-mile, then kill him.' Santee did just that, and 8,000 supporters in the stands roared their approval. Accelerating relentlessly after the first two laps, Santee floated away from everyone in the field. He hit the tape 12 yards ahead of the Finn in a new American record of 4:02.4. 'We're getting closer,' Bill Easton commented afterwards.

On 20 June, at the US Collegiate Championships in Lincoln, Nebraska, Santee tried again. This time he ran 4:03.7 and you could hear the sighs of relief back in Britain.

If you try to keep training on a pulled muscle it can last a season, with niggling doubts that nag you every time you try to run flat out. The only answer is rest, and Bannister was smart enough to know it. After a few days he was delighted to discover that his 'pull' was not as devastating as he had feared. The muscle fibres in the hamstring did not seem to be badly torn. He rested up for five days, then a masseur from the Amateur Athletic Association went to work, his strong thumbs breaking down and dispersing the adhesion in the leg.

'In eight days', said Bannister, 'I was dancing, and after ten days I was running gently.' In the middle of the following week, having done nothing but solo running since the injury, he was able to knock off two half-miles at four-minute pace without pain and without breaking down. He was full of the restless energy that follows enforced rest, and could hardly wait to return to his main quest.

The McWhirters were on the phone all the time. They suggested Bannister should test his leg and his speed over a paced time trial. He didn't need much convincing, particularly when they told him they had got wind that Wes Santee was planning a serious attempt on the record in Dayton, Ohio, on 27 June.

'The McWhirters were always stoking up his fears with a non-stop flow of information,' said Chris Brasher. 'The danger was that the record might cross the Atlantic before Roger could do it. There was a sense of desperation and hurry. We all knew Roger could do it – but time was running out.'

Norris McWhirter considered Santee stood a real chance with his attempt, and that, if Bannister was back to fitness, he should make his attempt ahead of him. 'Leave it all to us,' said Norris, adding that he would fix up something with Brasher.

Because of the time difference between Britain and America they decided to include the event secretly the following Saturday, just hours before Santee was scheduled to race, as a special invitation mile in the Surrey Schools AAA championship. The venue, Motspur Park, was a superb track, and in

June of 1953 its black cinders were dressed and rolled to perfection.

There Sydney Wooderson had won back the world mile record for Britain from Santee's boyhood hero, the American Glenn Cunningham. This was also the track where, the year before, Bannister had secretly run the greatest three-quarter-mile time trial of his life.

The June weather was perfect. The sports journalists who habitually hung around the heels of Bannister had plenty to occupy them elsewhere. At Lords, England's cricketers were battling in the Test. At nearby Wimbledon, it was the middle Saturday of a fortnight of fine tennis.

'I had no idea what would happen or whether I could last out the distance,' said Bannister. 'I only knew that the same afternoon, five hours later, Wes Santee was to run in Dayton, Ohio.'

'There were only three of us in the race,' said Chris Brasher. 'There was Roger, of course, Don MacMillan, and me. We decided to pace the whole thing and get Roger round in four minutes if we could. It was all a bit mad and had been fixed up on the hoof, very quickly. MacMillan reckoned he was fit enough to manage three laps. But that wouldn't be enough, so we got to thinking and came up with what we thought was a fiendishly clever idea.

'It was brilliantly simple really. While MacMillan and Roger covered three laps, I would take it easy and jog around for two. We hoped that just when MacMillan ran out of steam they would be coming up to lap me, and I could take over to tow Roger round at sub-four pace.'

As a solution to the pacing problem it was ingenious, beautiful, outrageous even – a typical Brasher ploy that he had hatched up with Norris McWhirter. And it very nearly worked.

The race went according to plan. MacMillan galloped through the first two and a half laps before he tired badly, leaving Bannister briefly out on his own. But coming up to the bell he caught the waiting Brasher, who was so full of running and enthusiasm that he was able to shout encouragement to Bannister over his shoulder as he ran. When Bannister made his strike for the tape, the schoolchildren – most of whom were politely sitting cross-legged on the grass around the track – cheered wildly, caught up in the excitement of it all.

The first three-quarters of a mile had been run in 3:01.8. Urged on by Brasher, Bannister ran the last lap in 60.2 to cross the line alone in 4:02 – missing the magic target time by only two seconds, but still running the third fastest mile in history.

'My feeling as I look back', said Bannister, 'is one of great relief that I did not run a four-minute mile under such artificial circumstances.'

When the British Amateur Athletic Board met a couple of weeks later to consider ratification of several new British record marks, they were faced with the problem of what to do about Motspur Park. They issued the following statement:

The British Amateur Athletic Board does not accept the 4:02.0 mile by R. G. Bannister at Motspur Park on 27 June as a record. The Board wish to draw attention to the fact that it has unfettered discretion whether to accept or refuse to recognise a record. The Board has carefully considered all the circumstances and regrets that while it has no doubt that the time was accomplished, it cannot recognise the performance as a record.

It has been compelled to take the view that it was not done in a *bona fide* competition according to the rules.

The Board wishes it to be known that while it appreciates the public enthusiasm for record performances and the natural and commendable desire for athletes to accomplish them, it does not regard individual record attempts as in the best interests of athletics as a whole.

The Board then went on to recognise Bannister's earlier 4:03.6 mile as the new British record, even though that had also been pretty blatantly paced. But at least it could be argued that it had happened during a bona fide competition, and at least in the case of the Oxford mile the event was printed on the programme. The decision caused lively debate in the press, but Bannister accepted it and said as little as possible. After all, he had the British record, and neither race had brought the four-minute mile, so the ratification of the 4:02 was not that significant. What *was* important was that he and his friends would have to rethink their pacing strategy.

Bannister went with Chris Brasher for a few days' climbing in North Wales, glowing with the certainty that he could cut those two seconds which stood between him and athletics history.

Just five hours after Norris McWhirter had stopped his watch at 4:02 in the obscurity of Motspur Park, Wes Santee, in the ballyhoo of a widely publicised record attempt in Dayton, Ohio, ran 4:07.6. The prize was safe for a little while longer.

Six weeks later, on 8 August, Wes Santee was in London for the Emsley Carr Mile – the centrepiece for the British Games at the White City stadium. The *News of the World* had heavily publicised the event and were rewarded by a massive crowd and a high-quality field.

Before the contest began there was a lap of honour in an

open-top Aston Martin carrying four legendary milers – Sydney Wooderson; Paavo Nurmi, the Phantom Finn; Joe Binks, then aged 79, who had set a British record of 4:16.8 back in 1902; and Gunder Haegg of Sweden, world record holder since 1945.

With John Landy at home in Australia, and Bannister declining an invitation to compete, the star attraction and favourite was Wes Santee. His opponents included Invar Eriksson of Sweden, Olaf Lawrenz of Germany – who, said knowing fans, was there as a pacemaker – and both Bill Nankeville and Chris Chataway from Britain. At the last minute Josy Barthel dropped out and the organisers allowed Gordon Pirie, whose speciality was longer distances, to make up the numbers.

Over 30,000 turned out on this August Bank Holiday, confident that Wes Santee would make the mile hard and fast. Only two days before, in Oslo, Santee had run 800 metres in 1:48.4, and that had followed a 1,500-metre win in Gothenburg on 23 July in 3:44.2. With the year's fastest officially recognised mile of 4:02.4 already under his belt, the Kansan was fizzing.

Lawrenz, as expected, made the early pace, but at the bell, with one lap to go, the time was 3:08.4, with Pirie in the lead. Santee charged to the front, looking impressive with his choppy high-stepping action. He seemed a certain winner on the final bend, but in the long home straight Pirie closed the gap, and as the White City crowd screamed their throats raw, he passed the tiring Santee 50 yards from the tape, and held him off to win in 4:06.8.

Hats, programmes, umbrellas, all were thrown into the air in celebration. 'It was', says Stan Greenberg, Britain's leading track statistician, who was rendered temporarily deaf by the cheering, 'the most exciting mile race I have ever seen.'

'Pirie', said Gunder Haegg, 'is magnificent. Had Santee run seconds faster Pirie could still have beaten him. He is a very great runner.'

For the moment, Gordon Pirie was king of the White City, and Wes Santee, the king of America's milers, was a beaten and exhausted man. To some it was hardly surprising. Santee had pursued a gruelling college relay season, sometimes grinding out three or more races in a weekend, and a European tour that included 26 races in 44 days. He was running on empty, yet he never seemed to know when to stop.

Even when he returned to the States, Santee didn't hang up his spikes for the winter. On the very last day of 1953, at the Sugar Bowl Meeting in New Orleans, the American unleashed another fearsomely fast mile – 4:04.2, with an amazing last lap in 55 seconds. Surely at last, even for Wes Santee, the season was over.

John Landy, rested and conditioned through the Australian winter, had seen the four-minute barrier survive and now believed it was his for the taking. In September he surprised the athletics world by announcing that he would not be available for the Empire Games in Vancouver in July 1954 because he intended to retire earlier in the year. Nevertheless, he said, he hoped to set a new world record for the mile early in the Australian 1953–54 track season – which was due to start in November. Then he would quit. He'd simply had enough. He complained that the grind of training two hours every day left him no time for other activities.

Landy opened his season with an easy mile in 4:15 on the grass track of his old school, Geelong Grammar. Then, on 5 December, in bad weather and against a head wind, he ran the mile in 4:09.8. A week later the weather improved, and on 12 December, an almost perfect day, he ran 4:02 on the

Olympic Park track in Melbourne, knocking 0.1 seconds off his previous best to set a new British Empire record.

'Two little seconds is not much,' he observed wryly afterwards. 'But when you're on the track those fifteen yards seem solid and impenetrable – like a cement wall.'

If Landy had doubts, they weren't shared by the Australian press and public. In race after race he trembled on the edge of the impossible, recording a series of times unmatched by any man before him. In half a dozen attempts he had ducked under 4:03, and the tension rose every time he missed the target. All he needed, said some, was good weather. Others believed the time would come with better tracks. Still more argued that the perfect mile would be possible only with the stimulus of international competition.

In the United States, Denis Johansson had fired up Wes Santee to run a 4:02.4 mile. Perhaps, said Australia's track elite, he could do even better for John Landy. They flew the Finn to Melbourne to see if it might do the trick.

Johansson delighted the press and enraged the public by scoffing at his opponent's achievements and promising that he, not their John Landy, would be the man to run away with the prize. Their race at the Sydney Cricket Ground on 11 February was built up into a two-man battle as if nobody else were taking part. The press conferences made it sound like a bare-knuckle prize fight as the grudge element was played up to the full.

An inch of rain fell on the grass track over the 24 hours before the race, and the surface was damp and spongy. As soon as Landy tried out his spikes he knew that a fast time was out of the question. The partisan Australian crowd bayed for him to murder his bumptious opponent, and he took the lead as usual, though Johansson stuck closely to him and even attempted to pass him on the last lap.

But Landy had not come to be beaten, and he pulled well away as Johansson broke and faded, to the delight of the jeering crowd. Landy's time, though, once again was treated as a failure. He had slipped and slithered his way round a greasy track, buffeted by wind, to record 4:05.6, and still it wasn't good enough. Johansson, generous in defeat, told the press, 'No one else in the world could have run the time Landy did in those conditions. He is the greatest miler in the world, and on a fast cinder track in Europe he would easily break the world record.

'Come to Turku,' he suggested to the Australian. 'I'll get you invited, and there you can run this four-minute mile that everyone wants so much.'

22

Will it Be Britain?

We shared a place where no man had yet ventured – secure for
all time however fast men might run miles in the future.

Roger Bannister

The months of January and February in the Britain of 1954
were bleak. Sleet, snow, ice and the muscle-stiffening grip of
winter made training for running difficult and dangerous.

'Those months', said Chris Brasher, 'must have been agony
for Roger. Every day we expected to hear news from Australia
that Landy had done the four-minute mile.'

The Australian had launched attack after frustrating attack.
He never seemed to bother with pacemakers and still his times
were amazing. He even ran 4:02.6 on a grass track at Bendigo
in April with a heavy leather football-boot stud caught under
his spikes.

Landy found the volume of racing, the relentless training,
and the weight of expectation almost impossible to bear. He
had said he would quit before the Empire Games in 1954, but
then he changed his mind, believing that the super-fast tracks
of Scandinavia might give him the edge he needed. By that
winter of 1953–54, Roger Bannister was in his final year as a
medical student at St Mary's Hospital, Paddington. Chris
Chataway was working as an under-brewer at the Guinness

Brewery in Park Royal, west London, and Chris Brasher was a junior executive for an oil company.

Bannister was still running during his lunch hour at the track near the hospital. But instead of training there alone, he now ran with a group of friends who had taken to calling themselves the Paddington Lunchtime Club. In his toughest training, Brasher was his constant sparring partner, urging him on to complete the demanding interval sessions that had been prescribed by Stampfl.

Whatever benefits Bannister may have derived from following these schedules, there was no doubt that both Chataway and Brasher were profiting. Brasher particularly, through the winter months, found a speed and fluency that he had never previously possessed, and improved from just under two minutes to 1:55 for the half-mile.

As the dark winter days eased into early spring, there was the ever-present danger for Bannister and his camp that the barrier might fall to someone else before they were ready. John Landy, they knew, was flying to Finland, where the tracks and competition might make anything possible. In the United States, Wes Santee too remained a threat. He raced fast and he raced frequently. He was capable of amazing performances. At one meeting in Michigan he ran a 4:02.6 mile, followed 40 minutes later by a 1:51.8 half-mile for the Kansas relay team. An American sports writer reckoned it was the greatest double ever seen on the track.

'So some time in March', said Brasher, 'the date for the attempt was set. It would be during the first match of the athletics year – the Amateur Athletics Association v. Oxford University at Oxford on 6 May. Chris and Roger, being ex-Oxford athletes, would almost certainly be picked for the AAA team in any case, but I, being an ex-Cambridge man, would have to make special arrangements. The tactics were decided on as well – even-paced running for the first two laps by me, the third lap by Chris, and then Roger stretching out for the tape.

'But then one evening, a week or two later, after a hard session at the Duke of York's, we went for a cup of tea at the Lyons Tea Shop in Sloane Square and Franz started having doubts about the tactics. We had originally planned the first two laps by me in 1:58, but Franz asked if I could manage two and a half laps, and if Chris could manage three and a half laps, leaving Roger to burst for the tape with only 220 yards to go. I had my doubts, but Franz was a very convincing man. He told me I could do it and by the time he had finished we all believed it.'

The three training partners had started a routine of running 10 quarter-miles several times a week. They began them in December, covering each quarter-mile in 66 seconds and taking a two-minute easy jog between each effort in order to recover. Every week, through January and February, they increased the speed of the quarter-miles, keeping the pattern and rest period the same. It was classic interval training and gave them a good indication of their progress. By April the trio could manage their quarters in 61 seconds, but there they stuck. Try as they might, they could not hit their target of 10 in 60.

'Something was wrong with the training. We seemed to be marking time,' said Brasher. 'However hard we tried – either Roger alone on the dusty Paddington track or together with us at the Duke of York's – we couldn't manage 10 repetition quarter-miles in under 60 seconds.

'Stampfl thought we needed some relaxation and so we did something that Moyra, Roger's wife, still believes was crazy. Roger and I went climbing in Glen Coe – cadging a lift from my doctor, who had an ex-Le Mans Aston Martin. The journey was 10 hours each way, and we took it in turns to crouch on a lilo in the luggage space between the bucket seats.'

The two finely tuned athletes walked and climbed for three days, and Brasher came close to wrecking all their carefully laid plans when he slipped and fell off Jericho Wall in Clachaig Gully. 'Luckily,' he said, 'the fall was broken by a running belay of nylon rope which broke, but in doing so it absorbed most of the fall. But Roger got soaked to the skin and throughly frozen.'

It was a crazy training programme with the race so close. But three days after another cramped 10-hour car journey returning from Glen Coe, the trio of Bannister, Brasher and Chataway, timed by Stampfl, ran their 10 quarter-miles at an average of 58.9 seconds each.

With less than three weeks to go to the planned race at Oxford, Bannister throttled back from the severe training of the previous months to concentrate on gaining speed and freshness. 'I had to learn to release in four short minutes', he said, 'the energy I usually spent in half an hour's training.' Each training session now became part of an extended rehearsal for what was to come. Stride length, style, pace judgement: all had become automatically ingrained.

On 24 April Bannister and Chataway ran a three-quarter-mile time trial at Motspur Park. They crossed the finish together with the watch showing three minutes. Later that afternoon Geoffrey Dyson, the AAA Chief National Coach, turned up to watch a schools meeting at the White City and said to George Smith, the AAA treasurer, 'The world's one mile record is doomed. I have just come from Motspur Park. Bannister and Chataway, finishing together, ran three-quarters of a mile in three minutes dead, and both were as fresh as paint at the finish. Believe me, my friend, great things are about to happen in the near future.'

The great things included another three-quarter-mile time trial at Paddington four days later. This time Bannister ran alone, with Norris McWhirter holding the watch. He ran 2:59.9. Two days later an easy half-mile in 1:54 put the finishing touch to his preparations, and Bannister calculated that five days' rest would bring him nicely to a peak.

Resting up for an athlete is not as easy as it sounds. After months of pumping weariness into your legs on a daily basis, your body is thrown by the sudden change in routine. Your legs flood with vigour in place of fatigue but the overflow of restless energy can have you pacing and pawing for the release that only a run can bring.

Then your mind starts to race with uncertainty. Have you trained too much? Or not enough? It's too late now and you know it. The best you can do is to take what comfort you can from what's written there in your training diary. For Bannister the build-up made good reading:

14 April	¾ mile solo time trial	3:02.0
15 April	880 yards solo time trial	1:53.0
16 April–19 April	Climbing with Brasher in Scotland	
22 April	10 x 440 yards – average of	58:9
24 April	¾ mile time trial with Chataway	3:00.0
26 April	¾ mile 3:14.0, 8 minutes rest, ¾ mile	3:08.6
28 April	¾ mile solo time trial	2:59.9
30 April	880 yards time trial	1:54.0
1 May	easy 4 mile striding	
1 May–6 May	rest up for the race	

The hard work was over. Now all Roger Bannister could do was to wait and pray the May weather at the Iffley Road track would be fine.

Things were not going so smoothly for Santee. He was not only isolated from the action in Europe, but because of a row with officials, he was trapped. He had returned from his tour of Europe in the summer of 1953, his training diary stuffed with fast times and victories, his luggage swollen with medals and prizes, to find he was facing an inquisition from the athletics authorities.

Santee never had a problem collecting prizes. He ran to win. But with the strict laws on amateurism still being rigidly enforced, no prize was supposed to be worth more than $20. 'One time,' Santee said, 'I won 54 wrist watches. It was crazy.' So, while on tour in Germany in 1953, he asked an official if instead of yet more watches he could pool his prizes for the next three races and get an Agfa camera worth $125 instead. 'The official said, "fine", and I went out and won three races,' said Santee, 'but when I asked him for the camera he changed his mind. He wanted to force me into running yet another race and then said it was all against the rules anyway. I got real mad and I guess I used some foul language.'

The official wrote a lengthy report to Dan Ferris, the secretary-treasurer of the Amateur Athletic Union, calling for Santee's suspension. 'The German guy reckoned I had hit him over the head with a chair,' said Santee. 'That was a lie. The whole thing was unfair but I had blown my top. I was only doing what the other guys on the tour were doing. They were all trading several small awards for a big one.'

Dan Ferris was unmoved by the explanation. As a punishment, Santee was banned from competing overseas for a year. He was furious. 'They were robbing me of my chance to run four minutes,' he said. 'And it wasn't just me that was going to lose – they were robbing the whole of America.'

In England, another American had four minutes on his mind. On the afternoon of 6 May, George Dole left his room in a little terraced house in Oxford's Parker Street, clambered on to his battered bicycle and pedalled off towards the track at Iffley Road. There he was due to run the mile for his university against the AAA.

Two months earlier the 22-year-old Dole, a Rhodes Scholar from Yale, at University College studying Hebrew, had won the Oxford–Cambridge mile at the White City. He knew this May race was going to be special. For weeks there had been gossip and rumour around Iffley Road that this was the big day for Bannister and Franz Stampfl's elite squad. Derek Johnson, the OUAC Secretary, had made a secret date with the groundsman to ensure the track was well rolled and that runners kept clear of churning up the cinders on the precious inside lane. Though Stampfl had told the students to tell no one, everyone knew.

But one student athlete, Nigel Miller, also at University College, where he was studying medicine, did not know all the details. He joined the straggle of spectators, drawn by whispers of a record attempt, walking up the Iffley Road. He arrived at the track shortly after 5.30, just in time to see Ian Boyd win the half-mile. He paid sixpence for his programme, settled down to study it and noted that the big event was starting at six o'clock. Then, to his amazement, he saw that he was down to run in it.

He looked at his watch and swore. He had come straight to Iffley Road from a medical lecture, and had no running kit with him. 'I knew I couldn't get back to college fast enough to get my kit in time for the race,' he said. 'In panic, I went into the changing room to see if I could borrow some kit, but it was hopeless. There wasn't a pair of spikes to be had.'

Nigel Miller's invitation to race had gone astray. The club's president blamed the secretary, the secretary blamed the president – and the mile that Miller always remembers is the one mile he never ran.

For that other medical student, Roger Bannister, the day had begun at St Mary's Hospital in London, where he was a junior houseman. That morning, though, the only thing on his mind was the race. He sharpened his spikes on a hospital laboratory grindstone and rubbed graphite into them. A runner sentenced to race becomes obsessed with the strangest of details. He walked the short distance to Paddington to catch the late morning train to Oxford. He wanted to be alone to think, and, above all, to be away from the press.

'I didn't know what time Chris Brasher and the others were going to Oxford,' said Bannister, 'but at Paddington I found by chance that Franz Stampfl was on the same train.' It was a vital meeting. The two sat together, sensing the tension, each understanding the unspoken anxiety about the trial to come. When Englishmen can't voice their fears they talk about the weather. Bannister looked out at the grey sky, the trees in the scudding wind, and said, 'It's hopeless to try it today.'

Stampfl reckoned the wind might cost Bannister half a second a lap but no more, and as he was capable of running 3:56, he could do it anyway. 'If you have the chance and don't take it,' he warned, 'you may never forgive yourself.' There would be pain of course, said Stampfl, but 'The mind can overcome any adversity.'

Bannister's fears about the weather grew worse as the day progressed. 'The wind was gusting, it was a dank, wet, cold and miserable day,' said Norris McWhirter. 'One was very conscious that the attempt was on the edge of possibility and in the conditions it seemed it would be unwise to try.'

There was a small army of sports writers and photographers at Iffley Road, mobilised by McWhirter, who had also tipped off BBC television to cover the meeting. When Milton Marmar, an American journalist based in London, called to ask if it was worthwhile going to Oxford, McWhirter told him not to miss it.

Bannister was met at the station by his old friend and fellow athlete from his freshman days at Oxford, Charles Wenden. They drove straight to Iffley Road to look at the track. The flag on the nearby church lashed wildly in a wind that would surely slap down any hope of a record. Still Bannister tried out both of his pairs of spikes. He had a new pair which had been specially made with the help of a climber and fell walker, Eustace Thomas. The weight of each running shoe had been pared from six to four ounces.

Bannister tried to relax after a salad lunch prepared by Wenden's wife, Eileen. But the weather made it impossible. 'The wind's hopeless,' said the old record holder Joe Binks as they walked to the track around 5 p.m. A few minutes later the rain, which had eased at the start of the meeting, returned with a heavy shower. The competitors in the early events splashed on. In the changing room Bannister pinned the number 41, slightly askew, just below the AAA badge on his vest.

'The rain stopped again,' said Chris Brasher. 'And there was a rainbow. We kept running in and out to see if Roger had made up his mind. It was he who had dreamed of reaching beyond a man's grasp; only he could know whether he was ready, whether he was mentally prepared to break the psychological barrier.'

'No one could persuade me,' said Bannister. 'The decision was mine alone.' As they lined up for the start Bannister glanced at the flag again. It fluttered more gently now. The wind had dropped and the six o'clock sun was strong enough to cast shadows on the track. Bannister had made up his mind. The attempt was on.

Seven names were listed in the programme to run the mile. Six shook their legs nervously at the start line: R.G. Bannister, C.J. Chataway, W.T. Hulatt and C.W. Brasher for the AAA, while G.F. Dole and A.D. Gordon wore the shorts and vest of an Oxford Blue. T.N. Miller, the man with no spikes, gripped his stopwatch forlornly on the infield.

All the attention, though, was on one athlete: Roger Bannister, the true blue amateur, the Oxford man who had helped create the very track on which the race was being run – tall, angular, elegant, anguished with nervous energy. He seemed to run with the shadows of Strode-Jackson and Jack Lovelock at his heels, and the hopes of all Britain on his shoulders.

A false start from Brasher, then they were away, Brasher taking the lead as prearranged. Bannister and Chataway tucked in behind him, gliding in his slipstream. After five days of rest, they were schoolboy-fresh. 'I was like a coiled spring crying to be released,' said Bannister.

Norris McWhirter had got the local electrician to rig up two speakers, one each side of the track, so that as the race announcer he could inform the athletes of their time for each quarter. Brasher ran the first 220 yards in a fraction over 27 seconds, which was fast. Bannister mis-heard the crackling speakers. 'Faster, faster!' he shouted at Brasher.

'I don't think I heard him,' said Brasher, 'but in any case, without getting up on my toes and sprinting flat out, I was going as fast as I could.' At 1:58 for the half-mile, the pace was just fine.

As the three men came in single file down the home straight for the second time, Stampfl leaned out from the inside to yell at Bannister, 'Relax, take it easy.' By the back straight, Brasher knew that his work was done. Every step hurt, and he longed for Chataway to take over. At last Chataway barrelled past with Bannister in tow.

The pace was good, and Chataway reckoned the record was on. 'That Roger could do it, I didn't have the slightest doubt,' he said. 'I believed that from the moment of that three-quarter-mile trial before the Helsinki Games. At the half-mile Chris was pretty well spot on, and the three-quarters at around 3:01 was fine, but I was worried going around the next bend because I must have been slowing by then. Roger could do a last lap in 57 if he had to, but getting round that last bend at four-minute-mile pace was one hell of an effort for me.'

The watches showed that Bannister had to complete the last lap in 59 seconds to break the barrier. He kept his nerve and clung to his pacemaker until just 300 yards from the finish. Then he struck – all long arms and legs, the stride massive, hands pumping with power, his hair streaming behind him.

Bannister wrote later of a moment of mixed joy and anguish. He says he felt that the moment of a lifetime had come. 'There was no pain, only a great unity of movement and aim. The world seemed to stand still or did not exist. The only reality was the next 200 yards of track under my feet. I felt at that moment that it was my chance to do one thing supremely well.'

The crowd were roaring their man on. Other athletes screamed as he passed, their clenched fists beating the rhythm of his strides. As he neared the tape it seemed to drift away from him and he wondered if he would ever reach it. 'The arms of the world', he said, 'were waiting to receive me if only I reached the tape without slackening my speed.' If he faltered, he knew the world would be 'a cold, forbidding place'.

He crashed through the tape, eyes closed, mouth gasping, his old friend Charles Wenden crouching by the finish, a hand over his face, not daring to look. Exhaustion flooded his every pore. For a runner it is far worse when you stop than when you are racing. The moment you stop, everything hurts. The pain that smacks through your legs, your shoulders, your neck, your fingers even, is too much. All you want is air, space, time, oblivion.

Bannister sagged like a beaten heavyweight into the arms of another friend, the sprinter Nick Stacey. Around him was a hubbub of excited speculation. Did he do it? Did he do it?

The loudspeakers crackled and the crowd went silent. Norris McWhirter seized the microphone. Like a bit-part schoolboy in the annual play, he was not going to miss this chance to milk every word, every line of the drama.

'Ladies and gentlemen,' he said slowly, 'here is the result of event number 9, the one mile. First, number 41, R.G. Bannister of the Amateur Athletic Association and formerly of Exeter and Merton Colleges, with a time which is a new meeting and track record, and which, subject to ratification, will be a new English Native, British National, British-Allcomers, European, British Empire and World Record. The time is three . . .'

Pandemonium drowned the rest of the announcement. Bannister hugged his two pacemakers and waved in triumph to the crowd. The swarm of well-wishers, reporters and photographers threatened to back-slap him to the ground. Franz Stampfl in his flat cap and duffel coat looked on and beamed.

The long quest for the four-minute mile was over. Time had stopped for Bannister at 3:59.4.

'We had done it,' said Bannister, 'the three of us. We shared a place where no man had yet ventured – secure for all time: however fast men might run miles in future, we had done it where we wanted, when we wanted, how we wanted. In the wonderful joy my pain was forgotten. No words could be invented for such supreme happiness.'

The offical result of the race had Bannister first in 3:59.4, Chataway second in 4:07.2 and Tom Hulatt, the Northern Counties mile champion from Derbyshire, third in 4:16. Alan Gordon, in his first year at Oxford and also from Derbyshire, finished fourth but was untimed. Behind him, Brasher and Dole had to barge their way to the finish through the spectators swarming on to the track to congratulate the winner.

Harold Abrahams declared he felt 'as if an atom bomb had just gone off', and Franz Stampfl, seeing Bannister's distressed state at the finish, muttered to the sprinter Sylvia Cheeseman, 'Bannister is not very fit.' Geoff Dyson, the Chief National Coach, congratulated Bannister, but added, 'Now for God's sake go and learn something about athletics, because from now on your word will be gospel.' A local newspaper reporter grabbed one of the McWhirter twins and asked, 'Is this the first time anyone has ever run a mile in less than four minutes?'

As soon as he recovered, Bannister embraced his mother and then went over to Walter Morris, the Iffley Road groundsman, to thank him for having the track in such good shape. He quickly told journalists that it had been a team effort and that without the help of Brasher and Chataway the barrier would never have been broken.

Norris McWhirter then whisked him off to Vincent's Club, just off Oxford's High Street. Fifty years on, even the also-rans get handed electrolyte replacement drinks at the finish. At Vincent's, Roger Bannister had to make do with a sprinkling of salt and sugar stirred into a wine glass of water.

For the man who had just made history, there was no better drink in the world. The champagne would come later, and with it the giddy intoxication of what he had done. When word got through that evening to the Oxford Union, the proceedings were interrupted by a proposal that 'This house shall adjourn for 3 minutes 59.4 seconds.' It was all too much for the new Indian President of the Union, who protested that no notice of the motion had been given.

Chris Brasher said he always believed the record would be broken that day in Oxford. So confident was he that before leaving London he reserved a table for a celebration that evening at Clement Freud's club above the Royal Court Theatre in Chelsea, and, he said, lined up three girlfriends to share the dinner.

'In the small hours of the morning, when the club kicked us out,' he said, 'we were driving in Piccadilly Circus and we stopped to ask a policeman the way to a nightclub that was reputedly still open. He peered into Chris Chataway's old pre-war Austin, saw the three of us jammed in with the girls and said, "You gentlemen are not gentlemen if you take these ladies to that club."

'Then he started to take out his notebook, and I thought, "We can't be booked for asking the way." But then he handed us the notebook and said, "Perhaps I could have your autographs, gentlemen?"'

It was when the morning newspapers were delivered to the nightclub that the full impact of what they had achieved struck home. There was the story, blazoned on every front page, and it wasn't just in Britain. It was a long time since the American journalist Milton Marmar, who had wondered if it was worth travelling to Oxford, had placed a front-page story from London. Now he had a by-line splash on the front of 1,600 American papers.

The *New York Herald Tribune* declared that Bannister had achieved 'the track's wildest dream. Bannister wanted that four-minute mile. He would never admit it but those who saw him working in the bitter wet winter on an isolated running track in London felt that if any man was going to get there, it would be the shy, gifted youth.

'The four-minute mile – this has been the Holy Grail of foot racing, this is the vision that has governed men's minds, fired their imagination, inspired more dreaming and more argument, more speculation and prophetic debate than the way of an eagle in the air, the way of a serpent upon a rock, the way of a ship in the midst of the sea, the way of a man with a maid.'

The day after the race, Bannister needed a suitcase to carry all the telegrams and messages of congratulation. Among them there were tributes from the giants who had themselves flirted with the dream mile. Gunder Haegg said, 'Bannister uses his brains as much as his legs and I've always thought the four-minute mile more of a psychological problem than a test of strength.'

'It is absolutely wonderful,' said Sydney Wooderson. 'I always thought he would be the first to do it.'

And from Finland, the land of runners, arrived the simplest tribute of all. 'Well done Britain,' it read. It came from Paavo Nurmi.

23

The Great Mr Second

Buzz Aldrin, Tenzing Norgay and me. It's nice we haven't been
completely forgotten. Perhaps we should have had some sort of
club named after the men who got there second.

John Landy

From America and Australia Wes Santee and John Landy
were quick to send their congratulations. 'It was a great
performance,' said Santee, 'but the time is still not as low as it
can be run.' Landy went along with the verdict. 'This is great,
great, great,' he said, 'and I think the brilliant achievement
will be bettered.'

But for the moment Bannister had the record. He found
that it had turned him into more than a front-page story. He
had become a household name and a national institution
overnight. He was learning rapidly that the pressures of
training could be as nothing compared with the pressures
of fame.

The British had a new folk hero, and the press and public
swelled with national pride. Yet when asked to comment on
the fulfilment of a lifelong dream, Bannister played the achievement down. 'I think the four-minute mile has been over-rated,'
he said. 'After all, it's only a time. But I am immensely happy
at having been able to win the four-minute mile for Britain.'

The British government, and particularly the Foreign Office, were quick to realise the potential value to the country of this young amateur sportsman. Within a week Bannister was whisked off to the United States on a 'goodwill visit', fixed up by the Foreign Office. His mission was to tell America by coast-to-coast television and radio how he had become the first to break the record, and to be held up as an enviable example of the achievement of post-war Britain.

Amid all the media ballyhoo, Foreign Office officials made attempts to keep Bannister's travel arrangements secret. He was booked to fly under the name of Richard Bentley. But news of his arrival leaked out, and when he stepped from the BOAC plane in New York he was greeted by a scrum of photographers and reporters.

A tobacco company tried to claim that they had sponsored the whole visit, and a member of the Olympic Committee of Southern California turned up in New York with a trophy for Bannister worth $300 – way above the amateur prize limit. Soon Bannister found himself on air and on camera fielding aggressive questions about his amateur status.

'I had never earned a penny and never expected to,' said Bannister. 'Sport tends to become complicated when money enters. I would not, I think, have wanted to be involved. The Americans wanted to give me a trophy, a huge ornate thing. I thought it looked expensive. We were restricted to accepting prizes up to $15 at the time and this could have been a snare to make me a professional. I said, "Thank you very much but no."' He insisted on accepting only a small replica trophy, 'the size of an egg cup,' he said, 'but it avoided the Santee trap'. And the initial schedule of television interviews was scrapped, to be replaced by a series of unsponsored broadcasts monitored carefully by the Foreign Office.

The American press and public loved what they saw. 'He is as impressive in his interviews as he is on the running track,' they wrote. And when there was a lunch given in his honour at the Yale Club in New York, they drew comparisons with that other long-striding Oxford miler sitting there at the table – Arnold Strode-Jackson. What, they wondered, might have happened if these two legends had been at Oxford at the same time? 'Oh, Roger Bannister would have beaten me easily,' said the old 1912 Olympic 1,500-metre winner, 'but it would have been a hell of a race.'

Percy Cerutty was highly critical of the way pacemakers had been used in the Oxford race. He preached that to run records you had to learn to lead from the start, and would snort, 'I'm waiting for it to happen in a proper race.'

Twenty-three days after Bannister's race in Oxford, Santee ran in his own home town, Kansas City. Without the aid of planned pacing, he ran 4:01.4 to equal the second best mile time ever – the world record set by Gunder Haegg at Malmo back in 1945.

Two days later John Landy had his first race since arriving in Finland in early May. In Turku, the original home of Paavo Nurmi, he tried to front-run the mile according to the gospel of Percy Cerutty, with a first half of 1:55.8. He finished in a personal best time of 4:01.6 – but still the magic four minutes eluded him. To many it seemed a mystery. Why couldn't John Landy do it? If ever there was a man made to break the four-minute barrier it seemed to be him. Not only was he a wonderfully gifted runner, but he was one of the hardest-training athletes of the 1950s, by his own reckoning often doing up to 20 miles a day.

The powerful hype and aura of the four-minute quest would not leave Landy or Santee alone, and every time they raced the world looked for faster times. At Compton, California, on 4 June, the conditions were perfect, with fine weather, a fast track and a large crowd. Wes Santee felt good as he warmed up, and after covering the first quarter in 58.1 he felt energy and confidence coursing through his legs. Running magnificently alone for much of the race, he finished with the second fastest mile in history at 4:00.6 – just six-tenths of a second shy of the magic barrier. In the course of the race he had gone through 1,500 metres in 3:42.8, and at last Wes Santee had a world record of his own.

He followed it up in Los Angeles on 11 June with another attempt, against Josy Barthel. This time the pace was ideal, 1:59.5 at the half and 3:00.2 at the three-quarter-mile mark. As Barthel tied up, Santee battled on alone to finish in 4:00.8. The American press went wild. Their own four-minute mile now seemed a formality. But already the AAU were delving deeply into allegations that Santee had taken illegal appearance money.

'The whole case against me, and the lifetime ban that eventually followed, was a farce and a miscarriage of justice,' said Santee years later. 'It was common knowledge among top-notch track athletes that most of them got expense money way above what was permitted by the Amateur Athletic Union rules. I got more than most of the others because the mile was the big feature event. If a meet promoter was without a leading pole-vaulter or sprinter he could still have a big show, but it was the mile that pulled in the crowds.

'I was not the first to receive padded expense money in the little brown envelopes. The practice had been standard for years. I was from Kansas, not part of the East Coast set-up. Both me and my coach Bill Easton were pretty outspoken and I think the AAU unfairly singled me out for suspension. I was never money mad, but what is someone who must support his family supposed to do when money is given to him? The AAU officials knew exactly how much I was getting, they were the guys who were giving it to me.'

By his own reckoning, Santee calculated that he had been offered and taken more than $10,000 for running the mile in the year after Bannister broke the barrier. The hearings that followed were to result in his suspension from amateur competition in 1955. Though his lawyers tried to fight it through the courts, and he kept training hard while serving in the US Marines, Wes Santee, still the fastest miler in America and their best hope for the 1956 Olympic 1,500 metres, was finished.

Just two days after Santee's last effort, Chataway and Brasher were together racing the 1,500 metres in the Netherlands Olympic Day meeting in Amsterdam. After he had won a slow tactical race, Chataway told Roy Moor, the athletics correspondent of the *News Chronicle*, that he wanted to race against John Landy, who again had just failed to break four minutes in Stockholm.

'Maybe', said Chataway, 'I could help him to get the four-minute mile which has been escaping him by such a tantalising margin. I would not go there just as a pacemaker, I would prefer to make a real race of it.'

It was an offer Landy couldn't refuse.

When Chataway arrived at Turku airport less than a week later, he found Landy and Denis Johansson there to greet him. And on 21 June, just 46 days after the history-making run at Oxford, Chataway was ready to participate in another attempt for a place in the record books.

It was a beautiful evening. Runners love the cool, crisp feeling of the Finnish tracks. The black cinders of Turku were famously fast. The crowd of 6,000 had learned their love of athletics at the feet of Paavo Nurmi. The air was still, with the fresh scent of pine needles.

A local hero, Aulis Kallio, took off from the gun, roared on by his home crowd. But before the half-mile point Landy floated to the front, relaxed and balanced, pattering through the 800-metre mark in 1:57.9 with Chataway breathing heavily down his neck. The crowd chanted, 'Landy, Landy, Landy' to the rhythm of their steps, and on the first bend of the final lap, Chataway made a spirited bid to kick past the Australian. But it was hopeless. Landy was a machine. There was no slowing down, just a relentless rapid piston stride.

Landy had stretched his lead like this in miles before. He had seen the tape, drawn strength from the crowd, raced the clock and missed the record too often to be sure of fulfilling his lifelong dream. But this time Chataway might still be lurking – a hunter waiting yet to pick off his prey. This time fear mixed with lactic acid in Landy's legs. And this time the mile was his.

He'd done it in 3:57.9. They rounded it up to 3:58 – but still it was nearly a second and a half faster than Bannister's run. Along the way Landy had smashed Santee's 1,500-metre world record, running 3:41.8. Wes Santee's record had lasted 17 days, and Roger Bannister's just 46.

The crowd went berserk and heaved Landy shoulder high. They all wanted to touch him, to share his glow of happiness. The press fought to get words from him and then fought again for the phones to spread those words around the world.

Back in London Roger Bannister said, 'It is a wonderful achievement. Landy has tried so hard and I'm so glad that he has now succeeded. It shows that times can always be broken. I am looking forward very much to racing against him in the Empire Games mile at Vancouver in August.'

In America Glenn Cunningham commented, 'The delay in achieving the goal was simply a mental one. The sports writers built up a psychological barrier that the four-minute mile just never could be run. When it finally came the time was a result of the mental attitude one builds up to keep doing things better. The milers shook off the notion that it couldn't be done and they gained confidence as they got closer to it. We're still a long way from the best that can be done now that the psychological barrier has been cleared. Even I don't have the psychological outlook to visualise a 3:50 mile, but then I remember when they told me that a 4:05 mile was impossible.'

Chris Chataway was hailed, fêted and toasted by the Finns, who since the days of Nurmi had been the most knowledgeable and enthusiastic of athletics fans. They appreciated and admired his part in the race. He had all the qualities of the cavalier English amateur they respected and loved. He was the first to reach for a cigarette after the race, the first to lift a glass in celebration.

They were well aware that he was the one athlete who had been involved in both the sub-four-minute miles. He'd finished second in both, this one in 4:04.4. 'The record', said Landy, 'would not have gone if it had not been for Chataway chasing me round the track. I knew he would pass me if I slowed down.' For his part, Chataway complained that he would rather have won one of the races. In London the *Evening Standard* labelled him 'the Great Mr Second'.

The party that followed the four-minute mile in Turku was bibulous and rowdy, ending with a typically Finnish session in the sauna. The Finns could be as competitive in the sauna as they were on the track, delighting in watching visitors from other lands wilt in the overpowering heat. They would laugh, lift the pinewood floorboards and reach for ice-cold bottles of beer stowed in the cool of the forest floor. The Finnish athletes loved it. The sauna kept their muscles loose, they claimed, and it meant that no summer's day had ever been too hot for people like Paavo Nurmi.

Roger Bannister's phone was hot with calls from Fleet Street and the world's press chasing his reaction to the news that his record had fallen so soon. He was, he admitted, shocked at how much Landy had knocked off his time. Of course the track conditions and lack of wind in Turku would account for some of the 1.4 seconds, but Landy's time was still a startling improvement.

Bannister's reaction was understandably ambivalent. He admitted it would have been nice to hang on to his record for a little longer, and there was perhaps a twinge of annoyance that his friend and training partner Chris Chataway had played such a key role. But records were there to be broken. Bannister knew, too, that this would add a distinct edge to the coming confrontation at the Empire Games in Vancouver.

The quest for the four-minute mile might have ended at Iffley Road in May, but the quest to decide who was the greatest miler was only just beginning. 'The world', said Bannister, 'seemed almost too small for us – we must meet and settle the score.'

24

The Showdown

The great thing about athletics is that it's like poker. Sometimes you know what's in your hand and it may be a load of rubbish, but you've got to keep up the front.

Sebastian Coe

Head-to-head battles have made for exciting spectacles since the days of bare-knuckle fights and duelling. It was the head-to-head battle between Walter George and William Cummings in 1886 that started the long quest for the four-minute mile. It involved just two men over the classic distance, with no pacemakers to help them out, and it produced the mile of the nineteenth century. Now Bannister and Landy, the two men who had ended that long quest, were meeting in their own mile of the century.

Back in the eighteenth century, it was gambling that had prompted the milers to run against the watches. Now, in Vancouver in the golden days of the amateur, the bookmakers had Landy down as a 4–1 favourite.

The contrast between the physiques, personalities and race preparations of the two rivals could hardly have been greater. Bannister was tall, thin, pale, reserved, deep-thinking. He believed that running was as much about the mind as the body. He harboured and gathered his mental and physical strength for just two or three peak performances in any season. He was unnerved by the amount and quality of training that Landy was said to be doing. He could read reports of it every day in the Canadian newspapers.

Landy was almost his opposite. He was stocky, suntanned, muscular, with short curly black hair and a bouncing, friendly personality. While Bannister agonised over his running, the Australian seemed to relish it, both on and off the track. He trained hard and he raced hard. He preferred to lead from gun to tape, killing off the opposition with his sustained and relentless pace.

The press and the other athletes who watched Landy's prodigious training sessions in Vancouver, during which he often ran barefoot, were convinced they were witnessing the preparations of the next Empire Mile champion. Any training Bannister did he kept secret. You might catch him shyly unveiling those thoroughbred legs on the springy grass of a secluded golf course, or sheltering in a swimming pool, but he kept well away from the men with their fingers on the buttons of the cameras and the stopwatches who hung around the crowded tracks of Vancouver.

The press were quick to interpret his behaviour as showing a lack of confidence, and many wrote him off. 'They all thought Landy would run the finish out of him,' said Chris Brasher, 'but they didn't realise that beneath that diffident exterior there lurked a fierce competitor and that he'd thought a lot about how he could win it. He knew Landy would run from the front and he'd talked about it with Franz Stampfl. Franz had this theory about having invisible contact with the man in front. If you fell back more than 10 or 12 yards, Franz warned, the invisible contact would be broken and you'd probably lose.'

The Empire Games (nowadays the Commonwealth Games)

were run like a cosy version of the Olympics. The inspiration behind them even seemed to pre-date the modern Olympic revival of 1896. In 1891, the Reverend Astley Cooper wrote in the *Greater Britain* magazine and in the London *Times* suggesting that a 'pan-Britannic pan-Anglican contest and festival be held every four years as a means of increasing the goodwill and good understanding of the British Empire'.

It was another 20 years, though, before Richard Coombes, President of the Amateur Athletic Union of Australia, started actively lobbying for the idea. And it was not until 1930 that the Games got up and running in Hamilton, Canada.

Now, in 1954, the Games, already re-styled the British Empire and Commonwealth Games, were back in Canada and the eyes of the world were on them because of the mile. The hype and expectations were enormous. Millions around the world were expected to follow the race by wireless and it was being covered by television throughout North America.

The two great milers hadn't met in a race since their heat in the Olympic 1,500 metres in Helsinki in 1952. There had been so many rumours about their retirement that many feared they would never meet again. But here, in August, in Vancouver, the classic clash was on. The problem for John Landy as the supreme artist of front running was to draw the sting from Bannister's devastating finish. The problem for Roger Bannister was to hang on long enough to be able to unleash his final effort.

Both Bannister and Landy went into the race with nagging problems. Bannister had developed a cold, possibly, he thought, as a result of spending too much time in the chilly water of a swimming pool, and Landy had cut a foot badly on a piece of broken glass, probably a photographer's discarded flash bulb, the night before the final. Both kept their troubles secret.

Landy was forced to have stitches in the foot. Bannister took potions for the cold.

The day of the mile final, Saturday 7 August, was hot, sticky and humid. Every ticket for the afternoon session had been sold long before the day arrived. The Duke of Edinburgh sat in the royal box, Lord Alexander of Tunis, former Governor General of Canada, at his side. The crowd of 35,000 sweltered as they waited in the stadium. Out on the roads of Vancouver the sun was blazing down on the marathon runners, who were already wobbling in the baking 80° heat.

In the cool of a London evening, track statistician Stan Greenberg, like hundreds of others, coaxed a signal from the glowing dial of his wireless.

They came to the start, the tall, pale-skinned Bannister looking frail beside the tanned, dark-haired Landy. The gifted amateur up against the well-tuned machine. The hunter against the hunted. England against Australia.

Landy wore the green vest of his country; Bannister was in white with the red rose of England. But it was Bill Baillie, in the black vest of New Zealand, who took off like a sprinter at the start.

As if running to script, though, Landy seized the lead before the lap was out and was through the first quarter in 58.2, with Bannister already five yards back. 'You've got him, John,' they screamed from the stands, as with short, staccato strides Landy stepped up the pace and increased the lead. With the half-mile passed in 1:58.3, Bannister found himself a dozen, perhaps 15 yards down. Landy looked confident, determined; Bannister looked anxious. The gap looked far too big.

Slowly on the third lap, Bannister hauled himself back towards the Australian as if joined by an invisible rope. But still, as the bell clanged with 2:58.4 on the clock, Bannister was four or five yards down.

Crouched by his wireless in London, Stan Greenberg turned the volume up full. 'I wasn't worried when Landy opened up a yawning gap early in the race,' he remembered. 'But when Bannister failed to close it at the bell, I was panic-stricken. As they entered the final bend. I found myself yelling. "Now Roger, now!"'

On that final lap, Landy was still motoring economically, urgently, efficiently, while Bannister seemed to take giant, gangling strides. Landy passed the 1,500 metre mark just 0.1 of a second outside the world record that he had set in Turku.

Coming off the final bend, the Australian glanced for a moment over his left shoulder. If Bannister had learned one thing from poring over the diaries of Jack Lovelock, it was to make a move the moment your opponent least expects it. 'Nobody expected to be passed on a bend in a mile of this calibre,' Bannister recalled. 'Landy didn't, and in a few strides I was past him.'

Bannister turned on his legendary finish. Over the final 80 yards he stretched his lead to an amazing five yards before hitting the tape and collapsing in the style which had become his trademark. The time was 3:58.8. Landy crossed the line in 3:59.6.

This time both men had smashed the four-minute barrier in the same race – but once again, Roger Bannister got there first. In the stadium the crowd rose with a roar to salute the two men. Back home, Stan Greenberg discovered that he had torn his *Radio Times* to shreds.

The spectators were still buzzing about the result when, 20 minutes later, the English marathon runner Jim Peters came staggering into the stadium. It was a pitiful sight to see this greatest of marathon champions reduced to an uncoordinated shuffle by the heat of the sun that had beaten down on him throughout the 26 miles and 385 yards of the race. Half of the field of 16 runners had already given up because of the oppressive conditions, and the heat was soon to claim another victim.

Over the next 10 minutes, during which Peters covered only 200 of the 385 yards remaining before the haven of the finish, he fell to the ground six times. Each time he heaved himself to his feet. He staggered, scrambled and crawled, zig-zagging impossibly, thrashing the air with his arms. Eventually he collapsed across what, in his confusion, he took to be the finish line. But the actual finish was still 185 agonising yards away on the far side of the track.

The horrified onlookers were frozen with uncertainty – not daring to touch him, lift him or help him in any way. They feared he would be disqualified. Way back in the 1908 Olympics in London, a little Italian, Pietro Dorando, had collapsed four times inside the White City stadium while leading the marathon. Eventually two officials helped him across the line. Although he had finished first, Dorando was disqualified and robbed of his gold medal.

Eventually the unconscious Peters was carried away on a stretcher. He was put in an oxygen tent for seven hours, and hung between life and death on a saline and glucose drip. He never raced again.

For Roger Bannister, now undisputed master of his distance, just one race remained.

He approached the European Championships 1,500 metres in Berne three weeks later relaxed and confident as never before. In the 1950s these championships were reckoned to be second in importance only to the Olympics, and once again Bannister was in the high-pressure position of favourite. But here, at the end of his career, he found a calm that had eluded him at the Olympic Games and throughout most of the races of his career since his first days at Oxford.

The tortured, sleepless nights, the anxious hours bathed in the sweat of fear and anticipation were behind him at last. This time, although the race was world class, Bannister knew that he was ready for anything. 'I no longer wanted to be wrapped in cotton wool,' he said. 'If my spikes had split now, I should have run in bare feet. If I were knocked over I should not feel martyred but would draw new impetus from my anger.'

Those who watched the race say that Bannister dominated the field as never before. He seemed to control it all from the back. On the final bend he hit the front with the speed of a quarter-miler. He won in a championship record of 3:47.2.

His old friend Harold Abrahams was there to draw a line under Bannister's career. 'Had Bannister required to run two seconds faster, he could have done it,' he said. 'If this be – as well it may – Bannister's last international race, it was a fitting climax to a wonderful season.'

In the space of 115 days, Roger Bannister had broken the four-minute mile, beaten John Landy in the Mile of the Century, and carried off the European title in Berne. More importantly than any of this, he would say himself, he had also qualified as a doctor. His running days were over.

25

Fame Never Fades

Now you will not swell the rout
Of lads who wore their honour out,
Runners whom renown outran
And the name died before the man.

A. E. Housman, 'To an Athlete Dying Young'

They are old men now. Fifty years and four minutes on, they have run their races. They may, like Chris Brasher, have had their time. But in the history of the quest for the four-minute mile they are frozen for ever in 1954, three high-stepping English boys doing what they loved on a track that was theirs.

The day after they had made history, the three of them, Bannister, Brasher and Chataway, walked together near Bannister's home. 'We sat on the grass on Harrow Hill,' Bannister remembers. 'We were wondering what was going to happen to us all and what we planned to do. Clearly that day we all had some vision that our lives would be changed, very changed.'

'All fine runners, through success, have to deal with the question of acclaim,' said Kenny Moore, an Olympic marathon competitor himself. 'Some are given a little recognition and allowed to get back to normal, some, whose achievements take on a symbolic resonance, find their lives absorbed in the public imagination. None more inextricably than the world's first four-minute-miler, Roger Bannister.'

The immediate question for Bannister was how he would spend a lifetime handling four minutes of fame. 'A good day for Roger', reflects Chataway, 'would be a day when nobody mentioned the four-minute mile. He's never been petulant about it, never said "Oh for God's sake, I'm a doctor", never brushed aside the endless questions.'

What was it about the four-minute mile that captured the imaginations of so many and held them for so long? Chataway wonders. Was it really a fantastic achievement, a milestone in sport? Or was it just another record?

Harry Wilson, who was the coach of world record holder Steve Ovett, thought the achievement overrated. 'I think it's bloody silly to put flowers on the grave of the four-minute mile,' he said. 'It turns out it wasn't so much like Everest as the Matterhorn. Somebody had to climb it first, but I hear now they've even got a cow up it.'

The Australian Herb Elliott, arguably the greatest miler ever, scoffed at the idea that there was ever a psychological barrier. He believed that the reason that milers such as Wooderson, Haegg, Andersson and Santee didn't break four minutes was because they weren't good enough, or rather that they lacked the high degree of physical fitness and mental inspiration necessary to achieve the goal.

'Since Bannister's success, there has been such a spate of sub-four-minute miles that they no longer rate headlines around the world. This has nothing to do with psychology,' said Elliott. 'It simply means that new standards of efficiency have been set for the mile as they've been set in every other athletic event. I make only one exception to my theory – John Landy, who allowed himself to be mesmerised by the four-minute mile. The mental pressure was too overwhelming. Never could he step on to a track without the whole of Australia standing by with bated breath saying, "This time he'll do it."'

But if John Landy and the world were mesmerised by the four-minute barrier, the public were equally captivated by the character and the philosophy of the man who broke through it. The fascination of the four-minute mile has endured because Roger Bannister, the shy student doctor in spikes, captured the imagination of Britain 50 years ago, and captures it still.

He tapped somehow into a deep reservoir of pride in Britishness and Britain's achievements, and the memories of those minutes at Iffley Road have passed into myth. Hundreds of old men who were duffel-coated boys in the 1950s swear they were there, that windy evening, watching the tall, angular golden boy on the damp black cinders of Iffley Road.

There was national delight at the achievement. Half a century ago the country took a simple, uncritical pride in the belief that in Oxford and Cambridge the nation had two jewels of education and achievement. There was more applause than resentment at the lifestyle of their meritocracies in those austere post-war days. The tradition of amateurism in sport, particularly in miling, the legends of Jack Lovelock and Sydney Wooderson, still exerted a powerful and romantic pull on the public. They admired, but were uneasy about, the more brash and professional approach of runners like Gordon Pirie. Bannister seemed to embody ideals that went beyond his running, and when he and the mile met he was magnificent. He was tall, long-striding, exciting to watch. 'He always ran', said Olympic 800-metre silver medallist Derek Johnson, 'with a degree of suppressed anguish.'

Bannister would hit the tape apparently at the threshold of unconsciousness, close to collapse in a way that would be scoffed at by the fit, hard, professionally trained men who were to follow him. After him – with synthetic tracks, tough training schedules, the lure of money and the doubt of drugs – the mile moved rapidly on.

Thirty years later, two of the greatest and fittest miling duellists the world has ever seen between them ran no fewer than 265 sub-four-minute miles. They were Steve Scott of the United States and John Walker of New Zealand. By the standards of the 1950s, their achievements seem superhuman. Walker, the first man to better 3:50 for the distance, ran 128 miles inside four minutes. Scott broke the barrier on 137 occasions. At the height of their powers their track-tuned bodies seemed indestructible.

Walker and Scott became caught up in a bizarre competition to be the first man to complete 100 sub-four-minute miles. They would race anywhere against anyone, haunting the commercial circus of Grand Prix races in Europe, living out of suitcases and subjecting their bodies to more excessive demands than any before them had dreamed of. They were the first of a new breed, athletes who turned their running into a job.

In previous eras, milers – Lovelock and Bannister among them – would carefully harbour their physical and mental energies for one or two supreme efforts each season. Walker and Scott would turn out such performances routinely, sometimes as often as two or three times a week. Their idea of a peak – a world-class effort – might come around every Wednesday and Friday.

As with Everest, when the tourists start getting to the top, the mountain loses its mystery. On one May day in 1992, no fewer than 30 climbers from five expeditions conquered that once 'unconquerable' peak. And since that May evening in

1954, close to 1,000 runners have broken the once 'unbreakable' barrier in the mile. On 8 August 1980, 13 men ran sub four minutes at London's Crystal Palace, and on the same day another 13 did it in Berlin.

'*Après moi*', Bannister predicted, '*le déluge.*'

But most of those who have followed have lost the happy knack of combining sport and living. Athletes run for money now, and know that a record time can bring a lucrative contract, a dashed-off ghost-written autobiography. They know it's a short leap to the TV commentary box, to highly paid TV commercials, to endorsements, to selling shoes or opening supermarkets. One of the modern characters missing from that Iffley Road meeting in 1954 was the agent – the man present at every great athletic event today, who is quickly on hand to spot a new and charismatic star, or to point out how a world-beating performance can quickly be turned into a million dollars.

Even when there were opportunities to cash in during the 1950s, athletes were wary of snapping them up. 'Immediately I retired,' said Chataway, 'I wrote some articles for *John Bull* magazine for which I got £2,500. It was a very substantial sum of money in those days and probably added up to an awful lot more than what most athletes who had been expelled from the sport had ever earned.

'Roger Bannister, I'm sure, could have made much more. After that I was offered £5,000 to become a Brylcreem boy. It was a hell of a lot in those days, but I don't think even for that kind of money I could have stood seeing my hair smeared back and pictured on the advertising hoardings. I did daydream about taking the money and going off to live in Australia for a while, only coming back when everyone would have forgotten the whole thing, but none of my friends and contemporaries would have approved.

'In our attitude and our training we were', said Chataway, 'a bit like Neanderthal man existing alongside a new breed who were going to inherit the athletic earth. We were the last of our kind and we wanted to prove that we could still put up a good show, still take on the best. It was the English dream of the amateur beating the world at a time when that dream was still just possible. Sport for us was an interlude, a preparation for life. We always expected there would be bigger challenges to come.'

What continued to fascinate the public, and make the appeal of the four-minute mile live on, was what happened next – what these athletes achieved after they stepped off the track.

If Roger Bannister sometimes betrays a mild frustration at being eternally characterised as the man who broke four minutes, it is easily understood. 'Sport was part of my childhood and youth,' he says. 'Athletics had been wonderful but I was looking forward to 40 years of medical life. I realised that all athletic performances and achievements are in fact ephemeral and soon forgotten, and I always knew I should retire once I had qualified as a doctor.'

Of course no one was going to ignore what Bannister had achieved on the track, though he says he found some of the recognition hard to handle. 'There were some minuses in my early career,' he said. 'To be given a CBE at the age of 25 raises eyebrows in some quarters when you're supposed to be a junior doctor. You get a few comments, too, as a national serviceman in the army when your battledress has a CBE ribbon. But I was working as hard as I could without asking for any special treatment.

'There were many pluses,' he added. 'There was an instant link, a lowering of the barrier between myself and other people. There was a sort of shared vision and memory which means

that people would say things to me that they wouldn't necessarily say to other people. So the four-minute mile was a bridge,
both at home and abroad in America. All that's been tremendously enjoyable and it led to a series of invitations to serve
on various committees and councils.'

The man who had won the Mile of the Century found there
were other prizes in life – doctorates, fellowships, scientific
degrees, a knighthood, the respect accorded to a neurologist
of international distinction, and the invitation to become Master
of Pembroke College, Oxford, a post he enjoyed for eight
years.

As the first Chairman of the Sports Council, Bannister
became a prime mover in the war against anabolic steroid
abuse, and he kept up an active interest in running through
orienteering, a sport to which he was introduced by Chris
Brasher. In 1975, the same year that he was knighted by the
Queen, Bannister almost lost his life in a car accident. One
ankle was permanently damaged.

'I was six months in plaster and I've never been able to run
since then, or ski or orienteer or take long walks, so it did
change my life. I had to rethink. I decided to do more research
as I wasn't able to leap around London.' Bannister set up a
centre for research into autonomic function and wrote a standard work on the autonomic nervous system. 'I do try to make
the most of opportunities,' he says.

Chris Chataway, too, with a carefree, restless energy, was
determined to seize every opportunity life threw at him. The
man who had once been labelled 'the Great Mr Second' went
on to carve out a running legend of his own in the darkness
of an October evening in 1954 at London's White City.

There, before a 40,000-strong crowd, and in one of the first
live televised races in Britain, Chataway took on over 5,000

metres the Russian Vladimir Kuts. Probing white searchlights tracked the figures around the darkened stadium. It was London v. Moscow, the swashbuckling dilettante in white against the red-vested machine-like product of Iron Curtain state training. Kuts ran like a boxer, desperate to deliver a knock-out blow on every lap. But somehow Chataway stayed on his feet. The Englishman clawed Kuts out of victory right on the line. It was a new world record, and with this rousing climax, Chataway tossed aside his athletics career.

He established a new one in TV current affairs, becoming ITV's first newsreader. Soon he tossed that aside too, for a new life in politics, becoming a Cabinet minister and Privy Counsellor. He moved on yet again to banking and the world of big business and was knighted in 1995.

Even as a world record breaker he enjoyed a cigar and a drink, and in his seventies the gravel-voiced Chris Chataway still runs and is still remarkably fit. 'I enjoy it enormously,' he says. 'I think I get more pleasure running slowly now than I ever did running fast in my twenties. It is pure enjoyment these days, there is no stress, no agony.'

Chris Brasher, the man who led the first two and a half laps of the four-minute mile, said the fame that followed left him feeling a bit of a fraud. 'The four-minute mile was Bannister's achievement really,' he said. 'Roger was extraordinarily generous after the event, the way he said it was a team effort, but it wasn't really, it was a one-man effort. That is why I pushed myself so hard at the Melbourne Olympics in the steeplechase. I wanted and needed to prove something to myself.'

By winning the gold medal in Melbourne, Brasher proved that determination and single-mindedness can be an athletic talent as great as any God-given ability. After he collected his Olympic gold – 'blind drunk,' he said, 'totally blotto from trying to keep up with the British press' – he went on to enjoy a life in business, in newspapers (as athletics correspondent and sports editor of the *Observer* he was twice voted Sports Journalist of the Year), as a television executive, and, above all, as the founder of the London Marathon.

Brasher's buccaneering life was dominated by an unquenchable love of sport and the outdoor life. He was a passionate environmentalist and would pour fortunes into saving a meadow or a mountain. He made fortunes, too, from devising the lightweight Brasher boot for walking in rough terrain, and from establishing stores and businesses geared specifically to the needs of the new hordes of recreational runners.

Chris Brasher died in February 2003, but he left a lasting legacy to sport by bringing hundreds of thousands into running their own marathons – into conquering what he called 'the Great Suburban Everest'.

Wes Santee kept training for the 1956 Olympics in the vain hope that he would be allowed to race again, but with no prospect of a return to sport, he set about earning a living in the insurance business. In retirement he still runs a couple of miles almost daily and is fiercely proud of his fitness. 'Get Chataway, Bannister and Landy over here now,' he says, 'and we'll have it out once and for all.'

Santee still works part time too, tending a monument to Dr James Naismith, the man who invented basketball. There, in the shadow of the memorial to one of America's founding fathers of sport, other great sportsmen can choose to be buried. Wes Santee will line up the plot. The man who missed the four-minute mile by inches now sells others a promise of sporting immortality.

John Landy, the Australian who was the second man to run under four minutes for the mile, went on to finish third in the

1,500m in the 1956 Olympic Games. But today he is very much the first man in the city of Melbourne. There he works as Governor of the State of Victoria. An agricultural scientist with a lifelong interest in butterflies and the environment, Landy was also for many years a senior executive of ICI in Australia.

As a runner John Landy pioneered modern miling. He ran five times below the four-minute barrier and demonstrated that a middle-distance runner could improve by daring to train year round at an intensity and volume undreamed of by the Corinthian amateurs who ran both before him and alongside him.

'We never trained like Landy,' said Chris Chataway, 'but in truth we trained ridiculously. Even on the evidence that was around at the time, the known details of what men like Zatopek and Landy were doing, we should have applied a little bit of intelligence and done more. Roger always says that half an hour was all that he could spare from his medical studies, but obviously that is nonsense. If you want to train for two hours instead of an hour, however busy you are, it can be managed. We could have done more without it interfering with our lifestyle. It was dim that we did so little.

'The price we paid was that our races were very painful. What we were outstanding at was dragging the last available ounce of energy from ourselves. All that suffering and near collapse at the end of races was never simulated. The public saw the effort we put in and the agony. It all became part of the mystique that made the breaking of the four-minute mile an event that has been so well remembered.

'You have to ask', says Chataway, 'what it was about this moment that made it endure. Why is it so remembered 50 years later? Why has the magic of this particular race worn so well? Because if you are looking back at the twentieth century

for great middle-distance runners, you'd name Paavo Nurmi,
Gunder Haegg, Seb Coe – the people who broke lots of world
records, got lots of important medals, who won the Olympics.
By that yardstick none of us begin to measure up to the real
greats of the twentieth century. We had just one good season
and a couple of good races.

'But it is remembered', says Chataway, 'because it is seen
now as the last flowering of amateurism. It was our lifestyle
that enchanted the watching world. They fell in love with the
idea that running was just a part of our lives. We were the last
flickering of the illusion that world athletics might still be
dominated by young undergraduates from Oxford and
Cambridge.

'Along with that there was the seductive mathematical
appeal of four laps and four minutes, the hypnotism of the
round numbers. Put that into an era of barrier-breaking with
Everest, the sound barrier and talk of a new Elizabethan age,
and you begin to glimpse why it has endured.'

Chataway picks out a volume from his well-stocked book-
shelves. 'Take a look at this,' he says, 'as an illustration of what
has happened. I bought this at Los Angeles airport. It's a book
called *1,000 Years and 1,000 People* – ranking the men and
women who shaped the millennium.

'These are the thousand most important people in the past
1,000 years. It lists St Thomas Aquinas, Charles Darwin,
Winston Churchill. John Kennedy doesn't get in and Ronald
Reagan doesn't make it – but Roger Bannister does. It's
supposed to evaluate how famous a person is: what is his or
her legacy to posterity, how they changed history and influenced the millennium. And there is Roger Bannister at
number 963 – towards the end admittedly, but none the less
he's there. Isn't that wonderful? There he is with William

the Conqueror and all the great old lags from the history books.

'Somehow what happened that day has passed into legend and into the language. When a Pakistani fast bowler launched the first 100-miles-per-hour delivery, I heard the commentator refer to it as "the four-minute mile of cricket". Then I went to a lecture at the Royal Geographical Society, given by the youngest Englishman to climb Everest, talking about the significance of barrier-breaking. He said, "Before Roger Bannister ran the four-minute mile, people believed you would die if you ran that fast." When I looked around there was nobody laughing or questioning what he'd said. I realised then how very big the legend had grown.'

And it's a legend that has continued to grow with the passing of the years. Half a century on, shortly after the death of Chris Brasher, his running clubs, the Thames Hare and Hounds and Ranelagh Harriers, got together to salute him in a relay along the length of the Thames, from its source to the meadows at Petersham where Brasher would sometimes run.

Chris Chataway, into his seventies, took the baton for the Oxford stage of the relay, lapping en route the old Iffley Road track and trying to keep pace with his memories. At the end of the leg, there on the riverbank was Roger Bannister, waiting in the sunshine to buy the drinks.

They smiled the smiles of old friends that brimmed with a lifetime of memories, and they laughed when Chataway spoke of the start of his run at Oxford's Folly Bridge. Waiting there, stripped to his shorts for the incoming relay runner, he was approached by a lady, her sharp old eyes undimmed by the passing of time.

'Excuse me,' she said, 'but are you Chris Chataway?'

'I used to be,' he replied with a grin.

'Ah, fame,' she said, her eyes now flickering as if watching a replay of that long-ago four-minute mile. 'You know, fame never fades.'

Index